Idealized Design

UU Wharton School Publishing

In the face of accelerating turbulence and change, business leaders and policy makers need new ways of thinking to sustain performance and growth.

Wharton School Publishing offers a trusted source for stimulating ideas from thought leaders who provide new mental models to address changes in strategy, management, and finance. We seek out authors from diverse disciplines with a profound understanding of change and its implications. We offer books and tools that help executives respond to the challenge of change.

Every book and management tool we publish meets quality standards set by The Wharton School of the University of Pennsylvania. Each title is reviewed by the Wharton School Publishing Editorial Board before being given Wharton's seal of approval. This ensures that Wharton publications are timely, relevant, important, conceptually sound or empirically based, and implementable.

To fit our readers' learning preferences, Wharton publications are available in multiple formats, including books, audio, and electronic.

To find out more about our books and management tools, visit us at whartonsp.com and Wharton's executive education site, exceed.wharton.upenn.edu.

IDEALIZED DESIGN
Creating an Organization's Future

Russell L. Ackoff
Jason Magidson
Herbert J. Addison

Wharton
UNIVERSITY *of* PENNSYLVANIA

Vice President, Editor-in-Chief: Tim Moore
Wharton Editor: Yoram (Jerry) Wind
Acquisitions Editor: Paula Sinnott
Editorial Assistant: Susie Abraham
Development Editor: Russ Hall
Associate Editor-in-Chief and Director of Marketing: Amy Neidlinger
Cover Designer: Alan Clements
Managing Editor: Gina Kanouse
Senior Project Editor: Kristy Hart
Copy Editor: Keith Cline
Senior Indexer: Cheryl Lenser
Compositor: FastPages
Manufacturing Buyer: Dan Uhrig

Wharton
UNIVERSITY *of* PENNSYLVANIA

© 2006 by Russell L. Ackoff, Jason Magidson, and Herbert J. Addison
Publishing as Wharton School Publishing
Upper Saddle River, New Jersey 07458

Wharton School Publishing offers excellent discounts on this book when ordered in quantity for bulk purchases or special sales. For more information, please contact U.S. Corporate and Government Sales, 1-800-382-3419, corpsales@pearsontechgroup.com. For sales outside the U.S., please contact International Sales at international@pearsoned.com.

Printed in the United States of America

Third Printing October 2006

ISBN 0-13-196363-5

Pearson Education LTD.
Pearson Education Australia PTY, Limited.
Pearson Education Singapore, Pte. Ltd.
Pearson Education North Asia, Ltd.
Pearson Education Canada, Ltd.
Pearson Educatión de Mexico, S.A. de C.V.
Pearson Education—Japan
Pearson Education Malaysia, Pte. Ltd.

Library of Congress Cataloging-in-Publication Data

Ackoff, Russell Lincoln, 1919-
  Idealized design : how to dissolve tomorrow's crisis...today / Russell L. Ackoff, Jason Magidson, Herbert J. Addison.
    p. cm.
  ISBN 0-13-196363-5 (hardback : alk. paper) 1. Creative ability in business—Case studies. 2. Creative thinking—Case studies. 3. Technological innovations—Case studies. 4. Organizational effectiveness—Case studies. 5. Corporate culture—Case studies. I. Magidson, Jason, 1964- II. Addison, Herbert J., 1932- III. Title.

HD53.A28 2006
658.4'01—dc22   2005037715

DEDICATION

Russell L. Ackoff

In memoriam to Aron Katsenelinboigen

Jason Magidson

To my parents, who have always encouraged and empowered

Herbert J. Addison

To Gerry, my wife and life's companion

132183

CONTENTS AT A GLANCE

CONTENTS

ACKNOWLEDGMENTS

The authors thank the many organizations and managers who have undertaken idealized designs. Without their confidence that they would achieve their goals, the concept of idealized design would have remained just that—a concept without testing in the real world.

ABOUT THE AUTHORS

Russel L. Ackoff is Anheuser-Busch Professor Emeritus of Management Science, the Wharton School, University of Pennsylvania, and was the August A. Busch, Jr. Visiting Professor of Marketing, John M. Olin School of Business, Washington University, St. Louis, Missouri, 1989 through 1995. He received his undergraduate degree in architecture (1941) and his Ph.D. in philosophy of science from the University of Pennsylvania (1947). He was a member and former chairman of the Social Systems Sciences Department and the Busch Center, which specializes in systems planning, research, and design—both within the Wharton School. Dr. Ackoff is the author and co-author of 22 books, including *Redesigning the Future, The Art of Problem Solving, Creating the Corporate Future, Revitalizing Western Economies, Management in Small Doses, Ackoff's Fables, The Democratic Corporation,* and his most recent books *Re-Creating the Corporation, Ackoff's Best, Redesigning Society,* and *Beating the System,* the latter two with Sheldon Rovin. He has also published more than 200 articles in books and a wide variety of journals. A charter member and former president of the Operations Research Society of America, founding member and former vice president of the Institute of Management Sciences, he has received the Silver Medal of the British Operational Research Society and the George E. Kimball Medal of the Operations Research Society of America. He is also a former president of the Society for General Systems Research. He has received honorary Doctorates of Science from the University of Lancaster (UK), Washington University (St. Louis, MO), the University of New Haven (New Haven, CT), the Pontificia Universidad Catholica Del Peru in Lima, Peru, and the University of Lincolnshire and Humberside (UK), and has been elected a member of the Academy of Natural Sciences of the Russian Federation. He was recently honored (September 2000) by the establishment of the Ackoff Center for Advanced Systems Practices at the University of Pennsylvania. His work in research, consulting, and education has involved more than 350 corporations and 75 government agencies in the United States and abroad.

Dr. Ackoff played a key role at the University of Pennsylvania, both in the early history of the Operations Research Group and in establishing the Social Systems Sciences Graduate Group. Since becoming Emeritus, he has been honored by the establishment of the Russell L. Ackoff Endowment in the Wharton School and The Ackoff Center for the Advancement of Systems Approaches in the Engineering School, through which his legacy at the University of Pennsylvania continues.

Jason Magidson is currently director of innovation processes at GlaxoSmithKline, where he has engaged employees, suppliers, and customers in developing innovations, new insights, and breakthroughs in a wide range of processes. In the procurement function, he and his team used idealized design to help the company save hundreds of millions of dollars. For more than 20 years, Jason has engaged end users—the source of most innovations—in product, service, system, and organizational design. He has applied innovation methods with numerous Fortune 1000 organizations and nonprofits. Jason has also written for publications including *Harvard Business Review* and the *Journal of Product Innovation Management*. He received his undergraduate degree in Business Administration from the Wharton School of the University of Pennsylvania and a Ph.D. from the Union Institute & University.

Herbert J. Addison has spent his career in book publishing, the past 20 years of which he was a sponsoring editor at Oxford University Press specializing mostly in business and management books for practicing managers, business students, and business academics. In 2000, he formally retired and has continued to work as a consulting editor and writer in business. He has written a brief history of business that appeared in *The New York Times Guide to Essential Knowledge* (2004). That history, together with a glossary of business terms that he also wrote, constituted the entire entry in that subject. He is a member of the Academy of Management and serves on the Advisory Board of the Ackoff Center for Advancement of Systems Approaches at the University of Pennsylvania.

FOREWORD

Russell L. Ackoff, no doubt one of the greatest management innovators of our time, has been one of the most important influences in my understanding of management theory and practice, even though I discovered him late in my professional career. His application of systems thinking and his penetrating insights into human and organizational behavior have enriched my thinking about how to radically improve management processes and business results. None of his many contributions to management thinking is more important than the subject of this book, idealized design and interactive planning.

Idealized design has its greatest benefit when an organization or a part thereof finds itself at a crossroad, where incremental improvement of past business models and practices will no longer assure future success, and in fact, may even precipitate a crisis. Historically, the pace of business change was such that a formula for success, once discovered, would, with incremental improvements, endure for many years if not decades. Today, in many industries, disruptions occur at such a rate that there is little momentum to business success. As Andy Grove, former CEO of Intel, said, "Only the paranoid survive." In an environment of such radical change, a new approach to planning is called for where continuous innovation and breakthroughs in every aspect of business is a way of life. Idealized design is the best approach I've found to cope with latent, if not actual, crisis and to respond with radical change. But also in less-dramatic ways, this methodology can be applied to more specific challenges such as redesigning a compensation program, improving the business planning process, or turning around a troubled division.

At my company Analog Devices, in the late 1980s, after two decades of profitable growth that averaged 25 percent per year, we hit the wall as growth slowed to single digits and profits plummeted. We did not have a systematic way to diagnose why our formula for success was breaking down or how to manage the radical change that would be required. So, as a complex, billion-dollar company, we stumbled for more years than we should have in discovering the source of the impending crisis. That's when I learned about Russ Ackoff and his principles of systems thinking.

Until then, I believed in the KISS theory of management, "Keep It Simple Stupid." Our formula for success was to hire the best and brightest engineers, to focus on technical innovation for competitive advantage, to divide the company into small divisions differentiated by technology, and to give these divisions as much autonomy as possible and require that they stand on their own bottom line. These divisions, except for a shared sales organization, were run almost as independent businesses with their own manufacturing and ways of doing business. Competition between divisions for the best technical approach to designing and manufacturing a similar class of functional integrated circuits was seen as a spur to innovation. This formula worked exceedingly well for low-volume customers, in military, industrial, and scientific markets, who could afford to pay high prices for the very best performance. But as our business shifted to high-volume customers in consumer, communications, and automotive markets, where price and quality were more important, this approach was not working. As we thought about change, our beliefs got in the way. First, we believed that if every part of the organization were optimized for success, then the performance of the corporation as a whole would be optimized. We believed that in a technology-driven business, you couldn't be held accountable for P&Ls unless you owned manufacturing. We believed you couldn't manage engineers unless they were within walking distance from your desk. These beliefs seriously constrained our flexibility to consider other possibilities.

The first lesson I learned from Russ was that the performance of an organization depends more on how the parts work together than on how they work separately; and thus, if you optimize the performance of the parts, as we were doing, you systematically suboptimize the performance of the whole. I learned that collaboration is a more powerful force than internal competition and that the job of leaders is to manage the interactions of the parts, not their actions. I learned that solving one problem at a time doesn't work when radical transformation is required. The challenge was to dissolve the mess—that is, the system of interrelated problems that were precipitating the crisis.

Following the principles of systems thinking and the process of idealized design, we in fact "blew up" the organization (read Chapter 1, "The Stages of Idealized Design," and you will see what I mean here) and reassembled the parts and business processes to more effectively compete in markets that were very different from those in which we built our early success.

The changes we made were so dramatic and far reaching that we referred to the process as "Creating the New Analog." We centralized manufacturing and standardized business processes across the organization. We integrated competing product groups into worldwide, strategically focused, geographically dispersed product teams. It took many years to iron out the wrinkles, to unlearn our beliefs from the past, and to learn new skills, attitudes, and behaviors. But step by step, we restored the growth of analog devices and opened exciting new opportunities for future success. We avoided the crisis that could have destroyed the company.

Systems thinking embedded in idealized design played a powerful role in uncorking the potential synergy and collective energy that had been bottled up by the way we were organized and by the way we thought about value creation. The most important lesson we took from idealized design was learning to focus attention of the key players from product groups and functional disciplines on the purpose and mission of the company as a whole and then freeing and encouraging them to think collectively and creatively about the best way to structure the interaction of the parts to achieve shared goals and objectives. This requires new ways to think about roles in the organization. Implementing interactive planning and idealized design certainly does not mean abandoning the fundamentals of accounting, marketing, engineering, and other disciplines, nor does it mean failing to do the usual financial assessments of risks and returns for alternatives and initiatives resulting from interactive planning. What it does mean is subjugating these disciplines to the pursuit of broader organizational objectives that are meaningful in systemic terms and that fit with the organizational competencies and opportunities available. This does not happen easily or automatically because vested interests, experience, beliefs, fears, prejudices, and limited understanding and appreciation for how an organization functions outside an individual's sphere of influence get in the way of open, objective dialog about new ways for product groups and functional organizations to work together. So it takes nudging, facilitation, patience, and sometimes a little force to achieve alignment. A sense of crisis, real or envisioned, by the mess formulation process of interactive planning as described in this book helps to reach agreement.

In reflecting on my experience, if I had it to do over again, I would have stuck closer to the script of idealized design. At every step along the way, the framework and principles of idealized design guided my thinking and actions as we "Created the New Analog." But I did not formalize idealized design principles sufficiently in the company's top-to-bottom planning process. Had I done so, a larger number of people in the company today would be more skilled in thinking about the business as a system, more focused on dissolving messes than solving problems, and bolder in shedding shackles and constraints of what is and imagining a more ideal future, even when a looming crisis does not motivate behavior. It is one thing to mount a major idealized design process to address a significant corporate-wide challenge that threatens the underpinnings of the company. It is quite another to make interactive planning an enduring way of life in every aspect of business planning, large and small. Among other things, this requires the development of staff expertise to facilitate ongoing idealized design projects, and it requires an idealized redesign of the business planning process itself.

This book, through many applications, provides rich evidence of the effectiveness of idealized design as well as a guide to implementing the process itself. These case studies and step-by-step descriptions of how the process works make it possible for you to initiate the interactive planning process even without the benefit of an experienced facilitator. These examples also illustrate just how universal this methodology can be in tackling a very broad range of challenges. As discussed in Chapter 10, "The Urban Challenge," idealized design points to possible solutions and approaches to dissolving even the most daunting and perplexing messes in which the world finds itself today, such as education, health care, and poverty. The lasting benefit of studying this book is that it enables readers to better understand and improve the world in which we live and work through the lens of systems thinking and the practical, useful approaches embodied in the idealized design process.

Ray Stata

Chairman, Analog Devices

Chairman, Center for Quality of Management

PREFACE

No idea has had as much effect on the professional and personal lives of the first two authors of this book as idealized design. It has influenced everything we do in our professional lives—for one of us, as a former professor now emeritus, and the other, head of a staff unit at GlaxoSmithKline. In every case described in this volume, one or the other of us, or both, were directly involved.

What is idealized design? The answer is in the Introduction, in which we explain not only what idealized design is but also describe its extraordinary origin as a powerful tool of management.

The cases presented here constitute only a small sample of the cases on which we have had the opportunity to employ idealized design. We have tried to select as diverse a group of applications as possible to reveal how broad is the applicability of the process. We have never been confronted with a problem or opportunity to which idealized design has not been applicable.

In a sense, idealized design has been much more than a way of doing our work; it has been a way of life. There is little either one of us is called in to do that is not affected by the use of idealized design. There is no limit to its relevance where problems or opportunities are involved.

Idealized design has been described in a number of books but never in as much detail or with as many illustrations as we provide here. Unfortunately, words cannot convey the power of the procedure nearly as well as experiencing it. We hope that the vicarious experiences we provide here will entice the readers to explore the process on their own.

Involvement in the process is a liberating experience. Moreover, it is *fun*. It provides an opportunity to reactivate the creativity we had as children but lost on the "way up." It is a "soft idea" that lends itself to fashioning to suit specific situations. It is not a process cast in concrete. It involves at least as much art as science.

ABOUT THE AUTHORS AND THE "AUTHORS' VOICE"

This book has three authors who have contributed differently to it. Russell L. Ackoff is the central figure in the development of idealized design. Not only did he initially grasp the potential of the process to revolutionize how organizations can change today to better shape the future, but he has also been the leading thinker in developing the way the process is implemented in the real world of organizations that we describe in this book.

Jason Magidson was a long-time student and colleague of Ackoff's and participated in many idealized designs before he joined a major pharmaceutical firm. In his present position, he continues to use the process in a variety of applications. He has contributed examples of idealized design to the book, as well as helped to shape the advice we provide to managers about how to begin and implement the process.

Herbert J. Addison has spent his career in book publishing, with the past two decades devoted mainly to publishing books in business and management for practicing managers, business academics, and business students. His contribution is confined to helping to shape the final book for its intended readership of practicing managers.

Inevitably, when a book has more than one author, there will be a blurring of what is often called the "author's voice." The book you hold in your hands does not reflect the distinct voice of any one of its three authors—least of all the voice of Russell L. Ackoff. Thus it can be said to have an "authors' voice" that is a blend of the three. But there is one exception. In Chapter 1, "The Stages of Idealized Design," Ackoff steps forward and describes in his own distinctive voice how he first experienced idealized design— including mistakes he made and the amazing outcome of the experience. His co-authors recommend that you read one or more of Ackoff's books listed in the Annotated Bibliography for a full experience of the authentic Ackoff voice.

Russell L. Ackoff

Jason Magidson

Herbert J. Addison

January 3, 2006

INTRODUCTION:
THE BIRTH OF AN IDEA

"Gentlemen, the telephone system of the United States
was destroyed last night."
—CEO of Bell Laboratories

Idealized design is a way of thinking about change that
is deceptively simple to state: In solving problems of
virtually any kind, the way to get the best outcome is
to imagine what the ideal solution would be and then
work backward to where you are today. This ensures
that you do not erect imaginary obstacles before you
even know what the ideal is.

Nothing better illustrates the power of this idea in
action than the experience that one of the authors,
Russell L. Ackoff, had many years ago. The experience
both enlightened him and proved to him that the idea
could facilitate profound change in a major
corporation. To relate the experience, this author
"steps forward:"

In every life, there are seminal experiences that
exert their influence on a great deal of experience
that follows. The one that is responsible for this

book took place in 1951. I was then a member of the faculty of Case Institute of Technology in Cleveland, Ohio. (It had not yet merged with Western Reserve University.) On a consulting trip to New York, I drove down to Bell Labs in Murray Hill, New Jersey, to see Peter Meyers, a manager whom I'd met when he had come to Case to recruit promising graduate students for the labs.

It so happened that on the day of my visit he and other managers had been summoned to an important—but last-minute—conference by the vice president of Bell Labs. After some hesitation, Peter Meyers said, "Why don't you come with me?" I pointed out it was a meeting for section heads and I was not even an employee of the labs. He said that no one would know the difference.

We arrived at a typical classroom that held about forty people and was almost full. The vice president was not there yet. Nor did he appear on time. This was very unusual. He was a big man, extroverted, and voluble. He could not get near someone without punching, pinching, pushing, hugging, or pounding them on the back.

About ten minutes after the hour, the door to the room squeaked open. All eyes turned to it, and there he was. He was obviously very upset. He was a pasty gray and bent over as he slowly shuffled down the aisle without a word to anyone. He mounted the platform, stood behind the podium, put his elbows on it, and held his head in his two hands, looking down.

The room was dead silent. Finally, he looked up and in an uncharacteristically meek voice said, "Gentlemen, the telephone system of the United States was destroyed last night." Then he looked down again.

The room broke out in a hubbub of whispered conversations saying that his statement was not true. Many in the room had used a phone that morning. The vice president looked up and said, "You don't believe the system was destroyed last night, do you? Some of you probably used the phone this morning, didn't you?" Most of the heads in the room shook with assent.

The vice president began to tremble with rage. He shouted, "The telephone system was destroyed last night and you had better believe it. If you don't by noon, you'll be fired."

He then looked down again. "What was wrong with the VP?" everyone was asking each other. But because discretion is the better part of valor where one's boss is involved, the whispers stopped as all waited for further word from him and an explanation of his erratic behavior.

The vice president looked up and glowered at the group. Then he suddenly straightened up, his normal color seemed to return, and he broke out in a great big belly laugh. All those in the room also began to laugh. They did not know why they were laughing, but it released the tension that his unusual behavior had created. It began to dawn on all of us that his behavior had been a trick.

After the laughter died down, he said in his normal voice with his normal demeanor, "What was that all about? Well, in the last issue of the *Scientific American*," he said, "there was an article that said that these laboratories are the best industrially based R&D laboratories in the world. I agreed, but it got me thinking."

He reached into the inside pocket of his jacket and withdrew a piece of paper and said, "I've made a list of those contributions to the development of telephonic communications that I believe have earned us this reputation. Before I share my list with you, I'd like your opinions. What do you think are the most important contributions we have ever made to this development?"

Almost every hand in the room went up. He called on one of those with a raised hand. He said, "The *dial*." "Right," said the vice president. "This is certainly one of the most important. Do any of you know when we introduced the dial?" One in the room volunteered a date in the 1930s. The vice president agreed. He then asked, "When was it developed?" No one knew.

He said he had not known either but had looked it up before he came to the meeting. He said, "It was before 1900." We were surprised to say the least. He pressed on, asking for another candidate. The next one offered was *multiplexing*, a way of transmitting multiple conversations simultaneously over one wire. This yielded an enormous increase in the capacity of AT&T's network. "Right," the vice president repeated. He once again asked when it has been introduced. Someone knew it had been between the two world wars. The vice president confirmed this and asked, "When was it invented?" No one knew. Again he revealed that it was before 1900.

He asked for one more suggestion. The person he called on said, "The *coaxial cable* that connected the United States and Great Britain." The vice president agreed and asked when it had been built. Someone knew: 1882.

"Doesn't it strike you as odd," he said, "that the three most important contributions this laboratory has ever made to telephonic communications were made before any of you were born? What have you been doing?" he asked. "I'll tell you," he said. "You have been improving the parts of the system taken separately, but you have not significantly improved the system as a whole. The deficiency," he said, "is not yours but mine. We've had the wrong research-and-development strategy. We have been focusing on improving parts of the system rather than focusing on the system as a whole. As a result, we have been improving the parts but not the whole. We have got to restart by focusing on designing the whole and then designing parts that fit it rather than vice versa. Therefore, gentlemen, we are going to begin by designing the system with which we would replace the existing system right now if we were free to replace it with whatever system we wanted, subject to only two not-very-restrictive constraints."

"First," he continued, "let me explain why we will focus on what we want right now, not out five or ten years. Why? Because we know that where we say today we would like to be five years from now is not where we will want to be when we get there. Things will happen between now and then that will affect our goals and objectives. By focusing on what we want right now, we can eliminate that potential source of error."

"Second, why remove practically all constraints? Because if we don't know what we would do now if we could do whatever we wanted, how can we know what to do when we can't do everything we want? If we knew what we would do with virtually no constraints, we could modify it, if necessary, to become feasible and adapt it to changing internal and external conditions as time goes on."

"Now, here are the two constraints. First, *technological feasibility*. This means we cannot use any but currently available knowledge. No science fiction. We can't replace the phone with mental telepathy. The second constraint," he said, was that "the system we design must be *operationally viable*. What does that mean? Because we are not changing the environment, it means that the system must be able to function and survive in the current environment. For example, it will have to obey current laws and regulations."

The vice president then said, "This group is too large to operate as a single group. Therefore, I am going to divide you into six subgroups of about six each, each with responsibility for a subsystem. Each group will select a representative to meet with other representatives at least once a week to discuss interactions. Let me explain.

"Each group will be able to design whatever it wants as long as it does not affect any other group's design. If what a group wants to do does affect one or more other groups' designs, it must get their agreement before it can be included in their design. I can tell you in advance," he said, "that the groups will do little that does not affect other groups. At the end of the year," he said, "I want to see one completely integrated system design, not six subsystem designs. I don't even want to know what the individual teams came up with. Is that clear?" he asked.

He created a "long lines" (inter-city communication) team, a "short lines" (within city communication) team, a switching stations team, two other teams, and finally the telephone set team, on which I found myself with my friend Peter Meyers.

When the meeting was adjourned, the teams immediately gathered so that their members got to know each other. When

Peter introduced me to the other members of our team, they thought it very funny that an "outsider" had successfully invaded their meeting. But, they said, the vice president had not precluded their use of "outsiders." Therefore, they invited me to participate in the effort. As a result, I spent a great deal of time in the next year with that team. What a learning experience it was!

The first meeting took place after lunch that day. The seven of us, six from the labs and I, met in a small breakout room. After the amenities, we discussed where we should begin. We decided to list the properties we wanted a telephone to have. We noted suggestions on a pad mounted on an easel. The first few were as follows:

- Every call I receive is intended for me—no wrong numbers.

- I want to know who is calling before I answer the phone so I need not answer it if I don't want to speak to the caller.

- A phone I can use with no hands.

- A phone that comes with me wherever I am, not one I have to go to in a fixed location.

We continued to add to this list for several weeks, ending with just more than ninety properties we wanted a phone to have. These properties became very complicated near the end. For example, we wanted to be able to talk simultaneously to groups in multiple locations, see all of them, and be able to transmit documents or charts instantaneously.

But we ran dry. We noted, however, that we had designed nothing yet, so decided to try our hands at it. We decided to select the first property on our list—no wrong numbers—and see if we could design a phone that met this requirement.

At this point, I almost destroyed my credibility in the group by pointing out that there were two kinds of wrong numbers. One consisted of having the right number in one's head but dialing it incorrectly. The other consisted of having the wrong number in one's head and dialing it correctly. One member of the group immediately pointed out that if one had the wrong number in one's head and dialed it incorrectly, one might get the right number. Fortunately, the group decided this was too rare to be of concern but that the percentage of wrong numbers of each type was of concern.

Here I was able to save my credibility a bit because I knew the head of the psychology department at the labs. I called him using the phone in the room. After the amenities, I asked him if he had ever done any work on wrong numbers. He exploded on the other end of the line. It was minutes before I could understand him. It turned out that he had been doing work on wrong numbers for a number of years, and I was the first one to ask him about it. He wanted to unload all his results on me. I had to convince him otherwise. After he calmed down, I learned that four out of five wrong numbers were the result of incorrectly dialing the right number in one's head. We decided to go to work on this.

An amazing thing happened; in less than an hour, we found a way, conceptually, to reduce, if not eliminate, such errors. We replaced the dial by—what did not exist at that time—a small handheld calculator. There were ten keys, one for each digit, a register, and a red key in the lower-right corner. The phone was to be used as follows. Leaving the phone "on the hook," one would put into the phone the number one wanted to call by pressing the appropriate buttons. These numbers would appear on the register. If these numbers, on examination, appear to be correct, one would lift the receiver and the whole number would go through at once. If the number on the register was wrong, one would press the red button in the corner. This would clear the phone, and one would start over.

We were very pleased with ourselves, but nevertheless we recognized that we did not know whether such a phone was technologically feasible. (The handheld calculator was not yet available.) Therefore, we called a department of the lab that worked on miniaturization and asked for technical help. They sent two young men down to our meeting. They appeared to be fresh out of school, still wearing their intellectual diapers.

As we described what we were trying to do, they began to whisper to each other and were soon more absorbed in their private conversation than in what we were saying. This bothered us, but such behavior was not entirely unexpected in an R&D laboratory. However, they suddenly got up and hurried out of the room with no explanation. We were furious but decided to let it pass for the time being. We went on to another property.

Several weeks later, the two young men appeared at one of our sessions looking sheepish and apologetic. They said, "You probably wondered why we ran out on you when we were here last." We told them this was an understatement. They explained, "We were very excited by what you were doing but not for the reasons you were. We did not want to take the time to explain. That wrong-number stuff was not as interesting as the buttons."

They went on, "We went back and built a push-button telephone and tested it on a very large number of people. It turns out to take about twelve seconds less to put in seven digits by pushing buttons than turning a dial, and additional time is saved by not occupying a line until after the number is put in and the receiver is picked up. The combined saving in time is worth millions to AT&T," they said, "so we have started a project to develop that telephone. We have given it a code name that is being kept secret for now." They looked around the room to be sure no one was listening and then told us, "Touch tone."

Before the year was over, the groups had established the technological feasibility of each of our many design features. The group of design teams continued to work after I was no longer a participant, and they anticipated every change in the telephone system, except two, that has appeared since then. Among these are touch-tone phones, consumer ownership of phones, call waiting, call forwarding, voice mail, caller ID, conference calls, speaker phones, speed dialing of numbers in memory, and mobile phones. They did not anticipate photography by the phone or an Internet connection.

The impact of the design we produced was greater than the impact of any other effort to change a system that I had ever seen. As a result, I began to adapt and modify the procedure to fit such other applications that we describe in this book. As you will see, its use has been extensive and is still growing.

This experience is a convincing example of how *idealized design* can literally move mountains of change. However, applying the process involves not only discarding old mindsets that inhibit creative thinking but knowing the steps that we have learned work best in applying it. The book is intended to take you through the process with many examples of different organizations in different industries.

THE PLAN OF THE BOOK

The book is organized to give you a roadmap for finding the most valuable sections that match your particular interests and needs. Part I, "Idealized Design: The Basics," describes the basic ideas of idealized design and the steps that managers need to take to implement it. Chapter 1, "The Stages of Idealized Design," explains the basic stages of a fully implemented idealized design. Chapter 2, "Organizing the Process," describes how to organize a successful design. Chapter 3, "Preparing for an Idealized Design Process," makes the case for the importance of careful preparation and provides essential guidance about how to prepare. The object of these three chapters is to give you a comprehensive understanding of the design process so that in later chapters we can concentrate on the important aspects of each topic without having to repeat all of the steps that led to the outcome.

Part II, "Idealized Design: Applications—The Process in Action," describes idealized design in action and applied in a variety of organizations and processes. Chapter 4, "Business Enterprise," looks at entire business organizations that are forced to respond to market conditions and change or lose out to competitors.

Chapter 5, "Not-for-Profit and Government Organizations," demonstrates that idealized design is as powerful a tool for not-for-profit and government organizations as for business organizations.

Chapter 6, "Process Improvement," discusses processes and shows how idealized design can be used to improve processes in a widely diverse group of organizations.

Chapter 7, "Problem Dissolving," describes the four ways of approaching problem solving and demonstrates that the most effective approach is "dissolving" the problem. Dissolving a problem invokes idealized design and results in the problem going away permanently.

Chapter 8, "Facilities and Sites Design," looks at facilities and sites and combines the factors of function and space that need to be reconciled to produce the optimum arrangement of elements.

Chapter 9, "Take the Plunge," brings together our accumulated experience in working with idealized designs and provides hands-on practical advice for conducting a successful design.

Part III, "Idealized Design: No Limit—Applications to World Challenges," takes a wider view of what can be achieved using idealized design by applying it to some of the major challenges facing the world today. Chapter 10, "The Urban Challenge," addresses the challenge of urbanism and describes a small car that is ideally suited to operating in cities. The chapter then describes how idealized design was applied to a redesign of Paris—and the national system of which it is a part—in a project that has had a continuing impact on France to this day.

Chapter 11, "The Health-Care Challenge," explores how the seemingly intractable challenge of the health-care system can yield to the power of idealized design. The chapter first describes a national health-care system for the United States that would deliver care equitably to all citizens. It then explains how health-care malls can deliver care at the point of contact between patients and health-care professionals that is both humane and effective.

Chapter 12, "The Challenge to Government," looks at the challenges that governments face and describes how idealized design can be applied to deal with problems of a national and international nature. The chapter first examines a national elections system—as a part of a larger redesign of government—that would raise the proportion of eligible voters who turn out in elections and at the same time improve the quality of candidates for public office. It then describes a new international organization that could either replace the present United Nations or be formed in addition to it that would solve many of the problems of international wars and conflict that the U.N. has failed to achieve. Finally, the chapter addresses perhaps the biggest threat to nations today: terrorism. It applies idealized design to one of the root causes of terrorism and explains how if the causes were eliminated, there would be fewer terrorists and terrorist attacks.

Part IV, "Complete Idealized Design," provides three complete idealized designs. These are actual designs drawn from examples in the applications in Part II. We discuss these examples in the applications chapters but only reprint excerpts from their final idealized designs. Readers should find the details of the complete designs of value if they want to embark on an idealized design of the kind described in one or more of these chapters.

A SURPRISING INGREDIENT

If our description of idealized design so far sounds mechanical and dry, our experience with it is exactly the opposite. There is a very important aspect of idealized design that is not normally discussed: Participation in preparing such a design is great fun.

The removal of constraints, allowing the free exercise of imagination, is a liberating and exciting experience. To engage in it is to play god in a limited universe and to enjoy the creative experience that any creator must have. In every design exercise, there is a point, usually fairly early in the process, when an "aha" experience moves the design group through a threshold that takes them out of the existing system into the realm of the newly possible.

Adding to the pleasure, rank is irrelevant within design groups; there is no hierarchy. Rank is deposited at the door. This removes the fear of retribution for what is said in the sessions by subordinates. This relief is augmented by the fact that the effort is not directed at criticizing the current system or attributing blame for its deficiencies, but in conceptualizing a better one.

Because participation in idealized design is fun and liberating, it is usually easy to obtain and maintain. And because all who are involved, directly or indirectly, share ownership in the output, implementation is greatly facilitated. The plans directed at realization of the design or an approximation to it are not seen as a separate kind of activity but as an integral part of the design process. The fact that aspects of the design are seen as implementable long before the design is completed reinforces the inclusion of implementation as part of the design process.

USING THIS BOOK

We encourage readers to read this book from beginning to end. However, we know from our own experience—and through talking to others—that many, perhaps most, readers skip around in books looking for the most interesting parts, or the parts that relate to their immediate concerns.

So to help guide those who want to skip, let us suggest that you read all of Part I to get a firm grasp of the process of idealized design. Then skip to those applications chapters in Part II that are of most interest or importance to you.

We also strongly suggest that you read the chapters in Part III to open your thinking to the possibilities of using idealized design to address major challenges in the world today. We think there is no limit to what can be accomplished in the world using the tool of idealized design.

In Part I that follows, we take you through the process of implementing an idealized design. The emphasis is on the general application of the process, not on specific applications. That is the subject of Part II.

We welcome you to the journey you are about to begin.

IDEALIZED DESIGN:
THE BASICS

1

The Stages of Idealized Design

"It's tough to make predictions, especially about the future."
—Yogi Berra

In the Introduction, we saw how the startling declaration by the head of Bell Labs that "the telephone system of the United States was destroyed last night" liberated the creative thinking of an enormous corporation and allowed it to reinvent itself. Of course, the declaration was not true. However, the idea that planning should begin with the assumption that nothing now exists clears the mind to think creatively about the best possible outcome rather than be distracted by finding reasons that "it can't be done."

In this chapter, we look at the stages in idealized design because success requires a systematic approach to the process. We begin by briefly explaining how it evolved from organizational planning in general, and conclude by describing how it was applied in the recent past to solve problems of the OnStar system at General Motors.

The chapter, and the two that follow, are intended to give you a comprehensive understanding of how idealized design works in practice in virtually any kind of organization or institution. Later chapters describe specific applications in less detail—focusing instead on the most important elements—with the assumption that you already understand the full process from these three chapters.

THE EVOLUTION OF IDEALIZED DESIGN

Before idealized design was developed, there were three approaches to organizational planning:

- **Reactivism**—Reactive planners find the solution to their organizational problems in solutions that have worked in the past. They are often nostalgic about the past state of their organizations and speak about "the good old days."

- **Inactivism**—Inactive, or conservative, planners are satisfied with the way things are and hope that their present problems will simply go away if they do nothing. Some observers have compared this mode of thinking to Voltaire's character, Professor Pangloss in *Candide,* who believed that "this is the best of all possible worlds."

- **Preactivism**—Preactive planners do not look to the past or present for the solution to their problems but believe that the future can be better than the present. For them, the future is an opportunity for improvement to be exploited.

The weakness in this approach is in predicting what the future will be. Any prediction of the future ensures a poor outcome. As Yogi Berra wisely observed, "It's tough to make predictions, especially about the future."

These approaches sometimes worked, but more often they did not. They were especially ill equipped to help organizations adapt to rapid changes in their environment, whether of changes in the market, changes in technology, changes in competitors, or other factors that affect their organizations. Visionary planners began to develop a fourth approach that was to result in the process of idealized design on which this book is based:

■ **Interactivism**—Interactive planners reject the approaches of the other three planners. They plan backward from where they want to be to where they are now. They plan not for the future but for what they want their organizations to be at the present time. In so doing, however, interactive managers prepare their organizations for success in the unknowable future.

THE PROCESS OF IDEALIZED DESIGN

The process of interactive planning, called *idealized design,* has two parts:

■ **Idealization**
  1. Formulating the mess
  2. Ends planning
■ **Realization**
  3. Means planning
  4. Resource planning
  5. Design of implementation
  6. Design of controls

Here is how they work.

IDEALIZATION

1. Formulating the Mess

Every organization or institution is faced with a set of interacting threats and opportunities. These form what we call a *mess.* The aim of formulating the mess is to determine how the organization would eventually destroy itself if it were to continue doing what it is doing currently—that is, if it were to fail to adapt to a changing internal and external environment, even if it could predict the course of this change perfectly. This process identifies an organization's Achilles' heel—the seeds of its self-destruction—and provides a focus for the planning that follows by identifying what the organization or institution must avoid at all costs.

There are instances in which an organization or institution is faced with a crisis here and now—not sometime in the future. This present mess needs to be understood ("formulated") in the same way as a future mess before an idealized design can be undertaken to avert the possible destruction of the organization. In both cases, the process of formulating the mess is essentially the same.

Formulating a mess involves four steps:

1. **Prepare a systems analysis**—A detailed description of how the organization or institution currently operates. This is usually best revealed in a series of flow charts showing how material is acquired and processed though the organization. A similar chart for the flow of money and information is also helpful.

2. **Prepare an obstruction analysis**—Identify those characteristics and properties of the organization or institution that obstruct its progress or resist change (for example, conflicts and customs).

3. **Prepare reference projections**—Describe what the organization's future would be, assuming no changes in either its current plans, policies, programs, and practices, or changes of what it expects in its environment. This will show how and why the organization or institution would destroy itself unless it makes significant changes. This, of course, is not a forecast but a foresight of how the organization could destroy itself. This projection should reveal how the obstructions described in Step 2 prevent the organization from making adaptive changes to changing conditions.

4. **Prepare a presentation of the mess**—Combine the state of the organization and its reference projections into a scenario of the possible future of the organization, a future it would face if it were to make no changes in its current practices, policies, tactics, and strategies, and the environment changed only in expected ways.

2. Ends Planning

This stage of planning is at the heart of idealized design. It involves determining what planners would like the organization or institution to be now if it could be whatever they wanted. It then identifies the gaps between this idealized design and the organization as it is, thus revealing the gaps to be filled by the rest of the planning process. It is crucial to note here that the design must demonstrably prevent the self-destruction revealed in the formulation of the mess.

REALIZATION

3. Means Planning

This phase requires planners to determine what should be done to approximate the ideal as closely as possible to avoid the self-destruction projected in the formulation of the mess. Planners must invent and select courses of action, practices, projects, programs, and policies to be implemented.

4. Resource Planning

Implementing idealized design requires planners to identify and marshal the resources needed to accomplish the planned changes, including the following:

1. Determine how much of each type of resource—personnel; money; materials and services; facilities and equipment; and information, knowledge, and understanding and wisdom—are required. Also determine when and where to deploy the resources selected.

2. Determine how much of each type of resource will be available at the desired times and places and determine the difference between what will be available in any event and what will be required.

3. Decide what should be done about the shortages or excesses identified in Step 2.

5. Design of Implementation

Determine who is to do what, when, and where. Create a schedule and allocate resources to the tasks to be carried out.

6. Design of Controls

Determine (1) how to monitor these assignments and schedules, (2) how to adjust for failures to meet or exceed schedules, and (3) how to monitor planning decisions to determine whether they are producing expected results (and, if not, determine what is responsible for the errors and correct them).

These six phases of interactive planning do not need to be carried out in the same order presented here, but they are usually begun in this order. Because they are strongly interdependent, they usually take place simultaneously and interactively. Interactive planning is continuous; no phase is ever completed—that is, all parts of a plan are subject to subsequent revision. Plans are treated, at best, as still frames taken from a motion picture.

CONSTRAINTS AND REQUIREMENT

There are two constraints imposed on idealized designs and one important requirement. First, the design must be technologically feasible—no science fiction. This constraint does not preclude innovation, but it does restrict innovations to what we currently know we can develop even if we do not have it now. For example, it would be inappropriate in a design of a communication system to use mental telepathy to replace the telephone or e-mail. But clearly, we could increase the functionality of the mobile phone by having it unlock automobiles, turn on their lights, and turn on the heat or air conditioning in the house we are approaching.

The constraint of technological feasibility ensures the possibility of implementation of the design, but it says nothing about its likelihood. An idealized design, however feasible it might be technologically, may not be implementable for economic, social, or political reasons. For example, if all monetary transactions were electronic, a consumption-based tax system—in contrast to an income-based system—would be possible but very unlikely for political reasons.

The second constraint is that the design, if implemented, must be capable of surviving in the current environment. Therefore, it cannot violate the law and must conform to any relevant regulations and rules. It does not mean that the design must be capable of being implemented now. It does mean that if the design were implemented now, it would be able to survive in the current environment. For example, it would be possible to implement a system of all-electronic voting in elections, but it would not survive in today's world of computer hacking where voters cannot be sure that their votes are being counted. In the future, however, when voters can be confident of the integrity of the system, it will probably be implemented.

Finally, there is the important requirement that the process that is designed must be capable of being improved over time. If that which is designed is an organization or institution, it must be capable of learning and adapting to changing internal and external conditions. It should be designed to be ready, willing, and able to change itself or be changed. Therefore, the product of an idealized design is neither perfect, ideal, nor utopian, precisely because it can be improved. However, it is the best ideal-seeking system its designers can imagine now.

ANTICIPATING THE FUTURE

We have pointed out how difficult it is to predict the future. And idealized design stresses the need for planners to concern themselves with what they want now, not at some future time. However, this does not remove the need to take the future into account. It changes the way the account of it should be taken. In conventional planning, designers forecast the future in which the thing being designed is to exist. Unfortunately, as the rate of change in the environment continually increases, along with its complexity, accurate forecasting becomes more and more difficult and less and less likely. As we have observed, poor forecasts (or predictions) lead to poor outcomes. How then should the future be taken into account?

The future is taken into account in idealized design by the assumptions planners make about it. Contrary to what some forecasters claim, assumptions about the future differ qualitatively from forecasts. Forecasts are about probable futures; assumptions are about possible futures. We carry spare tires in our cars despite the fact that we do not forecast having a flat tire on our next trip. In fact, if anything, we forecast that we will not have a flat tire on the next trip. But we assume a flat tire is possible, however unlikely it may be.

Assumed futures can be taken care of in two different ways. First, there is contingency planning. When there are a relatively few and explicitly describable possible futures, planners can prepare plans for each possibility. This is called *contingency planning*. Then, when the truth about the future is known, the appropriate plan can be invoked. For example, an oil company can develop exploration plans based on the price of oil increasing, staying the same, or declining. When it is apparent how the price is moving, they can quickly move to the appropriate plan already developed.

The way of dealing with more contingencies than can be planned for separately is to design into the organization or institution enough flexibility and responsiveness so that it can change rapidly and effectively to meet whatever it encounters. Automobile manufacturers cannot accurately predict customer demand for all possible models, colors, and accessory packages. However, the best automakers have solved this problem by designing production lines that allow them to build different models and colors on the same production line as customer demand requires. Some manufacturers in a number of industries have created such flexible production facilities that they can customize each individual product based on an order just received. Boeing aircraft and Dell computers are examples. It is obvious that an additional benefit of such a system is that it allows for a rapid inventory turn and minimum idle capital.

EFFECTS OF IDEALIZED DESIGN

So far, we have described the way idealized design is put into practice. However, planners should be aware of an additional dimension to the process. It has a number of beneficial effects on those who engage in it and on their organizations, as follows:

- Promotes understanding of that which is designed
- Transforms the designers' concept of what is feasible
- Simplifies the planning process
- Enhances creativity
- Facilitates implementation

Let's look at each in turn.

PROMOTES UNDERSTANDING

There is no better way to gain an understanding of something than by designing it. Designing something as simple as a door handle on a car requires the designer to understand how the human hand grasps a handle and then turns (or pulls) so that the design produces a comfortable and functional handle.

Furthermore, in the design process, for example, one is forced to consider the assumptions on which the design is based. This consideration frequently reveals the irrationality of some of the features of the existing object and allows for their replacement. For example, in nearly all men's stores, clothing is arranged by type; a section for suits, another for overcoats, another for shirts, and so on. When a group of male planners engaged in an idealized redesign of a men's store, it became apparent to them that this arrangement was for the convenience of those who run the store, not its customers. They found that a far better arrangement for customers was to arrange the garments by size, not type of clothing, putting all the suits, coats, shirts, and so on in the same place so that each shopper—small, medium, or large—could find everything he might want in one place. Bookstores have always known this and arrange books by subject (because most browsers know what interests them, even if they do not know which books are available).

TRANSFORMS DESIGNERS' CONCEPT OF FEASIBILITY

The principal obstruction to what we want most is ourselves. The great American philosopher Pogo recognized this in his classic observation that "We have met the enemy and he is us." Our tendency, however, when we stand where we are and look toward what we want, is to see all kinds of obstructions imposed from without. When we change our point of view and look backward at where we are from where we want to be, in many cases the obstructions disappear.

Banking is a good example. Years ago, banks employed many tellers who handled transactions with customers. They received deposits and filled out deposit slips, cashed checks, and entered interest in savings passbooks. Bankers had to hire legions of tellers as their business grew. However, a few visionary bankers asked themselves what would be the ideal bank. They concluded that it would have few—perhaps no—tellers and would process all the same transactions. This vision led them to create automatic teller machines that allowed customers to do the work rather than the tellers. In turn, this led to online banking, where customers do not even have to go to the bank to manage their accounts. The obstruction bankers thought they faced—how to find and pay all those tellers—disappeared when they realized that banks could operate just as well with a decreasing number of tellers. Although some customers complained about this change, many more were pleased at not having to stand in line waiting to be helped by a human being.

SIMPLIFIES THE PLANNING PROCESS

Planning backward from where one wants to be reduces the number of alternatives that must be considered when making a choice of how to get there. It simplifies the planning process considerably.

An organizational example of simplification—requiring the details of planning backward and forward—is too long for our purposes here. So we offer instead an example drawn from a tennis tournament that nicely encapsulates how working backward greatly simplifies idealized design. If 64 players enter a tennis tournament, how many matches must be played to determine the winner? This is not hard to determine. There will be 32 matches in the first round, then 16, 8, 4, 2, and 1, successively. Added together, these equal 63 matches. However, if we start at the end and ask "How many losers would there have to be?" the answer is obviously 63, and no arithmetic is required. The advantage of working backward is even more apparent if we start with a number of players that is not a power of 2, say 57. The arithmetic now becomes complicated because some players must be exempted from the first round to make the number of players left after that round a power of 2. If we work backward, however, it is apparent that there must be 56 losers; hence this number of matches.

ENHANCES CREATIVITY

Human creativity is as old as humankind, but it was not very long ago that we began to understand what it is. We believe that it is a three-step process. First, it requires that we identify a self-imposed constraint, an assumption that we make consciously or unconsciously that limits the number of alternatives we consider. Second, we must deny or eliminate that assumption as too limiting. Third, we must then explore the consequences of this denial.

These steps are conspicuous in solving a puzzle (because a puzzle is a problem we cannot solve if we make an incorrect assumption). When the solution to a puzzle we have not been able to solve is revealed to us, we want to kick ourselves because we realize that we were the obstruction between the puzzle and its solution.

For example, consider the following puzzle that most of us were confronted with when we were youngsters (see Figure 1.1).

• • •

• • •

• • •

Figure 1.1

Then you are supposed to place a pen or pencil on one of the dots and, without lifting the pen or pencil from the paper, draw four straight lines that cover all nine dots. It cannot be done unless you deny an assumption of which you may not be conscious: that you cannot draw the lines outside the boundaries of the square formed by the nine dots. If you are not told that you can draw outside the boundaries, however, you must take it that you can. And when this assumption is put to rest, the solution is relatively easy (see Figure 1.2).

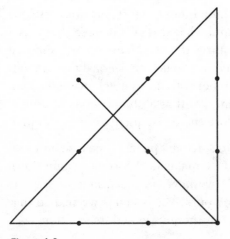

Figure 1.2

Furthermore, other possible solutions exist when all assumptions are ignored. If you fold the paper a certain way, the nine dots can be covered with one line using a felt-tip pen. An eight-year-old watching adults trying to solve this puzzle asked why they did not get a "great big fat pen that covered all the dots and just go blop." No constraints were imposed on the size of the pen used.

Creativity flows from this process.

FACILITATES IMPLEMENTATION

A major reason most plans are not fully implemented is that those people responsible for implementing it have no sense of ownership of it. This leads to resentment and subversion of its implementation. Idealized design, however, requires the participation of everyone who will be affected by it. Therefore, ownership of the resulting plan is widely spread among those who must implement it. This avoids resistance and subversion. Implementation of a design and plan based on it is usually carried out enthusiastically by those who had a hand in preparing it.

IDEALIZED DESIGN AT GENERAL MOTORS

In the Introduction, we saw how idealized design could be used to reinvent a major corporation, AT&T, and at the same time reinvent the industry in which it operates. However, it is likely that idealized design will be used more often in projects of smaller scope. At General Motors, in the late 1990s, the company faced a challenge with one of its new products, the OnStar safety and security system. Their actions illustrate the steps by which idealized design was applied locally in a huge organization through the determination of a few partisans of the method.

The example also illustrates that an organization going through a crisis of market-share loss and declining profits—that continues to this day—can nevertheless successfully remake parts of its business. The example was told to the authors by Nick Pudar, Director of the GM Strategic Initiatives group, who worked with Ackoff on problems at GM.

General Motors had introduced the OnStar system in its Cadillac line as a differentiating feature in 1996. Consumers could purchase the OnStar feature and have it installed on their vehicle at the time of purchase of the vehicle. OnStar was based on an electronic device installed in the cars that provided two-way cellular communication with a live advisor in a call center. The system delivered a range of services to owners: automatic two-way communication with the call center if the car is in an accident and the airbag deploys (at the same time, the car's GPS location is sent to the call center advisor who can dispatch emergency services to the car's location if necessary); if the owner is locked out of the car, the advisor can send a signal that unlocks it; if the owner cannot find the car in a crowded parking lot, the advisor can send a signal to the car to flash its lights and honk its horn; if the "check engine" light comes on, the owner can request the advisor to do a remote diagnostic check to determine how severe the problem is and what to do about it. These and other services that OnStar provided are, of course, of considerable value to owners.

But the OnStar system was expensive to install and maintain. Cadillac buyers could afford the car at a price that included OnStar. On the other less-expensive GM lines, however, the additional cost presented more of a problem. The system could not be included in the base price of the car without increasing the price beyond what planners believed buyers would pay. Therefore, installation had to be made by dealers who were able to sell the system as an "accessory" to those buyers willing to pay for it. It cost the customer almost $1,000, not including the cost of installation and dealer profit. In addition, buyers had to pay a monthly charge for cellular service and a subscriber fee for services provided by OnStar advisors. The result was that GM had more than 30,000 OnStar subscribers by 1998, far too few to consider the system a success.

It became clear to the people directly involved with OnStar that they needed to rethink their strategy if the system were ever to become widely adopted by owners and profitable. The OnStar leadership commissioned a small team to study the problem, and the team decided to use an idealized design approach. We look here at what they did at each stage in the process without going into all the details of the steps described earlier in this chapter. The object is to give an overview of a real-world application of a typical idealized design.

IDEALIZATION

1. Formulate the Mess

GM indeed had a mess on its hands if it wanted to expand the number of buyers who would pay for OnStar. The high cost of device installation and the high monthly fee of the combined OnStar and cellular service resulted in too few new customers for it to be profitable for GM.

The team formulated the mess. First, the device either added to the price of the vehicle and had an impact on sales, or, if it were offered below cost, it degraded the profitability of the program. Second, the team was concerned that dealer installation might potentially result in added quality and warranty costs because the vehicles had to be partially torn up to install the OnStar device. Third, the installation of OnStar bypassed GM's policy of lengthy testing to validate each new product, raising concerns about the quality of the system.

The team was concerned about the complexity of the business. Maintaining the availability of the right installation kits for each dealer was a daunting task. Each different GM vehicle required a different installation. Dealer training for the installation process was not a simple task either.

Dealers had their own concerns. Although they made a reasonable profit on each OnStar device they sold and installed, each dealer did not sell enough units to make it seem worth the time it took to install. Dealers also believed that selling OnStar to their customers created possible confusion and could interfere with selling the vehicle itself.

When the teams modeled the current business, they found that the same issues would be present regardless of how aggressively the business was pursued in the future. The economics and logistics of dealer installation could not be made into an attractive and lasting aspect of the business. Thus, the team realized that dealer installation was not sustainable. However, factory installation had its own problems. If the OnStar device was installed on a vehicle in the factory at no cost to the buyer, there was no guarantee that a customer would become a subscriber (and thus allow the subscription revenue to offset the hardware cost). Given the hardware costs at the time, it did not appear that factory installation would ever be a viable solution for the business.

2. Ends Planning

The team then came to the heart of idealized design, asking this question: "If you could have anything you wanted today, what would it be?" For the OnStar idealized design, the team's answer was simple: GM would have OnStar factory installed across the entire vehicle lineup for the 2000 model year. (The idealized design project was being conducted in the fall of 1998, and the 2000 model year vehicles would start being built by the next summer [1999].)

This design met the challenges identified in the original formulation of the mess. If OnStar were a standard feature on all vehicles, it would confer a distinctive and desirable awareness of GM to prospective buyers; factory installation would eliminate the need for dealers to "sell" the system and, instead, it would become a sales feature for dealers to use in closing the sale of a vehicle; factory installation would ensure quality control on installation and a lower installation cost; the final result would be a more aesthetically pleasing hardware package.

When the team presented this timing as the "ideal," they got uniform rejection from across the entire enterprise. The ideal was deemed to be ridiculously unrealistic, and completely disconnected from the reality of the extensive and lengthy vehicle development processes. At that time, typical product programs took up to five years to complete. The validation and testing process would never allow any vehicle features to be added late in the process. If new hardware such as OnStar was to be installed in the factory, it had to be added to a new product program and start from the beginning. The implication was that the earliest that OnStar could be factory installed in GM was for the 2005 model year, and on only one vehicle line to begin with. It would have to prove its value to the corporation, and then other vehicle platforms would decide whether it was warranted to add OnStar to their programs.

However, the team persisted and continued to describe and communicate the virtues of having a factory-installed solution across the entire line of GM vehicles. They presented a business simulation and financial model that showed a steady decline in costs through learning effects as well as economies of scale and scope.

Eventually, upper management became convinced of the value of factory installation but was unconvinced that it could be accomplished by the 2000 model year. The team was faced with finding ways to fill the gaps between the ideal and present reality.

REALIZATION

3. Means Planning

While the team was promoting the value of factory installation to upper management, it also turned its attention to finding the means of accelerating the expansion of factory installation of OnStar across all vehicle lines as soon as possible—shooting for a launch in the 2000 model year. The stages of idealized design do not always occur in lock-step sequence but often overlap as they did at GM.

The team identified five components of a successful business model to develop, based on Adrian Slywotzky's elements of a business model. First was this: Who were the *customers to be served*? These were to be every owner of a new GM vehicle. Spirited debate broke out over the question of including cellular phone service along with OnStar services. While some argued that cellular service was not in GM's product portfolio, others made the point that including it would generate revenue as GM became a "reseller" of that service. The team decided in favor of the opportunity to participate in the revenue from cellular service.

The second component of the business model to develop was the *value proposition* (what will be delivered to the customer that has value for that customer). OnStar would deliver a broad array of safety, security, and information services in a way that would be appropriate for different situations confronting vehicle owners.

The third component was *service delivery*; the team decided that the service would be "high-touch" and delivered directly by a live human advisor when required or requested by owners. However, an automated "virtual advisor" would also be available if the customer preferred that kind of service. Finally, the service would also be delivered and enhanced through the Internet at a personalized website for the customer. Setting up the system would take place outside the vehicle, and then voice recognition technology was used to navigate through the information when the customer was in the vehicle.

The fourth component turned out to be as contentious as any issue facing the team. This component was the extent of *strategic control* over the service. Should the design of the service be kept proprietary and exclusive to GM as a way of differentiating its vehicles to customers? Or should it be an open architecture across the entire automobile industry? The team concluded that the idealized design would have both open and closed aspects. The exchange of information to and from the vehicle would be an open architecture design with standard protocols. This would stimulate third-party developers to create service applications that could be used with the OnStar hardware. The team believed that the creativity and energy of outside companies would create "killer apps," or software applications that eventually dominate their markets, more quickly than if GM tried to develop everything in-house. However, the data and information that would be exchanged would have "controlled access" that was handled with encryption and authentication keys. The data would get "red, yellow, and green" designations. Things that were green would have encryption and authentication keys that were license free, and would have full read/write access to and from the vehicle. Such areas as radio control, seat memory control, heating, and ventilation would be candidates for the green designation. Things that were red would not have any access at all. Such areas as traction control, brakes, airbags, steering, and other safety critical systems would not be allowed to have read or write access by any non-GM application. However, there were other areas of the vehicle that had some economic value such as maintenance diagnostic data that would be designated as yellow, and would be made available through license arrangements.

All the data would flow through a single control point called the vehicle gateway. The team viewed this gateway as an important common interface for OnStar to connect to a wide array of vehicles. If the idealized design included other manufacturers' vehicles, it would be important that all vehicles had a similar gateway that functioned in the same manner for easy and standard communication for OnStar. The team recommended that an industry consortium be formed to drive toward a common approach to handling vehicle data exchange and set the appropriate standards. GM initiated the early discussions with other car manufacturers, and the Automotive Multimedia Interface Consortium (AMIC) was formed to address these very issues.

Finally, the team dealt with the fifth component of the idealized design business model, *value capture*. OnStar should make money from a variety of transaction types, including—but not be limited to—subscriptions, pay-per-use, supplier commissions, access fees, slotting fees, revenue sharing, reselling, and so forth.

4. Resource Planning

The team parceled out resource planning to a number of groups to determine how much of the types of resources—personnel, money, facilities and equipment, information and knowledge— would be required to meet the 2000 model year deadline. Groups determined when each resource would be needed and where it would be deployed. The groups also planned how to ensure that the resources would be available when needed. Specific focus was placed on design of low-cost and simplified hardware; development of the process of installation at the factory; design and negotiation of access to a system of non-geographic-based wireless phone numbers; redesign of the role of the dealer in the marketing process; change of the marketing approach from a *customer acquisition* focus (which would become automatic if OnStar was installed on all vehicles at the factory) to a *customer retention* focus (signing up owners for the OnStar service after their trial period was over); increasing the call center personnel to handle the huge anticipated volume growth; major redesign of the associated information technology applications to handle the business growth; renegotiation of many support contracts with outside vendors to take advantage of economies of scale; and development of a sales force to market OnStar to other vehicle manufacturers. Many additional details had to be identified and worked through to scale up the business in preparation for the increased volume of factory installation.

5. Design of Implementation

The team laid out a timeline specifying who was responsible for the completion of each phase of the implementation by the scheduled deadlines. It also specified the resources that needed to be allocated to each phase in order that the project move forward as planned. Each of the activities previously described had individual timelines that flowed into an overall timeline. The organization was small enough and concentrated enough to allow for regular meetings among the leaders in each area to track progress and to react quickly to deviations from the plan.

6. Design of Controls

Finally, the team designed control mechanisms to monitor the progress of the project. To succeed, each part of the system would have to be brought on line in time to make the 2000 model year deadline. If a scheduled completion of some part of the project did not occur on time, the final deadline would be in jeopardy. Having timely awareness of a slipped schedule would give project managers a chance for corrective action that might meet the ultimate deadline, or minimize the delay it might cause.

THE OUTCOME

This example of idealized design took place in the real world, and in the real world perfection is elusive. The idealized design called for OnStar to be factory installed on all GM models in the 2000 model year. The team did not succeed in full implementation, but it achieved enough success to prove that the concept of the project was feasible and that it would result in a significant increase in the sales of and revenue from OnStar.

Through hard work and determination, they were able to find solutions to launch OnStar as a factory-installed feature in half of GM's portfolio of 54 vehicles for the 2000 model year. Not every vehicle carried OnStar across the board. Some vehicles included OnStar as part of an "option package." Others offered it as an optional feature. A few did include it as a standard feature on each vehicle. Another important decision made was that the marketing divisions of GM would include one year's worth of OnStar service at the time of vehicle sale at no cost to the buyer as part of their differentiation strategy. The team expected that buyers who experienced the value of OnStar would sign up to continue the service. These decisions quickly launched OnStar's growth from 30,000 subscribers in 1998 to more than 3,000,000 subscribers in 2005. Table 1.1 shows the approximate monthly average of service requests by owners.

Table 1.1   Subscriber Interactions in 2005

Approximate Monthly Average

900 automatic airbag notifications per month	20,000 roadside-assistance requests per month
400 stolen vehicle location requests per month	35,000 remote door unlocks per month
13,000 emergency button pushes per month	293,000 route-support calls per month
23,000 GM Goodwrench remote diagnostics	7 million OPC calls per month (OnStar Personal Calling)
4,500 Good Samaritan calls	19 million OPC minutes per month
90 advanced automatic crash notifications	32,000 Virtual Advisor Traffic requests
62,000 Virtual Advisor Weather requests	

In addition, GM announced in 2005 that it would aggressively expand its OnStar delivery to be standard across all retail vehicles by 2007. By that time, GM plans to provide OnStar standard on more than four million new vehicles each year in the United States and Canada. In keeping with its important strategic decision to license OnStar to other automakers, in 2005 OnStar provided service to Lexus, Audi, Acura, VW, Honda, Subaru, and Isuzu. Some of these automakers installed the hardware in their factories before shipping the vehicles to the United States, and others installed it at the port of entry. None required their dealers to do the installation. Neither of the other two Big Three U.S. automakers licensed OnStar.

Many people worked extremely hard to make OnStar the success that it is, but at the beginning, OnStar's future was uncertain. The idealized design framework helped people focus on what the OnStar business "should be now" instead of focusing on the then-existing problems and constraints. It is safe to say that without idealized design, the partial launch in the 2000 model year would have been impossible and the full implementation in the 2007 model year would not be GM's mainstream plan.

SUMMARY

We have described the essential stages for a successful idealized design. We have also described the process in action in the real world. In the real world, some of the gaps between idealized design and today's reality can be filled, and some cannot. Without idealized design, however, most projects that seem impossible today will not be realized tomorrow.

The next chapter explains how, by organizing the design process, to increase the potential for success at each stage of idealized design.

2

Organizing the Process

"Desire must replace existence as a criterion of choice."
—The Authors

In Chapter 1, "The Stages of Idealized Design," we explained the stages involved in a successful idealized design. However, there is more to making the process work for you than just undertaking the process in defined stages. Our experience in assisting managers implement idealized designs has taught us the importance of organizing the process for an optimum outcome.

In this chapter, we describe who should be involved, the frequency and duration of design sessions, facilitators, recording the sessions, procedural rules, constrained and unconstrained designs, consensus design, and conference facilities and equipment.

WHO SHOULD BE INVOLVED?

All those who can be affected by the plan based on an idealized design should preferably be involved in the design process, giving "stakeholders" a sense of participation in the project. This includes those who must eventually decide whether to implement the design-based plan. When the number of those affected is very large—for example, in redesigning a complete business enterprise—it is possible to involve at least some of those not directly participating in preparation of the design. Planners can widely distribute drafts of the design, as they are produced, and solicit the suggestions for improvement from the "missing" stakeholders. It is important to acknowledge those suggestions that are used in subsequent versions of the design. The reasons for not using the others should be revealed to those who have submitted them. In some cases, all of this can be facilitated through use of a firm's intranet, its newsletters, and other internal communications media.

The greater the number of stakeholders who feel some ownership of an idealized design and the plan to implement it, the less resistance there will be, and the more likely it is to be implemented as intended. Participation in the design process often generates an enthusiasm—often even an excitement—that carries over to implementation. Furthermore, those who have participated, however indirectly, tend to become advocates who defend the design and its plan of implementation to others who did not participate in their preparation.

Planners should assure participants that no expertise is required to contribute to preparing an idealized design. Because such a design is concerned with what "ought to be," not what is or what can be, no expertise is relevant. The opinions of all those prospectively affected by a design and its implementation plan are equally valuable. Experts may have a critical role in planning for its realization after the design is produced and accepted. Only at this later stage is "what can be done" relevant.

Our experience leads us to suggest that design teams ought not to consist of more than ten people. Larger groups can be divided into a number of smaller teams working simultaneously or sequentially on the same design. When more than one design team is involved, frequent joint meetings of the groups are desirable (to enable planners to ensure that the broadest range of possible design options is considered). Furthermore, "cheating," borrowing ideas from others, should be encouraged. This enables designs prepared by different groups to converge on a consensus design. If more than one team is involved in producing an idealized design for the same system or problem, the facilitators (described below) should rotate among teams to accelerate the approach to consensus.

When more than one design team is working on the same system or problem, an "executive" team should be given responsibility for drafting a synthesis of the final designs of the various teams. This is the group that, working with the recorder (described subsequently), normally produces the written record of the individual sessions, distributes them, and collects and incorporates suggestions in revised versions of the report they have prepared. We have seen as many as eight groups working simultaneously and five groups working sequentially, all without difficulty. We have never encountered unresolvable problems in synthesizing the designs produced by different groups, but it can be a difficult task.

In those cases where design groups are of necessity larger than ten, some of those present tend to remain silent and not contribute actively to the process. This hesitancy can be overcome by a facilitator or chairperson who calls on the silent ones to express their ideas and opinions. In some cases, the facilitator or chair may have to tactfully ask a voluble participant to participate a little less. A dominant subgroup should never be permitted to take over a design session.

When possible, each design group should contain representatives of each type of stakeholder. For example, in forming two design groups that worked simultaneously to redesign the drug handling system at Johns Hopkins Medical Center, planners included doctors, nurses, administrators, administrative staff members, pharmacologists, pharmacists, and former patients in both groups. In a redesign project of residential roofing at the Certainteed Corporation, planners formed separate groups of architects, general contractors, roofing contractors, material suppliers, and individuals having homes built for themselves. To synthesize the resulting plan, an executive team was formed of company managers and staff personnel, together with personnel from an experienced consulting group.

It is particularly important to include relevant consumers in the design process. It is also important to recognize the difference in many cases between customers and consumers. Customers are the ones who pay for a product or service; consumers are the ones who use it. Although customers should also be included, it is more important to include consumers because unless they want what is produced, no amount of distribution and marketing will make it a commercial success. There are products or services that hardly anyone buys for themselves but which are frequently received as gifts (for example, Rolex watches and Montblanc pens). This is not only true of gifts, but also for household purchases made by the housewife but used by others in the family.

Market surveys may be of some use to a design team but not nearly as valuable as having consumers and customers participate in the design process. Surveys intended to find out what consumers or customers want are seldom useful because customers and consumers often do not know what they want. However, this does not keep them from answering the questions addressed to them in a way that unintentionally misleads. When engaged in the design process, customers and consumers have an opportunity to discover what they want, and they can make discoveries that surprise even themselves.

The idealized designers of the men's store referred to in Chapter 1 were surprised to discover that customers wanted sections of the store organized by size rather than by type of clothing. This discovery excited them as well as the owners of the sponsoring chain. In the idealized design of residential roofing just mentioned that involved multiple groups, it surprised each of them that every group wanted more contrast in shades and colors in residential roofs than was available.

It is especially important for the design team to include those who will eventually decide whether to implement the plan based on the design. The output of the design team should not consist of a recommendation made to others who have not participated in its preparation. Many such recommendations are turned down precisely because the decision maker(s) did not participate in the design and planning process. Therefore, they are usually less committed to the output than those who produced it.

Finally, each team should include either one of its members or an external consultant who acts as a facilitator of the design process. In addition, someone, a member of the team or not, should be designated as a recorder of the progress made. We describe these functions more fully later in this chapter.

FREQUENCY AND DURATION OF DESIGN SESSIONS

The frequency and duration of design sessions depend on the complexity of the object of design and the availability of the participants. In the design of a simple product or process, sessions as short as three hours may suffice. In the redesign of a corporation, as many as five to six full days may be needed.

We have found it difficult to get senior managers into a retreat for five or six days. They generally prefer several shorter sessions (for example, three two-day sessions about a month apart).

When the planning requires more than one session, selected members of the design team should issue a report after each session. Those who draft the report should circulate it and solicit comments and suggestions from as wide a relevant audience as they can reach. Then they should collect the comments and suggestions they have received and draft a revised version of the report in which the comments and suggestions they received are identified. This revised report should then be distributed to members of the whole design team before the next meeting.

After a design and an implementation plan based on it have been completed, the design team should meet for at least a few hours each quarter to monitor progress. They should make any adjustments in the design or plan that appear to be required. They should continue meeting even after implementation is completed to determine whether the expected outcome has been obtained in all respects.

FACILITATORS

The effectiveness of design teams is greatly increased with assistance provided by an experienced facilitator. The facilitator should be thoroughly familiar with the idealized design process and group dynamics. He or she should conduct an initial orientation session in which the design process is described and the scope of the design effort is established. In addition, he or she must establish the rules of procedure and subsequently see to it that these rules are followed. These rules are discussed later in this chapter. In addition, he or she must be able to move disagreements toward consensus, also discussed later.

It is entirely possible that a member of the firm or organization or institution can serve effectively as a facilitator. It is the hope of the authors that this book will give even a neophyte facilitator the tools to guide the design team to a productive conclusion. If the mess is of such size and complexity that the organization believes that it needs experienced help, however, it can call in an outside consultant to work with the design team. No matter who serves as facilitator, it is essential that the entire team accept and respect him or her so that the facilitator can control the team in its discussions.

RECORDING THE SESSIONS

Someone should be designated to record the proceedings of each session with an emphasis on progress made during the session. This person may either be a member of the team or an outsider who is present only to carry out this function (for example, a manager's secretary or administrative assistant). Although the teams normally work with flip charts, these are usually reworked so often as to make them usable only as reminders of what was discussed, not as a record of specific discussions. It is desirable to make a record of agreements, however tentative, and disagreements reached during the session. The recorder can do this most easily on a laptop computer as the session proceeds. It then becomes possible at the end of a session to print out a reasonably good record of what went on during that session.

This printout should be worked over by a designated small executive group to produce the report of the session that is distributed for comments and suggestions. Each report should have an introductory section in which the nature of idealized design is described to readers who have not participated in the process. Chapter 1 of this book can be adapted for this purpose.

PROCEDURAL RULES

The procedural rules that apply to the sessions should be described at the orientation session, and repeated during the design sessions as often as necessary. Repetition is usually necessary because the rules are difficult to follow for inexperienced team members and the discussion can easily digress into nonproductive avenues. The facilitator is responsible for enforcing the rules. There are three rules of procedure:

1. **The System Was Destroyed Last Night**

   It is difficult initially for members of the design team to leave what currently exists completely behind. They tend to evaluate design proposals in terms of feasibility in the current system. They also feel obliged to carry a great deal of the current system forward with them because they see no way to change it. It is not necessary to see how to change the existing system to approve a proposal. Individual team members may also be reacting to proposals in terms of the effect on their current positions and status and may be trying to preserve their present jobs. All these tendencies must be denied. This is part of the facilitator's job.

   Characteristics of the current system may be brought forward into the idealized design but only because the team decides that they are wanted in the design, not because they currently exist. *Desire must replace existence as a criterion of choice.* For example, a company may want to remain in its current location and continue to produce its current products even though it may want to expand production considerably. On the other hand, if the design team wants to change the location, the difficulty of doing so is not acceptable as a reason for excluding it from the design.

It is sometimes necessary to continually repeat that implementability is not an acceptable criterion for approving a design proposal. The final design does not have to be capable of being implemented. But approximations to it do have to be implementable.

2. **Equal Participation by Everyone**

In some teams, one or more members may tend to monopolize the discussion. The facilitator has a responsibility to stop or prevent this from occurring. He or she can call on the silent members to express their opinions, thereby drawing them out and involving them in the discussion. A discussion outside the group with the offenders often works to help keep them in control. Sometimes more drastic steps must be taken, as occurred in the following example.

The top management of Clark Equipment Corporation conducted an idealized design exercise directed at redesigning the firm. Because of the magnitude of the project, the CEO at the time, James Rinehart, participated. He was brilliant. Consequently, most of his subordinates waited to hear his opinion on an each issue raised before they expressed their own. These seldom departed significantly from Rinehart's. The facilitator asked Rinehart to hold back his opinions until other members of the team had expressed theirs. Rinehart apologized and said he would comply.

But he didn't. When there was a silence while others thought about the issue raised, he could not constrain himself. He burst out with his ideas. The facilitator then asked him to leave the room, explaining that the group was not operating as a team but as a claque. The facilitator also said that if Rinehart did not leave, he would. This shocked Rinehart, but he reluctantly left the room. The meeting then proceeded as it should. After about a half hour, Rinehart put his head through the doorway and asked whether he could return. The facilitator said he could if he sat in a corner and kept quiet. He did so.

After a while, he raised his hand and asked whether he could return to the table. The facilitator said he could but he could not speak. Again, he complied. After a short time, he asked whether he could express an opinion. The facilitator said he could but only after the others on the team had expressed theirs. Rinehart complied. He became an important member of that team and eventually took over its chairmanship, a role he filled extremely well.

3. **Positive Contributions Only**

Some team members tend to find something wrong with any proposal made. The rule should be that if a member of the team finds a suggested design feature undesirable he or she must offer an alternative that he or she prefers. In other words, fix it, do not tear it down. This rule ensures an accumulative effect of many suggestions and ideas. Repeated negative comments tend to put a lid on suggestions, particularly "wild and creative" ones.

CONSTRAINED AND UNCONSTRAINED DESIGNS

Team members should first produce a constrained idealized design. The constrained design is limited to the entity over which the team has, or has access to, control. Therefore, if the team is established by a division or department head, the design should be restricted to the division or department. When this is complete and the plan for its implementation has been prepared, the team should formulate an unconstrained design. In planning an unconstrained design, the team moves its focus up one level in the organization or institution from the constrained design. For example, a constrained design of a department would be followed up by an unconstrained design of the division that contains the department.

The unconstrained design should include changes in the containing organization or system over which the team has some influence but no control. These changes should modify the containing system but only in ways that benefit the design of the contained system. Thus, the unconstrained design of the division should facilitate the constrained design of the department. The team should then circulate the unconstrained design among those who control the containing system in the hope that it will induce a larger idealized design effort. It frequently does.

For example, Kodak had three computing centers, the smallest in corporate headquarters. The two larger ones were in the film and apparatus divisions. The head of the headquarters unit, Henry Pfendt, initiated and participated in an idealized design of his unit. When this design was implemented, the effectiveness of the unit improved significantly and conspicuously. It was conspicuous even to the heads of the other two computing centers. The design team then assumed it could combine all three computing centers and produced a corresponding idealized design. This was circulated within the other computing centers.

As a result, an idealized design team involving members of all three computing centers was formed to produce a design of an integrated center and determine whether it was desirable. The team that prepared this design, including heads of all three computing centers, recommended that its design be implemented by corporate headquarters. It was. The resulting combination delivered more useful information at a lower cost than the three original units had.

The telecommunications function at Kodak was similarly divided into three units. Observing the positive result of the computer project, the unit serving corporate headquarters initiated an idealized redesign of itself. It, too, then produced an unconstrained design incorporating the other two telecommunication units. A combined design team was then formed. It eventually proposed to corporate headquarters that an integrated telecommunication unit be created. It was also approved and implemented. Again, there was a gain in the quality of telecommunications at a lower cost.

Then the centralized computing center and the centralized telecommunication centers formed a joint design team and produced a design of a corporate technology center that incorporated both functions. This design was proposed to corporate headquarters, which accepted and implemented it. Even this was not the end of the story. Several joint ventures with appropriate companies followed that utilized idealized design to coordinate the activities of both organizations. Finally, top management set up an idealized design to study a possible joint venture with an outside vendor to provide these services at even lower cost and higher quality. This, too, was implemented, and the joint venture with IBM created an organization that provided career paths for its professionals that were not available at Kodak. This shows that unconstrained idealized design can lead to significant changes and improvements in successively larger containing systems.

CONSENSUS DESIGN

The design of the whole need not be taken to be the best possible by each member of the design team. They must agree, however, that it is better than retaining the status quo. This means that the designers need not agree that every design element is best, but only that the design of the whole is better than what is currently available. Nevertheless, the closer the team comes to consensus along the way, the more likely they are to achieve it in the end.

At one point, Jim Rinehart, CEO of Clark Equipment Corporation, had eight groups of managers work simultaneously on an idealized redesign of the corporation's structure. When each team had completed its design, they were brought together to present these designs to the whole group. Each group had used flip charts in making their presentations. These were taped to the front wall of the room. After all the teams had made their presentations, Rinehart asked the assembly how many thought the first design was best. About one eighth of the attendees raised their hands. The same occurred for the next two presentations. At this point, Rinehart turned to the consultant whom the company had used for the design process and said that he could not even get a majority, let alone complete agreement. The consultant told him he was asking the wrong question. Rinehart then invited him to ask it. The consultant rose and asked the assembly the following. "You have the following choice. Either I pick one of these designs randomly, or we keep the current corporate structure. How many favor my making the choice?" Every hand went up.

This forced the group to realize that they preferred any of the designs to what they then had, and they returned to the task and produced a synthesized design that was accepted by consensus.

It has been our experience that consensus is reached even on most design elements. For the relatively few for which it is not initially obtained, there are measures that tend to produce it. First, most apparent differences of opinion are based on a difference about what the underlying facts are. In such cases, the difference can be resolved by finding out what the facts actually are in a way that the differing parties agree to. They must also agree to comply with the outcome.

In another case, a company had 12 manufacturing sites. Division and top managers could not agree on whether the chief maintenance engineer in each plant should report to the plant manager or to the corporation's vice president of engineering. All the relevant managers agreed on a test in which the 12 plants were divided randomly into 2 groups of 6 each. In one group, the chief maintenance engineer reported to the plant manager, in the other to the vice president. The test revealed that neither was clearly the best and that results varied by plant. Therefore, everyone agreed to leave the decision to the individual plants.

In some cases, a test cannot be designed to reveal what the team wants to know, or cannot be done in the time available. Here a fallback is required. The CEO of a company that was an early user of idealized design developed a way to handle this. When it was clear that there was not an obvious resolution of a difference of opinion, the CEO asked each participant to summarize his or her position in a few minutes. This revealed sharply the members' differences. Then the chairman said what he would decide if agreement among team members was not reached. He then went back around the room calling on everyone to restate their positions, or revised positions. Now if two people disagreed with each other, they in effect agreed with the chairman because his opinion would then prevail. In this case, the participants changed their positions enough for there to arise a consensus design among team members that prevailed over the chairman's "threatened" design. In other cases, in our experience, when consensus was not reached, the participants had to settle for the chair's design. Whatever the outcome, when this procedure has been occasionally used, the team members have always thought it was a fair way to resolve differences that had to be resolved.

CONFERENCE FACILITIES AND EQUIPMENT

Design sessions should be held in a room that is large enough for the team but not too large. In a room that is too large, members tend to wander around during discussions. The participants should be seated so that each can see every other one. Long narrow tables do not serve well. Circular tables or tables arranged in a U shape work better. Each participant should have a surface on which to rest papers. Neither should there be a distracting view of the outdoors nor windows that allow blinding sunshine to enter the room. Use blinds to block glare.

Water should be within the reach of each team member. Snacks, coffee, and other beverages should be available in the room on a table off to the side or in the rear end of the room.

At least two easels and pads, together with a variety of markers, should be available and located so that everyone in the room can see them. There should be enough wall space on which to tape charts that have been completed. This enables the team to be able to see what has been covered. It is also useful, if flip charts are not available, to have a projector for transparencies available, together with a screen, blank acetate sheets, and appropriate markers. A third possibility is to have an LCD projector and networked computers so that participants can work collaboratively on the elements of the design. Such an arrangement permits team members to work together even if they are not all in the same room—as happens in some organizations.

It should be possible to lock the room(s) used so that notes and personal belongings can be left in it when the room is not in use. Use of telephones in the sessions should not be acceptable. Nor should outside interruptions for phone calls be permitted. There should be a facility for receiving messages to be delivered to participants when the group is not in session. Restrooms should be easily accessible.

If the sessions are held at a retreat, facilities should be available during off hours for participants to gather in small groups for informal discussions. The facilitator(s) should be available for such discussions.

Dress should be informal.

SUMMARY

All those who hold a stake in a design should be able to participate in preparing it. There is no limit to the number of stakeholders who can be given an opportunity to have an input to the process. The greater the percentage of each stakeholder group that has participated, the greater the chance of a successful implementation of the plan derived from the design.

Design sessions can be greatly facilitated by one who has had experience with many such design sessions. In addition, he or she should be acknowledged by the design team members as an authority on the design process. It is critical that the facilitator be acknowledged as an authority by the one(s) who must make the decision to implement or not.

Records of the sessions should be widely circulated and discussed to encourage as much participation as possible in producing the design. The design produced initially should be confined to the entity over which members of the design team (or, less preferably, its sponsor) has control. After completion of this design and partial completion of implementation of the plan based on it, the team should produce an idealized redesign of the next-level system that contains the one designed. It should focus on changes in the containing system that would improve the design of the contained system.

Acceptance of the final design should be by consensus. The agreement should not necessarily be that the design is the best possible, but that it is better than the system it is intended to replace. Consensus on individual design elements is not necessary but desirable.

The facilities in which the sessions are held should be as unobtrusive as possible. Participants should feel comfortable and "at home" in them. To the extent possible, there should be opportunities for informal discussions among subgroups of the design team. The facilitator(s) should be available for these.

The following procedural rules should be kept in mind throughout the sessions and reinforced frequently:

- **Keep constantly in mind that the current system (object or process) was destroyed last night.** This assumption is critically important because referring to the existing entity restrains designers from thinking about what they really want. Their minds tend to get caught up in the constraints inherent in the current entity and its environment.

- **Focus on what you would like to have if you could have whatever you want ideally, not on what you do not want.** The intention is to get the participants to shoot for the stars, not hold back. The facilitator can tell them they can always return to reality when the design is completed.

- **Don't worry about availability of resources required to implement what you want or whether it is even possible to implement it.** This is important because skepticism about whether the design will or can be implemented holds people back from letting their imagination soar. Furthermore, breakthrough thinking frequently makes resources available that previously were not. There are few exciting ideas that cannot attract the requisite investment.

- **If you disagree with someone else's design idea, do not criticize it; improve on it.** This does two things: It makes discussion accumulative, and it avoids excessive intrusion of egos into the discussion. This rule, probably more than any of the others, requires continuous reinforcement during the sessions.

- **Keep the system's larger containing system intact during the initial design.** Change it in the later unconstrained version but then only in ways that improve the first design. The containing system includes the system, contexts, processes, settings, and so on in which the entity being designed is normally located. This assumption enables participants to retain a focus on the purpose of each type of design.

The idealized design process should, above all, be fun. If it isn't, something is seriously wrong. Rather than continue, stop and redesign the process. Then resume.

A successful idealized design depends on more than planners' knowing the stages of the process (Chapter 1) and how it should be organized (this chapter). Careful preparation in the initial stages is essential to ensuring a successful outcome. The next chapter deals with this topic.

3

Preparing for an Idealized Design Process

"Blount County to Lose Alcoa Plant and 2,300 Jobs"
—Headline in simulated edition of a local newspaper

Given the high stakes involved in any idealized design, it is essential to prepare carefully for the project and to begin the initial stages correctly. In this chapter, we describe the steps to follow when preparing to conduct an idealized design of an organization or institution. Together with the stages described in Chapter 1, "The Stages of Idealized Design," the organization of the process described in Chapter 2, "Organizing the Process," and the preparation discussed in this chapter, we provide readers with a comprehensive understanding of the process of undertaking a successful idealized design in virtually any organization or institution.

Preparing to conduct an idealized design of an organization or institution requires the following three steps:

1. Formulating the mess
2. Preparing a mission statement
3. Specifying the properties desired in the design

Although an idealized design can be carried out without having taken any of these steps, our experience is that quality of the outcome of the design process is, generally, significantly enhanced by these steps.

FORMULATING THE MESS

We explained the process of formulating the mess in Chapter 1. In this chapter, we examine the process in more detail. You will recall that the mess is the future the organization or institution would experience if it were to continue doing what it is currently doing and its environment were to become exactly what planners expect it to be.

Of course, the assumptions of unchanging behavior and perfect forecasting are false, but they have an important function here. No organization or institution would go to the trouble of planning unless it expected to change its behavior in the future. And no organization believes its forecasts of the future are errorless. Therefore, it would be a mistake for an organization to assume that a projection of its future using these two assumptions would be an accurate forecast of that future. However, this is not the intention of the projection. The projection is intended to reveal the seeds of self-destruction in the current behavior and expectations of the organization. Any organization that does not adapt to changes in its environment, even ones that are expected, is bound to suffer, if not self-destruct. This much is known beforehand. What is not known is how it would suffer or self-destruct under the assumed conditions. Revealing this is tantamount to revealing the system's Achilles' heel, its point of vulnerability.

An example of an impossible future was revealed when the fourth district of the Federal Reserve Bank in Cleveland formulated the mess confronting it in the early 1970s. It concluded that if the number of checks cleared per year continued to increase as it had in the past 20 years, more check clearers would be required than could be provided even if every adult in the United States were to become a check clearer. The critical question raised by this projection was this: Would this situation be avoided by what was done *to* the bank or *by* what the bank did? The bank instituted an idealized design directed at determining what the bank could do to prevent such a future. The design team produced a plan for the electronic funds transfer system, now ubiquitous in banking.

Another example involved a successful insurance company, one that issued only large life insurance policies, therefore only to wealthy people who were generally financially sophisticated. Most of its policies had been in place for many years and allowed the insured to borrow on their policies at a rate fixed at the time the policy was issued. When the company realized that it was probably losing money on these loans, it formulated the mess that revealed just how much it was losing and why. It became clear that the rates at which money could be invested were much higher than the rate at which the insured could borrow on their policies from the company. An increasing number of those insured were borrowing from the company and investing the borrowed money at a much higher rate than they paid for borrowing it. This required the insurance company to borrow the money required to lend to its policyholders. The rate at which it could borrow money was much higher than the rate at which it was required by the terms of its policies to lend to its policyholders. The result was a negative cash flow. To terminate this problem, the company organized an ideal design that converted policies with fixed borrowing rates to ones with variable rates. In return, the company increased the value of the policies affected. Now policyholders were not able to borrow money from the company at lower rates than they could obtain from investing it, but they held policies with higher face values. This maintained the company's profitability and stabilized its cash flow.

An example of the formulation of a mess in a law firm illustrates how the mess can be defined in "soft"—that is, nonquantifiable—terms. In 1970, LL&D (a pseudonym of a Philadelphia law firm) was a 53-lawyer firm operating from one office with an annual income of $3.5 million. By 1980, LL&D was a $20 million operation with 54 partners, 74 associates, a supporting staff of more than 200 people, and offices in three cities. The transition had, for the most part, seemed to be successful. Many law firms going through the same era of expansion have not fared as well. Several have closed down or broken up into splinter groups. Others have become bureaucratized institutions in which the lawyers have lost personal satisfaction in the practice of law.

LL&D's managing partners realized that its transformation, despite its apparent success, had created new sets of problems and challenges that could lead to the same fate as some of its less-successful competitors if not properly addressed. Their projections showed that if trends at the time continued, average partnership share would be halved in ten years and would decline to zero by the year 2001.

The strength of the firm at the time was in the quality of its members as a professional group and the high morale and comradeship among partners. Therefore, despite the preceding indications, the firm was not facing an immediate crisis or threat. Much of what they saw was of a long-term nature. If left unattended, the problems of today could generate a crisis 10 years to 15 years in the future. They therefore decided in 1983 to undertake an idealized design to avert the looming crisis.

In planning for the idealized design, the team formulated the mess in many elements. Considered separately, none of the elements of the mess posed major difficulties. It was the reinforcing effect of the elements on each other that could become significant in the long run. The elements with which they had to contend included the following:

- There is a growing feeling among partners that the firm is becoming too much like a "business." There is a fear of loss of collegiality and cohesiveness. Some partners maintain that productivity, cost control, and strategic planning are not what lawyers are trained to do or should be doing. Others argue that this is a necessary evil of our times and the firm has no other choice if it is to survive the eighties. The dichotomous formulation of options leads to factionalization and a choice between unsatisfactory alternatives. This is a classical dilemma faced by many professional organizations. The solution lies in the creation of an organization capable of survival in the face of the realities of the market, while at the same time maintaining the essential characteristics of a professional group.

- The partnership has not found an optimal decision-making mechanism. The firm needs efficient and decisive leadership, but the very nature of a partnership cannot tolerate a "dictator." Absence of an autocratic leadership deprives many partners of the luxury of a single locus of blame for the firm's shortcomings. Partners do want to participate in the decision-making process and be involved in shaping the future of the firm, but they do not want to waste time in dozens of committees. Time spent on management is considered nonproductive.

- Communication is breaking down among major parts of the firm. Partners have different visions of the future direction of the firm, and few are aware of the firm's activities other than in their own group. The result is a growing feeling among the partnership of functioning as aggregates of departments and individuals rather than belonging to a synergistic whole system. This defies the very logic of forming partnerships.

- These conditions lead to a high turnover rate, low productivity, and high operating costs, which further exacerbate the major economic problem of the firm: expenses rising faster than income.

- Decreasing partnership shares create an atmosphere of shrinking business that can only lead to intensification of these problems. Morale will eventually decline, and the firm will lose its ability to attract high-quality professionals. LL&D, therefore, will lose its most valuable asset. It will then be only a matter of time before the firm disappears.

Good mess formulations such as these convince the idealized design team that there will be a crisis unless some radical changes are made. The team should take the formulation seriously and make sure their design precludes the future projected in the mess formulation.

THE MESS-FORMULATING TEAM

We recommend that the mess-formulating team differ from the idealized design team. Ideally, it should consist of three to five young professionals who have been with the organization or institution fewer than five years and who are considered to have high potential. The reason for using professionals who are relatively new to the organization is that they are more likely than old-timers to be critical of the organization and aware of its short-comings.

Our experience is that the team members are usually expected to spend about half their time on this task, spending the rest on their normal jobs. They should not feel their security is threatened in any way. In fact, they normally feel privileged rather than threatened. The team is given access to any data and information it requires.

The mess-formulating team normally begins its work before the idealized design team begins its work, and presents its findings to the idealized design team. Before an idealized design is considered to be finished, the design team must test it against the mess formulation to be sure the mess is averted by the design. This determination is normally made in a joint meeting of the mess-formulating and idealized design teams. When both teams are assured that the design can avert the mess, the mess-formulating team generally reviews the idealized design critically and makes inputs to the design team's deliberations.

PRESENTATION OF THE MESS

The success or failure of the idealized design project to get under way may hinge on the manner in which the mess is presented to upper management, whose approval is probably necessary for the project to proceed. Mess-formulating teams often develop ingenious ways to present their results. For example, at Metropolitan Life, the team prepared a video of a simulated evening-news broadcast on a major network. It was datelined several years in the future and included an announcement of the bankruptcy of the company. The newscaster told how the company got into the mess it was in, using conclusions developed by the mess-formulating team. This presentation was played to senior managers and executives. They were shocked by its realism. Not surprisingly, the idealized design that followed averted the history described in the broadcast.

The mess-formulation team at Alcoa's Tennessee Operations developed a similar strategy in 1979. The team arranged for a special issue of the local newspaper—dated April 1, 1984—that announced the closing of the installation. The copies of the paper were intended only for members of the idealized design team, but one copy got out. It was so realistic that a group of workers overlooked the date of the simulated issue and organized a protest of the closing. Here are excerpts from the story in the simulated issue of the *Maryville Times:*

Blount County to Lose Alcoa Plant and 2,300 Jobs

Economic disaster hit the Maryville town area yesterday.

The largest population center of Blount County lost 2,300 jobs and a substantial portion of the tax base when Alcoa announced it would close its fabricating plant operations in October of 1984.

The full extent of the closing will not be felt for months but the severity was apparent yesterday.

The $1,300,000 that Alcoa paid in property taxes is 60% of the township's taxes. Alcoa spends $400,000,000 a year in Tennessee . . .

A spokesman for the company denied that the closing is related to the current strike that has closed the Tennessee Operations down for the past six weeks . . .

The spokesman said that the energy costs and a metal shortage contributed to the decision to close. "The cost of energy to smelt aluminum has risen 200% in the past four years and, consequently, most of the metal ingots are used for manufacturing high-profit items by other divisions of Alcoa."

Most of Alcoa's smelting and manufacturing takes place outside the U.S., where energy and labor costs are significantly lower . . .

The closing will throw 600 management and 1,700 production workers out of jobs, in addition to those already laid off . . .

Alcoa Tennessee reported a loss of $10 million in the first quarter of its fiscal year. This was mostly attributed to the current protracted strike.

An anonymous source close to Alcoa said that the Tennessee operation had been in trouble for a long time. Management and the union were unable to work together on problems of productivity and competitiveness because of the high level of distrust, the source indicated. As a result, the corporate headquarters have invested little capital in Tennessee.

At the time this mess was formulated, the Tennessee operations were scheduled for closure five years out, in December 1984. The idealized design that was completed after the mess had been formulated called for a number of changes that were made in the operations and the way they were managed. The union realized that its survival at the plant depended on finding ways to cooperate with management to increase efficiency and lower costs. The design enabled Alcoa Tennessee to become profitable once again. Consequently, corporate headquarters retracted its decision to close the operations and made a large investment in modernizing its facilities and equipment. It became one of the most productive sheet aluminum producers in the world. Its creative presentation of the mess by a fictitious edition of a local newspaper was the catalyst in this transformation through idealized design.

PREPARING A MISSION STATEMENT

Most mission statements consist of platitudes, "motherhood" statements expressed with pomp and circumstance. They provide no guidance to the organizations to which they are supposed to apply and no inspiration to their stakeholders. A group of corporate executives was recently shown a set of corporate mission statements, including their own, with corporate identity removed. Few could correctly pick out the one belonging to their organization. These are not the mission statements with which we are concerned here. Our experience is that even the best of these prior existing mission statements seldom prove useful in the idealized design process.

A mission statement should formulate the organization's ideals in a way that inspires those who can participate in its pursuit. It should do so in a way that makes it possible to evaluate the progress toward these ideals. Without this possibility, a mission statement is useless. The statement should reflect the uniqueness of the organization and should be relevant to all stakeholders, not only to those who formulated it or approved its formulation. In addition, it should do three things.

First, it should identify the means by which the organization or institution intends to carry out its function in society. In the case of a corporation—whose societal function, we argue, is to produce and distribute wealth—it should identify the business with which it wants to carry out this function. This is not necessarily the business it is currently in. Most businesses identified in *effective* mission statements turn out to be major extensions of the current business. For example, we worked with a company that produces tapes of various kinds (audio, visual, and packaging) whose mission statement said that it wanted to be in the "sticking business." This declared a generic interest in joining any two things together. Clearly, this suggested new extensions and adaptations of its current product line.

In the case of a brewing company that was also in the entertainment business, its mission statement articulated its desire to produce products and services that enabled people to spend their leisure time in more satisfying ways. The company's then-current products and services addressed adults in their middle years. However, it is the senior and junior parts of the population that have the most leisure time, and their products therefore missed an important part of their intended market. The mission statement served to focus their attention on segments of the market they had not addressed and to consider a whole range of possible products and services they had not previously considered.

Second, a mission statement should excite and inspire those to whom it applies. For example, a Mexican company stated that it wanted to demonstrate that a publicly owned company could contribute significantly to national and local development. It was planning to locate a major new facility in a less-developed part of Mexico. It promised "to promote the region by enhancing its quality of life with special emphasis on creative and recreational aspects, and to do so in a way favoring local autonomy and self-sufficiency." This excited locals from whom most of the employees would come.

ALAD, the Latin American division of the Armco steel company, which integrated eight national subsidiaries, formulated a mission statement designed to challenge its employees to achieve lofty goals:

> To contribute significantly to the development of Latin America and to the viability of Armco Inc. by:
>
> Producing and/or marketing products and services that provide the most cost-effective solutions to current and emerging needs of Latin American industries.
>
> Providing conditions of work and a quality of work life to all its employees that will help them to achieve their personal aspirations.
>
> Developing technologies that are particularly suited to the social, economic, and cultural conditions of the countries in Latin America, and enable them to compete worldwide.

> Demonstrating that a multi-national company with roots in many Latin American countries can contribute significantly more to the development of each than can an organization centered in one country only.

This statement served to unite nationals of different countries, several of which traditionally had hostile relations. Although several of these countries did not permit the flow of currency between them, the ideal design the company undertook legally got around this limitation as well as constraints on the exportation of dollars to the United States by the creation of a trading company.

Third, a mission statement should formulate the function that the organization or institution wants to have for each type of stakeholder: employees, customers and consumers, suppliers, investors, and the public. For example, a major American automobile manufacturing company stated that it wanted to enable employees who left the organization voluntarily for reasons other than retirement to be more employable than when they joined it. In this way, it committed itself to the personal development of virtually every employee. In addition, it said it would protect their health and safety and strive to be in the vanguard of corporate democracy so as to encourage participatory decision making and entrepreneurial activity. Finally, it would develop a culture within which every employee could develop a proper balance between work and family life.

For its customers and consumers, another company committed to providing products and services of quality and reliability not equaled or surpassed by any of its competitors. For its stockholders, it said it would deliver economic performance superior to that of its peers and cause the equities markets to recognize this, thereby delivering superior total returns. It also committed itself to providing its suppliers with predictable demand for their goods and services together with the information required for them to meet the company's expectations, and to allow them to participate in making decisions that affect them. Finally, it would contribute positively and demonstrably to the quality of life and standard of living in every community in which the company had operations.

A meaningful mission statement is necessary, but not sufficient, in preparing for a successful idealized design.

SPECIFYING THE PROPERTIES DESIRED IN THE DESIGN

Before beginning the process of idealized design, the design team should draft a list specifying the properties they want to include in the idealized design. These will be specific to the organization or institution because there is no list of specifications that applies to every type of organization. However, we think that answers to the questions in the following list—applicable primarily to corporations—should suggest the kinds of properties of other types of organizations that specifications should include:

- What materials, goods, and services should the organization or institution provide? How and by whom should these be supplied? How should the requirements for them be determined and processed? Should servicing of the company's outputs be provided?

- How should inputs to the organization or institution be converted and into what products and/or services? How should the processing be organized and managed: autocratically or democratically, or some mixture of these? What type of structure should the organization have? How should the internal economy be managed: centrally controlled or by an internal market? How flexible should the organization be? Should organizational learning, knowledge creation, and adaptation be organized; and, if so, how? To what extent should the company be involved in the development of new products and services?

- How should the company's products or services be distributed and marketed? Where? Who should constitute the target customers and consumers?

- What should be done to promote the health, safety, and morale of the work force? How should the organization or institution relate to each of the communities in which it has operations? What should its environmental policies be?

This list is not exhaustive. However, we have found that there is seldom any difficulty in getting design team members to identify properties they want in the design. They generally find this much easier than creating a design that incorporates the properties they specify.

The following examples demonstrate the variety in form and content of specifications prepared by different types of organizations. The first is a department in a major corporation, and the other is an organization concerned with the way that health care is delivered to pets (or "companion animals"). Our hope is that you will be encouraged by these examples to think of similar specifications for your own organization or institution, whatever it may be.

A set of specifications were identified in planning an idealized design for the "think tank" at General Motors in 1998. This is the Corporate Strategy and Knowledge Development Department, and beginning in the early 1990s it was responsible for a number of strategic initiatives that helped GM avert a financial crisis at the time. Its director, Vincent P. Barabba, is the source for this example. The department had achieved considerable success, but its members realized that it could accomplish even more if it could embark on an idealized design. The following are just some of the specifications identified by the design team.

■ **What products and services ought to be provided?**

Identify strategic opportunities and threats and share them with appropriate decision makers. Where action is not taken, determine reasons, and make them the basis for research and action.

Collect internally and externally generated data, information, knowledge, understanding, and wisdom relevant to GM (not otherwise collected in GM), and make them (1) available in a timely fashion, (2) easily accessible, and (3) in the form wanted by those in GM who can benefit from their use.

Develop and facilitate continual improvements in GM's decision-making and implementation processes.

Encourage and facilitate creativity and innovation within GM.

■ **Who should be served?**

All internal decision makers, their supporting analysts, product and process designers, on a global basis.

A quite different list of specifications was identified when the Companion Animal and Family Health Council began a study of the North American Companion-Animal Healthcare System in the early 1990s. Its purpose was to look at the way that health care is delivered to pets and to produce an ideal design for the system. At an early stage, the design team specified an exhaustive list of desired properties of the final design, some of which follow:

■ The key driver of all professional activities (practices, education, research) should be a concern for the pet's and owner's well-being and their interrelationship. Animal health care should emphasize wellness and prevention of disease as well as treatment of disease and disability management.

■ An ideal system of companion animal medicine would consist of an integrated system of primary-, secondary-, and tertiary-care providers and centers. The secondary- and tertiary-care providers would fulfill a supportive role to the primary-care provider, who would be the pivotal entry point for the veterinary consumer.

■ There should be 24-hour access to emergency care for pets. The system should make appropriate use of professionals, paraprofessionals, and support staff.

■ The veterinary profession should recognize two pressing problems: a safety net for indigent pet owners and affordable pet health care.

■ Medical care should be based on current scientific knowledge. Research is needed to continually update that knowledge.

■ The remuneration for animal health-care providers should be commensurate with the level of education and professional dedication required. Primary-, secondary-, and tertiary-care centers should be profitable.

SUMMARY

Preparation of an idealized design benefits from preparing three things.

First, where the design is to involve an organization or institution, the mess confronting it should be formulated. The mess is the future the organization would be in if it were to continue doing what it is currently doing despite expected changes in its environment. That is, it is the future that will occur if it fails to adapt even to expected changes. This reveals the seeds of the organization's self-destruction. It serves as a checklist against which to evaluate a subsequent design. The design must avoid the destruction depicted in the mess.

Second, the design team should formulate a mission statement, unless the organization or institution already has a meaningful one (as described in this chapter). Such a statement should identify the function of the organization or institution in the larger system that contains it, and the means by which it intends to perform that function. It should be an inspiring statement that reveals the uniqueness of the organization or institution involved. Finally, it should state the obligation of the organization to each type of its stakeholders.

Third, the design team should specify the properties to be included in the ideal design of the organization or institution. This should precede the design stage to ensure that the design meets all the properties required of it.

This ends Part I. The three chapters in this part have provided a comprehensive guide to the process of idealized design that can apply to a wide variety of organizations and institutions. In Part II, we describe idealized design in a variety of specific applications and organizations. Depending on your interest, or organizational setting, you might want to skip to chapters that meet your immediate needs. We hope, however, that you will read the three chapters in Part III. Those chapters describe how idealized design can be applied to some of the major challenges in the world today.

IDEALIZED DESIGN: APPLICATIONS— THE PROCESS IN ACTION

4

Business Enterprises

"Management is doing things right, leadership is doing the right things."
—Peter F. Drucker

Although idealized design can be applied to a wide variety of organizations and institutions, it is not a one-size-fits-all process. Business enterprises, operating in competitive marketplaces and requiring a stream of profits for continued viability, present special challenges to planning teams. This chapter describes the application of the idealized design process in two companies in different industries to show some of the common design elements in business enterprises.

Before proceeding, however, we want to add an important qualification. This is not the only chapter relevant to business enterprises. Here we deal with large-scale idealized designs. However, the process works equally well in new product and process innovation, business problem solving, and facilities and site location, all of which are treated in later chapters.

There are two types of conditions under which corporations and other commercial enterprises might engage in idealized design on a large scale. One condition is a currently successful company whose leader is excited intellectually by the process and wants to try it because he or she thinks it will give the organization a significant competitive advantage. Or such a leader may wonder whether some possible change in the company's business environment might endanger its long-term viability. Our example is an energy company that was doing well but was concerned about possible changes in its market environment that might threaten its future.

The other condition is a company facing a crisis here and now that threatens its continued existence. Sometimes its managers have tried a variety of measures that have not worked. Under these conditions, they become desperate and willing to try anything, however slim they think the chances of success are. Almost as a last resort they turn to the process of idealized design. Our experience is that such efforts have usually been successful in averting the collapse of the enterprise. The example of this condition is a national supermarket chain in a state of decline within which idealized design was applied to a local area and turned it around. This example also demonstrates that idealized designs can be, and have been, applied to *parts* of organizations as well as to organizations as a whole; for example, to subsidiaries, divisions, departments, and even relatively small units in corporations. Whenever a design of a part has been prepared, it has usually been followed by an effort to affect the larger organization or system of which it is a part, as described in the example.

First, we look at the design features generally common to most business enterprises.

COMMON CONTENT OF DESIGNS

Our experience is that certain issues arise repeatedly in the many applications of idealized design to for-profit enterprises. Therefore, there is considerable overlapping content in the designs produced in the planning process.

The idealized designs of companies and corporations have normally included the following:

- Products and/or services it would supply
- Management style: the internal political system
- The internal economy
- Organizational learning and adaptation
- Human resource development
- Communications, internal and external
- External relations
- Equipment and facilities

This list is only meant to be suggestive. It can and does vary for different types of enterprises.

REPETITIVE DESIGN FEATURES

We will look more closely at several of the key features that we think are crucial to the success of the idealized design process. These are the *internal political system,* the organization of its *internal economy,* the nature of its *organization and structure,* and the way the organization intends to institute a process of *learning and adaptation* to changing internal and external conditions.

THE INTERNAL POLITICAL SYSTEM

Politics has to do with the way power is distributed in an organization. The internal political system of most enterprises is autocratic. However, for a number of reasons, there is increasing pressure on them to democratize. For example, the educational level of the work force has been rising continually. An increasing percentage of its members can do their jobs better than their bosses can. Under this condition, management by the exercise of authority, power over subordinates, becomes decreasingly effective. It becomes necessary for managers who want to increase productivity to exercise influence, power to, rather than authority over highly educated and capable subordinates. When this became apparent in the autocratically governed Soviet Union, its movement toward democratization, glasnost, became necessary. (Unfortunately, its current trend seems to be back toward autocracy.)

An organization is democratic to the extent that (1) everyone affected by a decision can participate directly or indirectly through representation they select in making that decision. (2) Everyone in a position of authority over others taken separately is subject to the authority of the others taken collectively. Power flows from the bottom up, not from the top down. (3) People can do whatever they want provided that it does not affect others; if it can affect others it requires their approval. (Children, future generations, those mentally ill, the infirm, and prisoners require special treatment.)

The design of a "circular organization" or "democratic hierarchy" has been developed to meet the requirements of a democracy. In this design, every manager is provided with a board that minimally consists of that manager, his or her immediate superior, and his or her immediate subordinates. Boards can add other members under conditions that they specify. They have six functions:

- To prepare plans and policies for the units whose board it is
- To coordinate plans and policies made at the level below it
- To integrate plans and policies with higher and lower level plans and policies
- To make quality-of-work-life decisions affecting board members
- To suggest ways of improving performance of the manager and his/her subordinates
- To control occupancy of managers' positions

To understand how boards work,[1] we look at how they were treated in the idealized design of Energetics, a company that produces, distributes, and markets natural gas. In April 1999, Energetics' total enterprise value was $39 million. At the end of 2003, it was $210 million. Its market capitalization in 1999 (adjusted for a reverse stock split) was $17 million. At the end of 2003, it was $165 million. In 2004, Energetics was acquired by another energy company at a considerable profit to its owners. The company's significant improvement was due in part to its planning activity, especially its idealized design.

The following excerpts from its idealized design demonstrate the company's understanding and acceptance of the workings of a democracy in a business organization:

> Nothing provides employees at all levels of an organization with as much opportunity to learn and develop as participation in decisions that affect them, nor does anything else raise their morale and dedication to work as much. Conventional organizations that provide such opportunities usually disrupt hierarchical relationships essential for effective management. The design that follows maintains the necessary hierarchy while providing the opportunity for participation in critical decision making to all personnel at all levels of the organization.

> Units that adopt the following type of organization—the democratic hierarchy—will be able to modify it to suit their needs and desires. For example, they need not initially give the boards all six functions identified below, but only a subset of them. They could later add functions initially omitted. Each unit would establish the frequency of its board's meetings, their duration, and its rules of procedure.

> The Company aspires to provide its users with the most advanced and cost-effective products and services. To do so, it must increasingly attract and retain employees with the most advanced, relevant knowledge and understanding. It has become increasingly apparent that the more educated and skilled a work force, the less effective a command-and-control style of management is. Participative democracy is necessary (but not sufficient) to attract and retain most of those who are on the leading edge of relevant technologies . . .

> Every manager will have a board that will minimally include that manager (as chairman), his or her immediate superior, and each of his or her immediate subordinates. Each board will be able to add additional members as it sees fit, as full or partial members, voting or non-voting, and so on . . . Subordinates must be a plurality of the voting members.

This means that every manager except the one at the top and those at the bottom will participate on boards at three levels: their own, their boss's, and those of each of their immediate subordinates. Therefore, most managers will interact with five levels of management: two levels above them, their own level, and two levels below.

Boards will normally meet once or twice per month for about two-three hours per meeting. Where the members of a board are geographically disbursed, meetings should be arranged to coincide with other normally held get-togethers.

Board meetings should reduce the number and frequency of other meetings by more than the amount of time they require [emphasis added]. Each board may have the following functions:

- *Policy making.* Each board will formulate policies [decision rules] that apply to units subordinate to it. However, it will not violate any policy made by a higher level board . . .

- *Planning.* Each board will prepare strategic, tactical, and operational plans for the units whose board it is. Its plans will have to be consistent with higher-level plans, but it can appeal to the appropriate higher board for a change in these. Every board and its unit will be able to implement any part of its design that does not affect any but its own subordinate units for which it has the required resources. Otherwise, it will have to obtain the necessary agreements and/or resources from higher-level units or boards.

- *Coordination and integration of policies and plans.* Each board will take steps to assure coordination of plans and policies of the lower level units for which it is responsible, and for assuring no violation by itself or lower-level units of higher-level plans or policies.

- *Quality of work life.* Each board will be free to make decisions that affect the quality of work life of its members provided such decisions affect only members of the board. If they affect others, approval of the others is required.

- *Performance improvement.* Each year the subordinate members on each board will meet to determine what their immediate superior can do to enable them to do their (subordinate) jobs better. They will prioritize their suggestions and present them face-to-face to their boss. The boss will have three options: (a) to agree, (b) to disagree but give the reasons for it, or (c) to ask for more time (not to exceed a month) to consider the issue. In addition, the manager whose board it is will also formulate suggestions to his or her subordinates as to what they could do to improve his or her performance. The subordinates will have available the same types of response to these suggestions as the manager has to theirs.

- *Tenure of managers.* Every board can remove the manager whose board it is from his/her position. It cannot fire him/her; only his/her boss can do that. This means that no manager can hold his/her position without the approval of his/her immediate superior and immediate subordinates.

Each board will formulate its own rules of procedure, but operate only by consensus . . .

Finally, each manager's responsibilities will include:

- Enabling subordinates to do their jobs better in the future than they can now; seeing to it that they develop continuously by encouraging and facilitating their continuous education and training.

- Managing the interactions (a) among those who report to them, (b) of their units with other units within the company, and (c) their units with relevant entities outside the company.

- Leading subordinates in carrying out the Company's mission.

Although it may seem to be a complicated system on first examination, the organization reduced the number of meetings, made them more productive, and simplified management. The circular organization worked smoothly and effectively at Energetics and contributed to its accelerated growth.

THE INTERNAL ECONOMY

Business organizations can be thought of as incorporating internal economies. The process of cost accounting, in which the company allocates the costs of materials, people, and other expenses against revenue, creates systems of "buying and selling" between divisions and departments that behave in a similar way to national economies. And, like national economies, with increasing size and complexity, organizational economies become increasingly difficult to manage effectively from a centralized position.

One difficulty that often confronts managers in conventional organizations is transfer pricing. This is the price charged to internal units for use of the output of other internal units. Such pricing almost always produces conflict between the internal units involved. The producing unit usually thinks it can sell its goods or services more profitably externally, and the buying unit thinks it can buy them for less from outside suppliers. In a sense, there is no such thing as a fair transfer price, one that precludes conflict between the affected units. Because conflict over transfer pricing is endemic to a centrally controlled internal economy, another type of economy is required to avoid its consequences.

Internally used services and goods in a conventional organization often are supplied by internal monopolies with no competitors—internal or external. If these monopolies are supported, as they frequently are, by subsidies supplied from above in the form of budgets that may hide their real costs, they tend to become bureaucracies and less responsive to the needs of their "customers," the internal units that they serve. As a result, the goods and services that are used internally and are provided by internal bureaucratic monopolies are often more costly than goods and services that can be obtained externally.

In an internal market economy, every organizational unit (with exceptions noted below) that serves more than one other organizational unit, or serves one or more external units, operates as a profit center. It is free to sell its goods or services at whatever price it wants and to buy whatever goods or services it needs from any source, internal or external, that it wants. However, these decisions are subject to an override by the manager to whom the unit reports. The overriding manager must compensate the unit for the profit it loses or the increased cost it incurs. This means that no internal unit will have to pay more for what it buys, or receive less for what it sells, than it would in a completely free market economy.

An internal unit that provides other internal units with goods or services that gives the organization a competitive advantage in the marketplace is generally prevented from selling its services externally. For example, a product-design or research unit could provide proprietary knowledge to competitors if allowed to sell outside the company. Therefore, such units are usually made cost centers and are often assigned to profit centers, which then must justify their added expense. The same is true of units that are confined within the organization for national security reasons.

Here is how Energetics partly described its internal market economy in its idealized design:

> As many units as possible will be profit centers; each of the others will be a cost center attached to a profit center. This does not mean that profit centers must be profitable. They may be retained because of some other type of advantage they provide (e.g., prestige). Where this is the case, the company will know and should attempt to know how much this advantage costs.

> Every unit will be able to sell its products or services to whomever it chooses at prices it establishes. Decisions to sell the products or services of input units to external customers can be overridden as described next.

Every unit will be able to consider the purchase of any product or service it requires from either internal or external sources.

Whenever an internal unit considers a quotation of a price from an external supplier of a product or service that is also provided by an internal unit, the internal unit will be given the option of meeting the external price before the external purchase is consummated . . .

Whenever a unit has a legitimate business desire to purchase products or services externally that a unit within the company provides, the manager to whom the unit reports can prevent that unit from using the external source. However, the overriding manager must compensate the buying unit for any increase in its cost that results . . .

Whenever a unit has a legitimate business reason for not wanting to sell a product or service to another internal unit at a price that is the only price acceptable to the buying unit, the lowest-level manager to whom both units report can override the decision but must compensate the selling unit for the difference in price.

The compensation allowed to the constrained unit by an overriding manager will be a cost to that manager . . .

The executive office of the corporation will also be a profit center. The after-tax expenses of this unit will be offset against its income. Since it is treated as the owner of the profit centers, it collects a share of their profits and interest on the capital it provides to them . . .

Every profit center will be allowed to accumulate profit up to a specified limit [set by the next-higher-level board at an amount greater than which the unit is not thought to be able to invest so as to obtain a satisfactory return on investment]. It will be permitted to use this money with the approval of its board and in a way that is consistent with higher-level policies . . .

Managers of producing and consuming centers at Energetics reported that they greatly enjoyed and benefited from the freedom to seek the best price—high or low—for the operation of their units.

ORGANIZATIONAL STRUCTURE

Many organizations reorganize every few years. This is often costly. It consumes large amounts of time, and lowers the morale of many of those affected. Nevertheless, such changes appear to be necessary for the organizations to adapt to internal or external changes. Given this state of affairs, organization planners have wondered whether it is possible to organize in such a way that does not require *re*organization later in order to adapt to such changes.

W. C. Goggin (1974), CEO of Dow-Corning, found a way to avoid reorganizations. It consists of organizing multidimensionally. Conventional organizational structures are represented in a two-dimensional chart, up and down (the allocation of authority) and across (the allocation of responsibility). Goggin's multidimensional organization had three dimensions. What follows is a significant variation on his concept, but underlying it is his original significant idea.

To organize is to divide labor functionally and to coordinate the divided labor. Regardless of the nature of an organization, there are only three ways to divide labor functionally: *inputs* (functions), *outputs* (products and/or services), and *users* (markets).

Input units consist of units whose outputs are primarily (if not exclusively) consumed within the organization (for example, accounting, research and development, purchasing, mailroom, computing, and human resources).

Output units consist of those units whose outputs (products or services) are principally consumed externally to the organization (for example, at General Motors, the Chevrolet, Pontiac, Buick, and Cadillac divisions).

User units are defined by classes of customers defined either geographically (for example, North America, Europe, Asia), or by the means by which they are reached (for example, catalogue, Internet, retail stores, television), or demographically (for example, by age, occupation, race, sex, and income).

In every organization, the relative importance of the three criteria used in dividing labor is expressed by the level of the organization at which they are applied. The first level below the CEO may be organized by using any one or more of the three criteria, the next level similarly, and so on. More than one criterion can be used at any level. The higher level at which one or more of the three criteria are used, the more important they are deemed to be by the organization. For example, in single-product companies, functional units are usually the most important; in multiproduct companies, product units are often the most important; in multinationals, particularly those in highly competitive markets, market units defined by countries or regions are commonly the most important.

Most reorganizations consist of a reordering of the criteria used in dividing labor so as to adapt to changing internal or external conditions. If an organization places units of all three types at every level of the organization, the need to restructure in order to adapt is eliminated (see Figure 4.1). Such an organization adapts by reallocating resources among the units rather than by reordering the criteria used in dividing labor. Put another way, the basic organizational structure at each level does not need to change over time, but managers can and do reallocate resources to each of the three types of units within each level to respond to changing business needs.

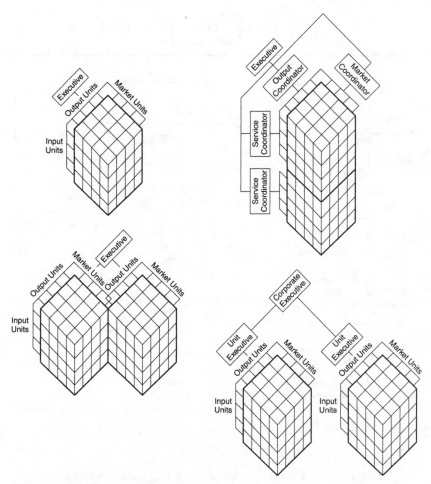

Figure 4.1 Multidimensional organization designs

Energetics provides an example in its idealized design of a multi-dimensional organization. Here are excerpts:

Energetics will be organized multidimensionally. Its units will have input (functional) units, output (product or service) units, and user (market) units. It will also have an executive office with appropriate staff support [see Figure 4.2].

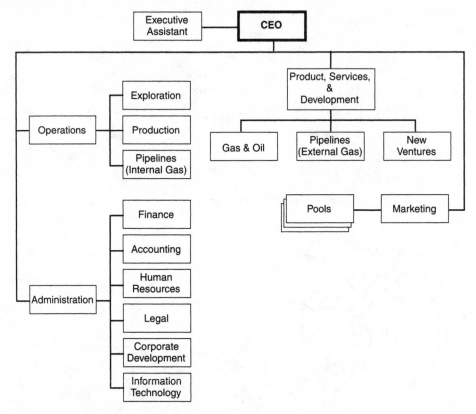

Figure 4.2 Multidimensional structure of Energetics

The Executive Office. In addition to a CEO, there will be four other executives in charge of (1) line input units (operations), (2) staff input units (administration), (3) output units (products and services), and (4) marketing. These four executives together will make up the CEO's board.

Output Units. There will be three output units: gas and oil, pipelines, and new ventures. These units will consist of management and a small supporting staff with scarce and uniquely required expertise and services. They will have fixed assets and operating capital.

Output units will be responsible for the profitability of their products and/or services. They will arrange all activities required for getting their products/services to the market and for receiving payment for them.

Input Units. Input units will develop and provide the personnel, facilities, equipment, and services required by output units. All input units will serve at least two output units. A functional unit that serves only one output unit will be part of that output unit [for example, a producing facility that produces only one type of product can be a part of that output unit responsible for that product] . . .

User (Market) Units. Initially there will be pool-defined [gas reservoir] units that will market, distribute, and transport the outputs of the Company and other companies to different customers in the areas in which the pools are located.

The user units can sell products obtained from other producers . . .

In the years after the implementation of its idealized design, Energetics found that it no longer needed to reorganize its basic structure.

ORGANIZATIONAL LEARNING AND ADAPTATION

It is important to the results of an idealized design that the design include a strategy for the business organization to continue to learn and adapt to what will certainly be a constantly changing market environment. Many books have been published in the recent past that have established the concept of the "learning organization" and described how to achieve it. In this section, we analyze the process of learning and adapting as we, in turn, have learned it working with many business organizations. Although we do not claim that this will exhaust the subject, we believe that it can help planners focus on the main issues involved in leaning and adapting.

We begin by making a distinction among some of the key terms involved in describing organizational learning:

- *Data* consist of symbols that represent the properties of objects and events. They have little value until they have been processed into information. Data are to information as iron ore is to iron. Little can be done with iron ore until it is processed into iron.

- *Information* consists of data that have been processed to be useful. It is contained in descriptions, answers to questions beginning with such words as *what, who, where, when,* and *how many.*

- *Knowledge* is contained in *instructions,* answers to *how-to* questions.

- *Understanding* is contained in *explanations,* answers to *why* questions.

- *Wisdom* is concerned with the value of outcomes, effectiveness, whereas the other four types of mental content are concerned with efficiency. Efficiency is concerned with doing things right; effectiveness is concerned with doing the right thing.

These five terms define categories of mental content and form a hierarchy of value in which data have the least value and wisdom has the most. Our experience is that too many organizations allocate their time inversely—spending too much time on data and information and too little on understanding and wisdom. An effective learning process requires more attention to the top of the hierarchy than the bottom.

One more concept is crucial to understanding the learning process. And it sounds counterintuitive. We argue that little is learned when an organization does something right, but that much can be learned when it does something wrong. When we do something right, it can only confirm what we already know. The corollary is that we can only learn from making mistakes, and then identifying and correcting them. However, all through school, and subsequently in most organizations, we are taught that making a mistake is a bad thing. Therefore, we tend to deny or hide mistakes. We continue to do things "right" even when the outcome is wrong because we have been told what is the "right way" and what is the "wrong way." We fail to learn that what we should be doing is the right thing. Peter Drucker summed up this distinction when he said, "Management is doing things right, leadership is doing the right things."

There are two types of mistakes from which we can learn. One is errors of commission, doing something that should not have been done; the other is errors of omission, not doing something that should have been done. For example, acquiring a company that creates a less-profitable company than the acquirer is an error of commission; not acquiring a company that would have created a more-profitable company is an error of omission.

Organizations are more likely to get into trouble because of errors of omission than errors of commission. American automobile makers that failed to produce low-cost and fuel-efficient cars when the price of oil spiked in the early 1970s found it almost impossible to catch up later. Now those that are not producing and selling hybrid vehicles—with combined gas and electric motors—across all of their vehicle lines will certainly have to play catch-up as demand increases. It is difficult to identify errors of omission because accounting systems identify only errors of commission. Therefore, in organizations that treat mistakes as bad and punishable, the best way to maximize job security is to do nothing. This is the major contributor to the reluctance of employees at all levels to initiate change. Unfortunately, in an environment that is increasingly complex and unpredictable, doing little or nothing is a sure path to the destruction of the organization.

Individuals within an organization can learn and adapt without their organization doing so, although their effectiveness is only felt if they are in positions high enough to do something about it. We have observed that the higher the status of an individual, the less likely they are to identify mistakes and learn from them.

An organization as a whole only learns when everyone in it has access to the learning of any others when they need it, even after the others may no longer be a part of the organization. This requires capturing what individuals learn and storing it in a memory accessible to others who have a need to know.

It follows from all this that an organization's ideal design for learning and adaptation requires the following types of support:

- Coverage of all five types of learning—from data to wisdom
- Coverage of errors of omission as well as errors of commission. Retention and provision of access to relevant learning to every member of the organization who has a need for it
- Identification of mistakes (of both types), determination of their sources, and correction of them

As discussed later, this can require the organization to set up an elaborate system to accomplish the learning and adaptation process. However, the results will justify the time and expense.

The system should provide a way that all-important decisions are monitored to detect deviations from their associated expectations and the assumptions on which these expectations are based. It should diagnose deviations to determine their causes, and then prescribe corrections. Because the corrections themselves involve decisions, these decisions should be treated as if they were original decisions. When correction decisions are monitored, and in turn corrected if necessary, deep organizational learning takes place. It accelerates the process of learning how to learn.

The planning team at Energetics designed a Learning and Adaptation Support System that embodied the requirements that we have described. A glance at the diagram of how it worked shows how elaborate some learning systems can be (see Figure 4.3). However, it is not necessary to understand this system in detail to get a sense of how it fulfilled its requirements. The following are highlights of the idealized design that addressed the four types of support just listed (the boxes represent functions, not individuals or groups; numbers are keyed to items on the diagram).

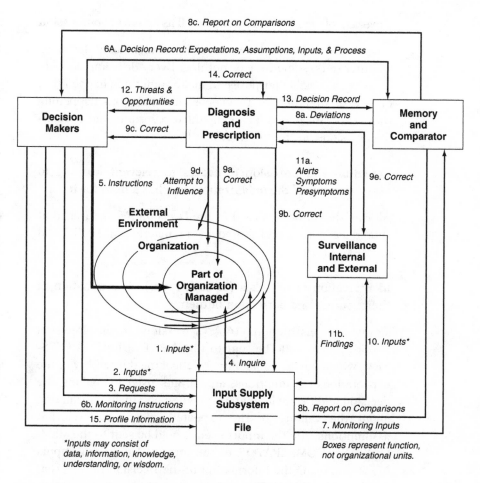

Figure 4.3 A learning and adaptation support system

Coverage of all five types of learning

We begin with the generation of *Inputs* (1) - Data, Information, Knowledge, and Understanding of the behavior of the ORGANIZATION being managed and its (internal and external) ENVIRONMENT. These inputs are received by the INPUT SUPPLY SUBSYSTEM. The inputs may come in a variety of forms, for example, oral or written, published or personal. [Although Wisdom is not mentioned, it was expected to be an input.]

Coverage of errors of omission as well as errors of commission

A *Decision Record* (6a) is required for all significant decisions whether to do something or nothing. Every decision has only one of two possible purposes: to make something happen that otherwise wouldn't, or to keep something from happening that otherwise would. [This included recording and evaluating decisions not to do something.]

Retention and provision of access to relevant learning to every member of the organization who has a need for it

All this should be recorded in the *Decision Record* (6a) that should be placed and stored in an inactive MEMORY and COMPARATOR.

Identification of mistakes (of both types), determination of their sources and correction of them

Monitoring Instructions (6b), a version of the Decision Record (6a), should be sent to the INPUT SUPPLY SUBSYS-TEM, which has responsibility for checking the validity of the expectations, assumptions, and inputs used in making the decision and its implementation. When obtained, information about the validity of the expected effects, the relevant assumptions, and the inputs used should be sent to the MEM-ORY AND COMPARATOR in the form of Monitoring Inputs (7). Then, using the information in the Decision Record (6a) stored in the MEMORY, and the Monitoring Inputs (7) a comparison should be made of the actual and expected effects, and the assumptions on which they are based [el] Such deviations indicate either that what was expected did not occur or what was assumed turned out to be wrong. A diagnosis is required to determine what has, and what should be done about it. The purpose of the diagnosis is to find what is responsible for the deviations and to prescribe corrective action. In other words, the diagnostic function consists of explaining the mistake, and therefore, producing understanding of it.

In addition, Energetics established ways in its idealized design to enhance individual learning through its human resources policies:

- Every employee will be given the opportunity to develop a career development plan with the help of his or her immediate superior. The Company will provide the time and money required to obtain certification, accreditation, or licensing of skills required by the company.

- Personnel at all levels of the organization will encourage, recognize, and reward innovation and be tolerant of failure of innovative efforts. Such failures will be regarded as opportunities for learning. Failure to learn from a mistake will be taken as a serious mistake.

- Every manager's evaluation by his or her superior will include an evaluation of his or her conduct of evaluations of subordinate performance and the assistance they provide subordinates in realizing their personal development plans.

- The Company will encourage development and acquisition of critical skills including those that will broaden and enhance its intellectual capital.

Subsequent to implementing the idealized design at Energetics, the company's performance improved significantly—beyond management's expectations before the design.

If you would find it valuable to have the full Energetics idealized design, you will find it in Chapter 13, "Energetics (Business Enterprise)."

We now look at the situation in a company in a state of national decline and how idealized design was applied to a local area that averted potential disaster. Comparison with the design of Energetics indicates how designs of different organization differ and where they are similar.

A SUPERMARKET CHAIN AT THE CROSSROADS

The Great Atlantic and Pacific Tea Company (A&P) had been in serious trouble since the early 1970s. Mounting losses had resulted in several changes in its management and ownership, and the number of its stores had been reduced from about 3,500 in 1974 to about 1,000 in March 1982.

The metropolitan Philadelphia area was a microcosm of the company's woes. Over a two-year period, the company had closed down about 60 of its 110 stores, two thirds of them in early 1982. The company cited high labor costs as its major problem. Because A&P's work force was completely unionized, and because of seniority clauses in its labor contracts, the layoffs were mostly among part-time, younger, and less-costly workers. This left the highest-paid workers still on the payrolls. In addition, the average length of employee service was twice that of other supermarket chains in the area. Therefore, A&P's labor costs were much higher than average (15 percent of operating revenues as compared with 10 percent for the industry). It was clear that A&P would eventually close most, if not all, of the stores in the area.

At this point, early in 1982, Wendell Young, president of the union local that would be most seriously affected, 1357 of the United Food and Commercial Workers union (UFCW), sought help from the Busch Center (a systems-oriented research center) in the Wharton School of the University of Pennsylvania. He wanted to discuss the imminent closing of more of A&P's Philadelphia-area stores and what might be done to prevent it. The outcome of these discussions, led by Jamshid Gharajedaghi, Director of the Busch Center, was that the union organized its members to buy and operate a small number of the stores being shut down. The main question on Young's mind was whether the union could succeed where the company had failed.

The union made its bid to buy several stores in early March 1982, even though there was opposition within A&P to selling the stores. Two weeks later, the union announced that 600 members had pledged $5,000 each as seed money to be used to build a purchase fund. The company agreed to sell several stores to the union.

After two of the union-operated stores had become successful, workers and union representatives began an idealized design for the operations of all the union-owned A&P stores. During the design process, it became apparent that the workers had a great deal of relevant knowledge that previous owners had never tried to use. When workers were engaged in an idealized design effort, their knowledge and understanding led to innovative organizational forms, participatory management, and some new training programs. All this involved a radical departure from traditional union roles, which had involved organizing, bargaining, pension administration, and so on. There was considerable skepticism among both managers and workers about whether this would be a proper role for the union, but the union moved forward with its idealized design.

The O&O (owned and operated) stores, as they were called, prospered and made A&P's management rethink its position and consider alternatives to mass closings. Together with the union and the university-based center, the company initiated what was called the "Quality-of-Work-Life Plan." Negotiations led to an agreement between A&P and the relevant unions that had the following four elements:

- A&P agreed to reopen at least 20 stores and give workers a chance to buy 4 more. This would be done under a new subsidiary of A&P called *Super Fresh*. The name was intended to create a new image centered on the display of fresh foods in each store. The logo was also changed from the familiar red A&P to the new green Super Fresh.

- The locals accepted shorter vacations and pay cuts up to $2 per hour.

- The workers would receive 1 percent of gross sales if the labor costs were held at 10 percent of operating revenues. This share was to be reduced if labor costs exceeded 10 percent and would be increased if they fell below 9 percent. In fact, labor costs did fall below 9 percent.

- The company committed itself to Quality-of-Work-Life Programs to be initiated immediately in the new stores.

With the increase in the number of stores, the union and workers realized that more planning would be necessary to ensure the success of the larger organization. By mid-June, three design teams had been formed containing a deep slice of the new organization, including the president of Super Fresh and workers down to the level of part-time checkers. Each team completed an idealized design of the whole organization. Representatives of the design teams synthesized the designs into a single version that was prepared and approved with few modifications by the whole group. In mid-September, the first new stores were opened.

The following are some of the relevant portions of their design:

> Super Fresh will be organized as a two/three level structure. The first level will be that of the corporation itself, which will incorporate five different dimensions.
>
> **Output Units.** Achievement of the organizational ends and objectives will be the responsibility of the output units (stores) of the system. The other units are created in order to facilitate the operation of the stores. These units will be self-sufficient and autonomous to the degree that the integrity of the whole system is not compromised.
>
> **Input Units.** Inputs are the services required to support the output units. Because of economies of scale, technology, and geographic dispersion, inputs can best be realized at the corporate level. These units will also be semi-autonomous.
>
> **Environmental Units.** The two main functions of these units are marketing and advocacy; that is, attracting the customers, making contact with the external stakeholders, and advocating their point of view within the company.
>
> **Planning Boards.** Planning is a process that provides the overall coordinating and integrating function for the input, output, and environmental units. Planning Boards are the main policy-making body of the organization and at all levels serve as the vehicle for the participatory management style of Super

Fresh. This enables the information, judgments, and concerns of subordinates to influence the decisions that affect them. One of the key functions of the planning boards is to constantly re-assess the progress that the corporation, store, or department is making toward its goals (via feedback from the management support system) and to chart new objectives when necessary. Planning at the store level is directed to those matters affecting the store. Planning affecting more than one store is done at the corporate level. There will be planning boards in every store and every employee will be involved in one.

The second level will be the internal structure of the store itself, which will be organized along the same concept as the corporation, having the same five dimensions as does the larger system.

As Super Fresh increases the number of stores it operates, a three-level structure will be created that groups the stores into regional units.

EFFECTS OF THE SUPER FRESH DESIGN

In an article that appeared in the *Philadelphia Inquirer* on Sunday, April 3, 1983, Jan Shaffer wrote the following:

> When the first Super Fresh food market opened here 8 1/2 months ago, it was hailed as a breakthrough in employee participation in management. In fact, the reincarnated food chain, a subsidiary of A&P, appears so promising that A&P is looking hard at the possibility of expanding it nationwide. . . . The Super Fresh format, first used to reopen closed stores, now is being used to convert existing A&P stores to Super Fresh Markets.[p. 1D–2D]

Today, Super Fresh has more than 128 stores in the United States. It has moved out of the Delaware Valley into other parts of Pennsylvania, and into New Jersey, Delaware, Maryland, Virginia, and the District of Columbia. It also has opened some stores in Canada.

SUMMARY

The examples of idealized design provided in this chapter reveal parts of such designs that different organizations have in common and parts that differ. Most frequently, they share a democratic organization, the internal market economy, the multidimensional structure, and the learning and adaptation support system. Even those parts that they have in common tend to differ in details, reflecting the uniqueness of the organization involved.

Not every organization will include in its design all or even some of the repetitive elements we have identified. Those organizations that do not include them should consider the problems these designs address and be sure that they are adequately dealt with in their designs.

The properties specified for incorporation into the idealized design should include those that would differentiate the organization from others of the same type. The list should be dynamic, changing as the design develops, and it is experienced after its implementation. The idealized design of an organization is a continuing process that should be both revolutionary and evolutionary.

In the next chapter, we show how idealized design can be undertaken productively in organizations other than business enterprises. Although they face some of the same challenges as for-profit organizations, they also must deal with issues unique to the environments in which they operate.

5

Not-for-Profit and Government Organizations

"The idealized design process legitimized everything. All of the stakeholders became 'owners' of what we all said we wanted to do in the session."
—Executive director of an opera school

Idealized designs for not-for-profit and government organizations differ from business enterprises in that they are applied to organizations that are widely varied in both structure and functions. Therefore, it is not possible to specify the content that their idealized redesigns should include. The content of such designs should take into account the unique functional requirements of the organization involved. Nevertheless, many of them can appropriately incorporate the basic designs that have emerged from the design of corporations: democratic hierarchies, internal market economies, multidimensional structures and learning, and adaptation support systems.

In this chapter, we describe two not-for-profit organizations and one government organization. They illustrate the variety of these organizations that can benefit from the process of idealized design. We turn first to a cultural organization that believed that it needed to take a bold approach to planning for its future.

AN OPERA SCHOOL REINVENTS ITSELF

In 1997, the Academy of Vocal Arts in Philadelphia, a small, premier opera-training school, considered itself among the elite opera schools but was aware that the opera world did not necessarily share this view. At the time, it relied on a small number of benefactors. Well-known graduates did not support or maintain significant connections with the school. The school had always been low-key, did not publicize itself, and so did not often get media attention. It did not aggressively pursue the best students, but admitted the good students who applied to it.

A number of those involved in the school agreed that for the organization to be recognized as world class, it would need to convince the very best prospective students that the school would be great for their careers, and this would require letting the outside world know about its unique programs and offerings.

The school's management and board discussed a number of initiatives and agreed that they wanted to increase the number of board members who would be actively involved in the institution. They also wanted to increase faculty involvement in, and cooperation with, the academy's management. Some wanted to involve students—who did not feel they had any opportunity to influence the organization to better meet their needs—in shaping school policies. Many ideas surfaced but were not widely discussed, so that they did not get the support required for their implementation. There was no shared vision of what the students or other stakeholders wanted the organization to become. Clearly, no breakthroughs would occur unless a fresh approach was taken to planning for the future.

The academy's management and board had learned of the concept of idealized design from members of INTERACT, the Institute for Interactive Management, and decided to involve the entire organization in an idealized redesign of the school. They started with an all-day session involving a team of nearly fifty stakeholders, including students, faculty, staff, alumni, board members, financial supporters, and management. They divided the participants into four groups, each consisting of every type of stakeholder and each assigned to draft an idealized design.

Midway through the all-day session, the groups reconvened and presented their designs to each other. Then they went back into their groups to incorporate aspects of the other teams' designs that they liked. The designs were subsequently synthesized into a single design by a strategic planning team of about ten people that included all stakeholder types. In the following months, this team added detail to the design and reviewed it with the wider organization. The resulting design addressed the main objectives sought by management and the board.

ATTRACTING THE BEST STUDENTS

The design called for offering to finance the best potential students and making it very attractive for them to come to the school. Rather than waiting for students to discover the school, it formulated a bold plan that used the media to make more potential students and the public aware of the academy. Its managers began to attend a variety of opera festivals and performances, scouting for the best talent. Faculty and staff became actively involved in recruiting students, and current students collaborated with them.

The school also arranged for prominent alumni and other talent to speak to potential students, describing life in the opera world, and how to get into that world.

Planners realized that media exposure and alumni participation were not sufficient for attracting the best students. New York's Metropolitan Opera, an extremely strong competitor for potential students, was paying students who participated in their apprentice program. Through the idealized design process, the school's managers came to realize that they would also need to offer at least full tuition plus cost-of-living stipends. In addition, they had to convince potential students that going to the academy was even more attractive than participating in the apprenticeship at the Met. One way to do this was to offer more principal roles in school performances and those of professional opera companies affiliated with the school. The new message was that the school would support student development while moving them more rapidly into starring roles and recognition than by participating in apprenticeship programs.

EXPANDING AND IMPROVING THE FACILITY

The planners made provision for providing a state-of-the-art facility that would enhance training and practicing. It was designed to provide individual training rooms, soundproof practice areas, and a large area for building scenery. At the end of the first design session, there was unanimous agreement by all 50 people engaged in it that to realize their design, the academy would have to buy the building next door. (The school is located in a row of brownstone buildings in Center City Philadelphia.) This would double the present size of the facility. A team of three people, including a real estate attorney, was formed to approach the neighbor for discussions. After a series of negotiations, the neighbor agreed to sell the building and lease back part of it for a specified period of time. Then the challenge was to raise the money required to buy the building. Armed with a detailed bold design of how they would use the new facility, management found out that it was easier then expected to raise the funds required. One source alone contributed more than $2.5 million for the project.

INCREASING THE NUMBER AND QUALITY OF PERFORMANCES

The designers knew that the school would gain media and public attention by producing well-attended opera performances. The design provided for increasing the number of performances and location of touring productions. The result would enhance the recognition of the school among the general public and attract more people to opera.

To generate media coverage, the school invited prominent singers to participate in its performances. Prominent alumni were also among those invited to participate. Their involvement attracted local and national newspaper and radio attention. A Philadelphia radio station began to broadcast the school's performances. In 2004, the school got national exposure when National Public Radio profiled a student who had recently made his debut at the Metropolitan Opera in New York.

RAISING MONEY

The school's idealized design included increased media exposure not only to attract better students but to attract the additional funds required to increase public performances and to provide fellowships to almost half of its students. The strategy paid off.

Because of their involvement in the idealized design process, various stakeholders—including board members, faculty, and staff—took ownership of the design and became strong advocates of its implementation. Board members were completely sold on the exciting possibilities the design presented, and their energy was evident to foundations and other potential providers of funds. The school not only increased the number of funded programs, but also was able to double its endowment. In the words of the academy's Executive Director, Kevin McDowell, "The idealized design process legitimized everything. All of the stakeholders became 'owners' of what we all said we wanted to do in the session. Everybody bought into it."

Five years after implementing most of the idealized design, the school repeated the idealized design process, updating their earlier design with what they had learned from its implementation.

Today the Academy of Vocal Arts has become an institution where admission to its four-year program is highly competitive. It now claims to be the only tuition-free school dedicated exclusively to teaching voice. Its latest initiative is to implement another part of its idealized design that is intended to increase its international presence. It intends to participate in more international festivals and performances that will give the school more exposure to potential students and give their present students more international exposure.

If you would find it valuable to have the full Academy of Vocal Arts idealized design, you will find it in Chapter 14, "Academy of Vocal Arts (Not-for-Profit)."

Next we look at an example of a health-care organization that undertook an idealized design to cope with its deteriorating financial condition.

VISITING NURSES FACE A FINANCIAL CRISIS

Health care for those who have no coverage and cannot afford to pay for service from private sources is a major national problem. Fortunately, a number of charitable institutions and hospitals partially make up for this national deficiency. Among them are visiting nurses associations. Unfortunately, these organizations are having increasing difficulty in maintaining themselves financially.

As of 1981, the Community Home Health Services of Philadelphia (CHHSP), a nonprofit organization, had provided nursing services in homes for more than 90 years. It was operating that year with a deficit of $520,000. The number of nursing visits they were able to provide had declined in recent years, and its bad debts from patients had more than doubled in the past year.

As CHHSP became increasingly unable to function adequately, the director of patient services resigned in despair. A spontaneous committee of supervisors called on the organization's board of trustees to protest conditions within the organization. Management responded by imposing rigid operating procedures, causing morale among the workers to decline. Reacting to this pressure, in September 1981 the staff of CHHSP became the first professional group in Philadelphia to elect the National Union of Hospital and Health Care Employees as its collective bargaining agent. Union affiliation held the threat of increasing the organization's expenses when it could least afford it.

CHHSP was financially dependent on cost reimbursement from Medicare and charitable contributions. In the past, it had had no competition, but the elimination of health-care licensing requirements in Pennsylvania opened the door to a number of competitors. These competitors provided services mostly to those patients who could pay—reducing the number of payers available to CHHSP who accepted patients regardless of ability to pay. By the end of 1981, CHHSP was on the brink of financial disaster.

The management team blamed much of their troubles on an inadequate management information system that, they believed, did not deliver the right kind of information for correct decision making. Early in 1982, the executive director asked for help from the Busch Center of the Wharton School of Business at the University of Pennsylvania, explaining that CHHSP wanted to develop a more effective management information system. After a preliminary study, the Busch Center proposed that, instead of addressing the management information system, an idealized redesign of the organization as a whole be initiated. Some at CHHSP resisted this suggestion but finally agreed, and a team of CHHSP and Busch Center personnel was formed under the leadership of John Pourdehnad of the center. The team initiated an interactive planning process, in which idealized design had a major role, to deal with the "mess."

Because there were more than 400 people in CHHSP, it was impossible to include all of them in the redesign. So, three design teams were formed—totaling more than 50 volunteers—that included a cross-section of all stakeholder groups. Although the union was invited to participate, it chose not to because of ongoing contract negotiations.

In formulating the mess, the teams identified problems embedded in the organizational culture at CHHSP. Over the years, the organizational culture had become bureaucratic, authoritarian, hierarchical in management style, detached from the field staff, and essentially concerned with paper shuffling and exercising rigid rules. This resulted in a lack of participative spirit and the absence of a common vision of the future, which in turn prevented a marshalling of employee energy in pursuit of CHHSP's stated goals and objectives.

In March 1982, after the mess had been formulated, the three teams began idealized designs independently. Within three weeks, each team had completed a preliminary design. They came together and synthesized their designs and then formulated a mission statement. The most important part of the statement was that it committed CHHSP to achieve financial independence, particularly by aggressively marketing its services to paying patients.

The teams then focused on improving the structure and functioning of the organization, including its bureaucratic culture. The teams proposed a series of changes in the organization of the area offices from which the agency's services were delivered. Central to these changes would be the creation of semi-autonomous health-care teams of five to seven members in each office that would be responsible for delivering patient care, case management, and coordination of the functional areas involved. Each health-care team would select its own leader, but it was assumed that the teams would eventually be self-directed and not require a designated leader. Incentives were designed to encourage cooperation within and between teams.

Each area office would be given its own support staff, including human resources, financial, information systems, and marketing. These would be a replica of these same functions at headquarters, and each area office would be a miniature CHHSP. Multifunctionality of individuals would be encouraged and facilitated by the creation of appropriate training programs. This would increase efficiency in the area offices by increasing flexibility in the deployment of workers. The effect would be to radically change the organizational culture, devolving central control to the area offices.

After the idealized design was completed, the teams identified the gaps between the real and idealized system. They worked through a series of initial approximations to the idealized design and decided that the final design should achieve four major objectives over the next five years: 1) build organization strength; 2) diversify referral sources and strengthen current relationships; 3) diversify services; and 4) network with other voluntary home health organizations. Taken together, these objectives should lead to a financial turnaround.

The idealized design teams formed a group of 16 volunteers, divided into 4 teams representing a cross section of stakeholders, to design the means for pursuing each of these objectives. Targets and schedules were set and a monitoring procedure was developed together with a way of correcting deviations from expectations and assumptions.

Following completion of the initial idealization, and during the realization process (see Chapter 1, "The Stages of Idealized Design"), fundamental changes were made, including the following:

- CHHSP was restructured by forming a parent company, Philadelphia Home Health Care, with for-profit subsidiaries.

- CHHSP changed its patient admission policy and now required seven paying patients from each referring source for each indigent patient they "provided."

- In addition to a substantial diversification of the services provided, there was an extension of service limited from 9 to 5 each day, Monday through Friday, to 24 hours, 7 days a week.

- Formation of a joint venture with a major supplier of medical equipment, and establishment of a consumer advisory board that included previous as well as current patients.

- A new labor contract with the union was negotiated, one that all stakeholders found favorable.

A complete financial turnaround was achieved through the new patient admission policy that offsets one nonpaying patient with seven paying patients.

By fiscal year 1984–1985, earned income doubled, reaching approximately $8 million. The agency went from negative to positive cash flow. Both operating and equipment funds increased significantly. Salaries and employee benefits increased. Productivity increased, and overhead decreased. Attrition rates and absenteeism significantly decreased.

The last example is a government agency based in the White House that responded to pressure to become more effective by designing a democratic structure.

REORGANIZING COMMUNICATIONS IN THE WHITE HOUSE

This White House Communications Agency is responsible for all communication going into and out of the White House. It is a part of the White House Military Organization, whose director is a presidential appointee.

Most members of this government agency are drawn from the five military services (Army, Navy, Air Force, Marines, and Coast Guard). Most are assigned to the agency for a four-year tour of duty. At the end of their tour, they are returned to the branch of service from which they came. Therefore, except for a small number of civil servants, none of the agency's members consider the agency to be a career choice. They have no permanent commitment to it. When the leadership of the agency decided to undertake an idealized design, this lack of commitment made it difficult to mobilize its members in the redesign effort. The story of the redesign and its eventual outcome provides insights into the opportunities and obstacles with which planners contend in a governmental redesign. Our description is based on slightly modified extracts from an article published about the design effort.[1] In addition to minor rephrasing, we omit ellipses in the interest of readability:

> The White House Communications Agency (WHCA) is the unit of the federal government responsible for fulfilling the communication needs of the President of the United States and his or her staff. From relatively mundane, nonsecure phone calls, to highly visible public speeches, to unique, encrypted messages, the agency supports the office of the President by fulfilling all communication needs instantly.
>
> In the narrowest sense, the agency's customers are the President, Vice President, and first lady of the United States. But it also supports the Chief of Staff, the Office of Administration, National Security Council, Defense Information Systems Agency, the U.S. Secret Service, the presidential staff, and "others as directed." In the broadest sense, the agency's customers are the citizens of the United States and the free world.

The transformational effort initiated at WHCA was intended to move the agency from one that was managed autocratically to one that was organized democratically. In the course of its journey, WHCA first explored [W. Edwards] Deming's approach to continuous improvement, engaging several of his prominent associates as consultants and trainers, and [subsequently] explored [Russell L.] Ackoff's approach to organizational design, engaging his associates and Ackoff himself as a consultant and mentor.

Total organizational redesign was not what WHCA had in mind originally. Like much of the federal government in the early 1990s, the agency was feeling pressure to improve its processes. Prior to hiring Dr. J. Gerald Suarez [in 1992 as director of the Office of Process Improvement] WHCA engaged external consultants to help start a process improvement initiative, but the nature of the agency limited the effect an external consultant could have. There were spotty stories of improvement, in administrative processes here, a personnel process there, but no significant systemic improvement. By 1994, the agency's process-improvement projects still were not having the desired [result].

In the fall of 1994, the Republicans took control of Congress. At WHCA, the budget-chopping attitude in Congress added pressure to the case for changing the agency's structure. In response, the agency chose to use the interactive planning and idealized design concepts articulated by Russell Ackoff. Suarez and the Office of Process Improvement facilitated the redesign effort; Ackoff and his associates, including John Pourdehnad and Jamshid Gharajedaghi, mentored the agency and provided strategic advice. The people within the agency, however, created the new structure.

The agency's commander, Colonel Joseph J. Simmons, and the executive office redesigned the structure of WHCA [through an idealized design]. It was organized into eight directorates, each with its own specialized mission that supports the agency's overall mission. The directorates were divided by inputs (skills/functions), outputs (products/services), and markets (customers/users). Input units provide mission support services (services used internally). Output units provide mission-fulfilling services (services used externally). Market units are customer-support units.

The concept of participatory management is not compatible with the traditional style of military management, which continues to be a key characteristic of WHCA's culture. That the agency, in 1997, could talk about having a participatory management style is an indication of how far it had come since 1992. Nevertheless, without an organizational mechanism to support participatory management, the agency might not hold any progress in this direction against an ingrained command-and-control culture. To provide such a mechanism in its redesign, the agency incorporated the use of management boards prescribed in Ackoff's concept of the circular organization, a democratic hierarchy (Ackoff, 1994).

Each person in a position of authority is provided with a board. [Its composition and functions were similar to what was described in the design of Energetics (Chapter 7, "Problem Dissolving.")] Initially, people tended to think that the number of boards would increase the number of meetings a person would attend to an impossible level. In practice, the board structure reduced the number of meetings, as well as the number of memos, e-mails, and miscommunications. Suarez says, "Team skills are necessary, but not sufficient, to manage interactions. The boards are how the agency manages interactions."

The redesign created a Customer Support Directorate to provide two-way liaison between the agency's customers and WHCA personnel. Creation of the directorate provides a centralized, proactive approach to understanding and fulfilling customer requirements.

The agency uses its board structure as a mechanism for performance evaluation, both up and down. Each year, subordinate members of the boards meet to determine what their immediate supervisors can do to enable them to do better. They prioritize their suggestions and present them to their supervisors who may agree, disagree (but give reasons for it), or ask for more (limited) time to consider the matter. The process also works in reverse——superiors suggesting what their subordinates could do to enable them to do their jobs better—with the same three options. Feedback from clients is also used in this process. (In the new structure, workers have only one boss but multiple clients.)

In the previous structure, someone who was good at a job could become locked into it. [In the newly designed system] job rotation was designed to assure individual development. Client feedback identifies skill gaps and triggers the agency's just-in-time approach to training. During the redesign, the agency also came to grips with the issue of how to deliver training to people who are constantly on the road. The result has been new instructional design packages that take the learning environment to the people wherever they are.

The agency now has a newcomer orientation program to introduce new personnel both to the information systems and to the agency's mode of interacting and participatory management. The orientation also serves as a bridge to help new people extend their existing loyalty to their branch of military service [Army, Navy, Air Force, Marines, and Coast Guard] to include loyalty to the agency.

It is hardly surprising to learn that, after accomplishing a total organizational redesign, WHCA is still engaged in continual process improvement activities, especially as related to standardizing its newer processes. The agency continues to improve its processes.

WHCA has made what appear to be fundamental system changes and Suarez is optimistic about the future. "The board structure has given a voice to the people. We have given people democracy. In a military structure, that is a profound shift. The board structure," he says, "makes people focus on what is good for the agency, not what is good for their units. Will it survive over time? I don't know," Ackoff says. "Even if it fails, there will be a great many lessons learned."

The implementation of the idealized design accomplished many positive results, including the following:

- Reduced the number of entities in the organization from 16 independent units to 8 interdependent directorates.

- Developed a two-week indoctrination for newcomers to orient them to life in the White House and to the functioning of WHCA.

- Documented, flowcharted, and streamlined critical processes.

- Increased the number of civilians from 5 to 12 to bring stability and continuity to key positions.

- Reduced the number of people and amount of equipment required to support travel missions while meeting the communications requirements of the president.

Despite its successes, the redesign did not survive a later change in top command. Colonel (later Brigadier General Select) Simmons's support as head of WHCA had been essential to the design process and its implementation. He was subsequently promoted into directing the White House Military Organization, WHCA's parent organization. He initiated a similar effort there, having taken Suarez with him to direct the effort. However, with a change in the administration in 2000, Colonel Simmons was replaced, and his successor chose to let the effort lapse and its results dissolve.

If you would find it valuable to have the full White House Communications Agency idealized design, you will find a full account of it in Chapter 15, "White House Communications Agency (Government)."

SUMMARY

There is no limit to the kinds of non-business and government organizations to which idealized (re)design can be applied.

An organization that is "not-for-profit," must nevertheless be profitable in the sense that its income, whatever its sources, must be equal to or exceed its expenses. Otherwise, it cannot survive. It is apparent that not-for-profit organizations that depend on externally provided subsidies are likely to be in a precarious financial state when the national economy is not doing well. They are much more secure if they can be financially self-sufficient. Even if an organization is self-sufficient, subsidies can facilitate its development and growth possible.

Because not-for-profit organizations often cannot charge the recipients of their services for the services they receive, they must either depend on subsidies or on developing additional activities for which they can charge. In the former case, involvement of potential or actual subsidizers in their idealized design is essential. In the latter case, involvement of their potential "customers" is. For this reason, stakeholder participation in the ideal design of not-for-profit organizations is even more important than it is in the design of for-profit organizations.

Essentially the same requirements hold true for government organizations as for not-for-profits. They must maintain a balance between their expenses and the funds allocated to them—from whatever sources—for their operation. They too must involve their stakeholders in the idealized design process to ensure a high probability of success.

In the next chapter, we will take you through the use of idealized design to significantly improve processes—often the root causes of organizational dysfunction.

6

Process Improvement

"Never before have I seen such a well-received system."
—VP of a major pharmaceutical company

Idealized design of a process differs significantly from reengineering a process. Reengineering focuses on improving a process without changing the system of which it is a part. We contend, however, that the principal criterion that should be used in changing any part of a system is its effect on the system, then secondarily on the part itself. In idealized redesign, the critical interactions between the process being redesigned and the system in which it is embedded are taken into account. Therefore, the relevant aspects of the containing system as well as the process are redesigned. Whereas reengineering leads to reform of a process and little if any change in its containing system, idealized design usually leads to a radical transformation of both.

In this chapter, we describe examples that illustrate the diversity of processes to which idealized design can be applied. They include an oil company and a company manufacturing electric motors—both of which involve creating internal economies (or markets)—as well as a major pharmaceutical company and an earth-moving equipment company. Because of this diversity, there is no set pattern or content to their idealized designs. The idealized design process and its content must be adapted to the nature of the process being designed. However, each shows the importance of including in the idealized design the system in which the process is embedded.

INTERNAL MARKETS TRANSFORM INTERNAL MONOPOLIES

The following two examples involve internally consumed services that were provided by internal monopolies. The idealized design of each significantly improved performance and reduced costs as a result of introducing internal market economies on a limited basis. Nevertheless, this produced a profound transformation of internal transactions in both cases.

OPENING A COMPANY'S COMPUTING SERVICES TO COMPETITION

This major oil company had an internal computing center that virtually all parts of the company were required to use. The center was subsidized by corporate headquarters. This meant that the units using the center did not pay directly for the services they received, but, of course, they still bore the costs indirectly through corporate overhead charges.

Units within the corporation frequently complained about the computing service they received. They said it was slow and generally unresponsive to their needs. On the other hand, the computing center complained about the unnecessary inflation of priorities placed on computing requests; these added to aggregated time demands it could not possibly meet. Furthermore, it argued, much of the computing it was required to do was not really needed but was requested because of the illusion that it was free to the user.

A new CEO noted that computing costs were rapidly approaching personnel costs. He requested a study to evaluate the services of the computing center to determine whether it was worth its cost. The initial investigation reached two conclusions. First, it was not possible to evaluate experimentally its principal outputs-schedules for refineries and shipping because they were changed liberally and frequently by receiving managers. They made no record of their changes. Second, the investigators concluded that as long as the computing center operated as a subsidized monopoly, it would not offer, or be perceived to offer, satisfactory services. Furthermore, it concluded that only the users should make judgments about its value.

An idealized design of the computing center's interactions with its users was initiated with representation of all the internal stakeholders. This ensured that the design would address not only the computing center but also the system of user units that it served. The principal characteristics of the idealized design produced involved 1) converting the computing center into a profit center that charged for its services, 2) permitting internal users of computing services to obtain them from external sources, and 3) permitting the internal computing center to sell its services wherever it wanted (including externally) at whatever prices it wanted.

In a very short time, the computing center significantly reduced the amount of equipment it used. Nevertheless, it was doing most of the internal businesses in a way that now satisfied its internal customers. In addition, it had developed a thriving and profitable external business.

Many of the internal users had initially rushed to external suppliers when they had to pay for the services of the internal center. However, they gradually returned to the internal service when they reduced their computing requirements to what was absolutely necessary (because they now had to pay for it), and they learned how good the internally provided services were perceived to be by its external customers.

When an internally produced product or service must compete with external sources, the need for benchmarking is removed. The internal source will not survive unless it can compete effectively against external sources.

SOLVING THE PERENNIAL PROBLEM OF TRANSFER PRICING

This company had two large divisions among others. The larger of the two manufactured motors that it sold to equipment manufacturers. The parts division supplied distributors with replacement parts for electrical equipment, including the motors of the type the larger division produced. Because both divisions were profit centers, a price had to be paid to the first division by the second. The corporation established the transfer price. As with many corporations that deal with transfer pricing, the result was animosity and bitterness resulting from the transactions imposed on the two divisions.

The transfer price was less than the price the manufacturing division charged external customers for its products. Therefore, its profit margin on every sale it was required to make to the parts division was lower than on external sales. On the other hand, the parts division could sometimes buy the motors it wanted from an external supplier for less than the transfer price, but was not permitted to. An external supplier who had unused capacity would frequently be willing to marginally price the product to fill its capacity. Therefore, the parts division often suffered an increased cost because it had to purchase motors internally.

The CEO asked the Busch Center at the University of Pennsylvania's Wharton School to look at the conflict between the two divisions and try to establish a fair transfer price. It took little examination of the problem to realize there was no such thing as a fair transfer price. Therefore, the research group initiated an idealized design of the interaction between the two divisions. The design produced permitted the manufacturing division to sell to whomever it wanted at whatever price it wanted, subject to an override by the vice president to whom it reported. The parts division was allowed to buy from whatever source it wanted, but such a purchase was also subject to an override by the same vice president. That vice president could require an internal transfer of the product but, when he did, he was required to pay the manufacturing division for the lost income from a low-margin sale and the parts division for whatever increased cost it incurred. In effect, the manufacturing division would never have to sell a motor at a lower price than it was willing to, and the parts division would never have to pay more than it was willing to.

Clearly, because the income of the vice president, who was also a profit center, was based on the profit of the divisions he managed, he had to weigh the cost to him of an override against the benefit of keeping the sale inside the corporation. At the end of the year, the corporation's executive committee reviewed the considerable amount spent on overrides and decided it was not justified. In the following year, the vice president significantly reduced the number of overrides he imposed. Both divisions then became more profitable and began to collaborate. The manufacturing division offered a reduced price (equal to that of external suppliers) to the parts division when it had unused capacity. The parts division would buy from the internal division whenever it met the external competition's price.

As we have contended, the idealized design was successful because it included the system in which the transfer pricing process was a part.

TRANSFORMING A PROCUREMENT PROCESS

In 1999, Gregg Brandyberry assumed leadership of the global group that supports procurement (purchasing) processes at GlaxoSmithKline, a multinational research-based pharmaceutical company. The group was responsible for creating and implementing systems and processes that support the overall procurement process, including management of contracts, placing orders, analyses of expenditures, preparing requests for proposals and quotations, assuring continuity of supply, monitoring supplier performance, collaborating with suppliers, and so on. The corporation spent $12 billion annually on supplies, and the group's performance had a significant impact on the company's bottom line.

When Brandyberry assumed leadership of the group, he learned that internal customers believed it was unresponsive to their needs. They found the systems in place to be irrational and time-consuming. They told him that they felt the systems had been designed by "experts" with little input from users.

The system for managing supplier-contracts that was in place was a prime example of what was wrong. It was so cumbersome that most of the procurement staff prepared their own contracts and stored them in their desk drawers. Consequently, there was no global way of knowing what contracts were in place. It took a lot of time and effort to track down contracts. When people left the company, contracts were often lost, and it was often necessary—and embarrassing—to have to call suppliers for contracts.

The procurement staff did not have systematic access to quality contract templates and drafted many contracts without consulting its legal staff. This ultimately resulted in the legal department being backlogged with a very heavy workload of correcting non-standard contracts.

Brandyberry wanted to turn the approach upside down so that the users would drive the design process rather than the "experts." He asked a member of his management team, who was thoroughly familiar with idealized design, to educate the others on his team and work closely with them. The team included the group's stakeholders in the idealized design. This not only changed the stakeholders' negative perception of the group but also substantially enhanced the resulting idealized designs.

The team turned first to redesigning the supplier-contracts process. Three groups of ten users were engaged in initial half-day design sessions. Over the next eight weeks, a core group of five people initiated mocking up display screens for computers and representations of flows. The group arranged for open-invitation luncheon-review sessions at which users were invited to provide their inputs to the design process. Twelve weeks later, a new Web-based contracts-management system had been programmed and implemented.

Here are some of the key features that were designed and implemented:

- The designers wanted to be able to quickly understand what a contract is for and what are its key terms without having to read 30 pages. To accomplish this, the designers created a standard summary page for each contract that included such information as start date, expiration date, annual contract amount, supplier name, contract manager, and description of goods or services contracted. This allowed for quick review of contract coverage, which facilitated consideration of interruption risks, strategic relationships, and negotiations with suppliers.

■ The designers wanted the system to include high-quality contract "templates" that had been preapproved by the legal department. The system that was implemented included a wide range of templates that cover, for example, consulting, advertising, contract manufacturing, temporary labor, and research services. These templates included language about payment terms, business-interruption plans, quality audits, delivery terms, intellectual property, fee schedules, and so on. The templates accelerate the contract-creation process and help ensure that the contracts are comprehensive and that they include the latest legal, regulatory, and business requirements. The templates also speed the contract review process, because attorneys can electronically compare edited drafts of contracts with the original templates. This enables them to quickly see the changes instead of having to review every page for subtle changes. This feature dramatically reduced delays in reviewing contracts. Additionally, because each contract manager starts fresh each time with an up-to-date template, there is less-frequent use of "watered-down" contracts. Previously, many managers who were creating contracts with a new supplier would look for, and then start with, a similar contract that was already in place. This was undesirable because they often started with contracts whose terms had been modified in ways that were not favorable to GlaxoSmithKline.

■ The new system also sends automatic alerts about upcoming contract expirations or automatic renewals. This helps ensure continuity of contract coverage, which protects against business interruptions.

■ Users can do focused searching of specific fields—for example, suppliers, products/services, contract managers, contract values, and expiration dates. This makes it very quick and easy to find contracts. It now takes seconds to locate contracts that had taken hours or days previously.

- There are also benefits to having a single globally accessible system. There is much better visibility of contract coverage. Contract managers around the world can see what contracts are in place and can often piggyback on those, resulting in substantially better pricing and terms.

This system was embraced and received praise throughout the wider procurement department. One vice president commented, "Never before have I seen such a well-received system."

Next, the management team directed that an idealized design be applied to create a system that could allow the procurement staff see and analyze how much GSK spends globally with specific suppliers, who is spending the money, what they are buying from each supplier, and the price paid for each good and service. This information is important because it assists in negotiating effectively with a supplier. In a global enterprise such as GSK that operates in more than 70 countries, acquiring and organizing this information requires a lot of effort—but the results should justify the time and costs. Before the system was in place, the procurement staff sometimes resorted to asking the supplier for this information. Not only did this embarrass them, they also believed it weakened their negotiating position.

Brandyberry's team engaged the procurement staff in multiple idealized design sessions in which they first specified the information they wanted. Then they designed computer screens that revealed how they wanted to access and view the information. The new system design was implemented and produced major improvements over the previous system. For example, a report was created that showed the consolidated global amount spent with a supplier and the trends over the past three years. In the new system, this report took about 20 seconds to run and view. Previously, it would take users about two hours to put this information together each time spending information was updated. Similarly, dramatic improvements were made in the time required to get such information such as expenditures by category, by country, by continent, and by operation.

GSK employees and procurement personnel also participated in sessions directed at designing their ideal process for buying goods and services. This enabled employees to buy from preferred suppliers using preferred purchasing and payment processes. The use of preferred suppliers saves GSK a lot of money because these are suppliers from whom the company generally receives good service, significantly discounted rates, and better terms and conditions. It also reduces costs that arise from dealing with many suppliers and increases company leverage in negotiating purchases. The use of preferred purchasing and payment processes reduces administrative costs.

One system created through idealized design guides employees to preferred suppliers and processes by use of a Web-based buying guide called the "Orange Pages" (after the color of GSK's logo). Employees enter key words for things they want to buy, and the system returns results (much like a Web search engine) that tell them from whom to buy, how to order, and how to pay. It is estimated that this system is enabling GSK to save $100 million a year.

Idealized design was also used to create a system called RiskTrak that helps managers put in place robust plans that mitigate risk of interruption to supply of raw materials, packaging, components, and such that go into the medicines. This system is helping prevent potential interruptions to the supply of medicines to patients while also protecting the company's revenues.

In 2003, the Chartered Institute for Purchasing and Supply (UK) awarded GSK the "Best Use of Technology Award," which recognized GSK as having the best procurement systems platform of any company operating in the United Kingdom. Between 2000 and 2003, the set of systems developed using idealized design helped the procurement department exceed its goal of saving more than $1 billion. In 2005, GSK won an "ROI Leadership Award" from *Baseline* magazine, the prominent publication focused on technology implementation. This award recognized GSK's implementation of an online procurement request-for-proposal and bidding tool that helps ensure that suppliers successfully meet GSK's key business requirements while promoting healthy competition through online bidding. This information technology project produced a three-year return on investment (ROI) of 5451 percent, the highest return of any project recognized not only at this year's award ceremonies but for the entire three years the award has been in existence.

Recently, a new program was launched in which procurement, key suppliers, and GSK internal customers of procurement engage in idealized design in order to generate business requirements, identify opportunities to improve service, quality, innovation, and savings, and enhance their relationships. There are currently three main variations of the program. In one, suppliers observe GSK employees designing what they ideally want from a supplier's product and/or service. In the second, GSK and supplier's employees jointly design any aspect of the ideal relationship. In the third variation of the program, suppliers take idealized design into their organizations and apply it to processes, improvement of which is hoped to benefit both organizations.

Finally, a number of managers in other departments have seen procurement's successes with idealized design and became interested in applying it to their processes. To date, it has been applied to other processes including R&D, accounts payable, sales support, marketing, finance, hiring, maintenance of plants and facilities, supplier diversity, and travel.

In addition to the many improvements that the use of idealized design accomplished, the GSK example illustrates one of the basic strengths of idealized design: An unconstrained idealized design can lead to significant changes and improvements in successively larger containing systems.

FACILITATING A JOINT VENTURE

We next focus on describing the process of an idealized design—on how the design of a joint venture was brought about—rather than on the details of the resulting design of that venture. It illustrates how formulating an idealized design can change planners' entrenched mindsets and release their creative thinking. This description is taken from Ackoff (1999).

In the mid-1980s, the Clark Michigan Company, a wholly owned subsidiary of the Clark Equipment Corporation, was in serious financial trouble. The Japanese company Komatsu had entered Clark's market with better mobile earth-moving equipment that sold at a lower price than Clark's. Clark reduced its prices to Komatsu's level with the hope of retaining at least some of its market share. During the time it hoped to gain, it intended to study the possibility of redesigning its products and its production processes so as to compete more effectively with Komatsu. In the meantime, it sold products for less than the cost of producing them. This resulted in negative cash flow. Clark's creditors threatened to put the company out of business and liquidate its assets to get their money out. Clark was not given enough time to modify either its subsidiary's products or production processes so as to become profitable. Therefore, it adopted the strategy of dressing up the subsidiary and trying to sell it.

Clark Equipment's board blamed its CEO for the mess its subsidiary had gotten into and relieved him of duty. It then had to find a new CEO quickly. Because of the rush, it did something unusual: It hired a good one, James Rinehart, who was then president of General Motors Canada.

After joining the company and familiarizing himself with the subsidiary's mess, he called a meeting of its managers. He explained the nature of idealized design to them—a concept with which he was familiar from his earlier experience as head of Packard Electric. He asked the assembled managers to spend several days producing an idealized redesign of the Clark Michigan subsidiary. They objected, pointing out their studies had indicated that there was nothing they could do to save the company within the amount of time available to them. Therefore, they argued, the new CEO was asking them to imagine they could do whatever they wanted when there was nothing constructive that they could do. They wanted to know why they should waste their time on such a task. He replied that they would find an answer to that question when engaged in the idealized design process. They turned to it reluctantly.

A week later, they reported their results to Rinehart, saying that now they understood why they had been asked to prepare such a design. For the first time, they had been able to use all they knew about their industry. As a result, they now believed that a company of their design could dominate its industry if it came into existence. But, they added, there was no conceivable way they could get from where they were to a realization of that design.

Rinehart told them that was not the right problem to consider. He said he wanted them to work back from their design to where they were, not forward from where they were to the design. They did not understand. He explained. He said there were a number of other companies in their industry in states similar to theirs. What combination of these companies with Clark Michigan would give them the closest approximation to their idealized design?

Again they objected, pointing out there was no way they could acquire another company because of their financial condition, and no other company would be willing to acquire them for the same reason. Again Rinehart pressured them to continue.

A week later, after completing their assignment, they expressed their surprise that by combining three companies with Clark Michigan—a German company, a Swedish company, and a Japanese company—they could get a close approximation to their idealized design. But again they repeated that they did not see how they could get close to realizing such a union. Rinehart argued that because the companies identified in their design had not seen the design, their reaction to it could not be accurately predicted. Therefore, he organized a visit by a subgroup of Clark Michigan's managers to the firms to discuss the design they had prepared.

At Daimler-Benz (D-B), they discussed the Euclid Truck Company, an American company D-B had acquired a while back. It had never been profitable. After seeing Clark Michigan's idealized design, D-B decided that survival of the Euclid Truck Company would be considerably enhanced if it became part of the joint venture envisaged in that design. Much to Clark's surprise, they offered to sell it to Clark. Rinehart explained that they could not buy it for lack of cash. D-B then offered to sell it for shares of Clark's parent company's stock. Clark accepted and acquired Euclid.

At the second company, AB Volvo, the discussion focused on Volvo BM, a subsidiary that produced earth-moving equipment. Volvo executives were impressed by the marketing potential of the joint venture designed, but expressed skepticism about the ability of a cross-cultural management to work effectively. Volvo was well known for its participative approach to managing factory employees. Rinehart admitted to such a possibility but suggested that a team of Volvo, Clark, and Euclid managers be formed to design the closest approximation to the four-firm joint venture Clark had prepared.

For legal reasons, the Japanese firm, the third company approached, was unable to become involved, although it was greatly interested.

In April 1985, the task force suggested by Rinehart was formed. It began work with the help of two professors from the Wharton School as facilitators. By September, a detailed design of a joint venture had been completed with no cross-cultural difficulties at all. A proposal to create the joint venture was made to the boards of Clark and Volvo, and they accepted it. In April 1986, the VME Corporation was created: Volvo, Michigan, Euclid.

Through idealized design, what was originally taken to be infeasible became feasible and was, in fact, realized.

SUMMARY

The processes covered in this chapter are different, and deliberately so. They reveal that idealized designs of processes have little or no content in common. Their similarities lie only in the design process itself.

In these examples, the designers had to be continuously aware of the effects of their design on the containing organization. For this reason, it is always desirable to have representatives of the containing organization as part of the redesign team. Objections from members of a containing system commonly obstruct implementation of the independent redesign of one of its parts.

Using participative idealized design to change organizations, processes, products, and sites and facilities, and to solve problems involves a cultural change. It is democratic and changes how people think, from analytic to synthetic thinking.

In the next chapter, we examine how idealized design can be used to solve problems by approaching them from an entirely new perspective.

7

Problem Dissolving

"If you can't solve the problem you are facing, you're
probably facing the wrong problem."
—An infrequently used principle of inquiry

In this chapter, we apply idealized design to problems.
We show that the four ways of treating problems form a
hierarchy of value. The highest value method we call
problem dissolving. This is followed by several quite different examples that reveal the applicability of idealized
design in dealing with a wide variety of problems.

THE FOUR WAYS OF TREATING PROBLEMS

The four ways of treating problems are absolution, resolution, solution, and dissolution. They form a hierarchy
of value, in which dissolution is the most valuable.

1. **Absolution** consists of ignoring a problem and hop-
   ing that it will solve itself or be solved by others. It
   deals with problems by default.

2. **Resolution** consists of two approaches. One is to
   examine past experience to determine whether a

similar problem has been dealt with in the past. If it has, it must be decided whether the treatment used in the past can be used or adapted to the present problem. The other approach is to look for the cause of a problem and remove the cause. This brings the situation back to a previous state when the problem did not exist. Both approaches seek an outcome that is good enough, that "satisfices"—satisfies and suffices. But, it usually is not the best possible outcome.

3. **Solution** consists of doing something that yields the best possible outcome or approximates it as closely as possible, that *optimizes.* Problem solvers take an analytical research approach to problems, employing quantitative methods and/or experimentation where possible. Operations research and management science exemplify this approach.

4. **Dissolution** consists of eliminating a problem, preventing it from arising again by redesigning the system that has the problem or its containing system. Problem dissolvers try to *idealize,* to do better in the future than the best that can be done today. They recognize that in a turbulent environment problems do not stay solved and that their solutions often generate a number of new and more difficult problems. Problem dissolution avoids both these consequences.

The advantages of dissolving a problem become apparent when we consider the fact that many, if not most, problems are not best treated where they appear. For example, when we get a headache, we do not try to solve it by brain surgery. Because someone understands how the human body works—how its parts interact to affect the whole—we swallow a pill. The pill contains a chemical that, when the pill dissolves in the stomach, enters the bloodstream. It is then carried to the pain center in the brain, where the headache is usually cured.

There are several lessons here. First, problems that arise in organizations are seldom best solved in the part of the organization in which they appear. To find the best or even a good way of treating them requires understanding of how the parts of the organization interact. Only then can one determine where to enter the system to get the "biggest bang for the buck" in getting rid of the problem.

It's important to realize that problems are not disciplinary; there is no such thing as economic, health, governmental, educational, physical, chemical (and so on) problems. The adjectives in front of the word *problem* tell us nothing about the problem. They tell us about the point of view of the person looking at the problem. It is clear in the examples that follow that the problems could be viewed in many different ways.

Idealized design plays a key role in dealing with many kinds of problems. Determining what to do at the selected point of entry to a problem, after it has been identified, can usually best be done by preparing an idealized redesign of either that point of entry or of the problem's containing system. The first example takes us through all the ways of treating a problem. After management failed using the first three ways, a consultant identified a way to dissolve the problem.

ENDING LABOR VIOLENCE ON CITY BUSES

A large city in Europe exclusively uses double-decker buses for public transportation. Each bus has a driver and a conductor. The driver is seated in a compartment separated by glass from the passengers. The conductor stands in the rear of the bus, where passengers enter and leave the bus.

In an effort to increase the productivity of the system, its management introduced incentives for both the driver and conductor. The closer the driver kept to a printed schedule, the more he earned. Most drivers liked the system because they made more under it than they had under the previous fixed-salary system.

The conductors collected zoned (hence variable) fares from boarding passengers, and issued receipts, which they collected from disembarking passengers, checking to see whether they had paid the correct fare. Unless the conductors signaled the drivers not to stop at the next stop, they would stop. They were also supposed to signal the drivers when the bus was ready to move on after a stop. Passengers who wanted to disembark at the next stop signaled the driver by pulling an easy-to-reach cord. Undercover inspectors rode the buses several times during a shift to determine whether conductors collected all fares and issued and checked all receipts. Incentive payments to conductors were reduced depending on how many times they were observed by the inspectors to have failed to collect fares or check receipts, the former being a more critical error. Conductors also preferred this system to the old one; they, too, earned more on average under this system.

To avoid delays during rush hours, conductors usually let passengers board the buses without collecting their fares, which they would subsequently try to collect between stops. Because of crowded conditions on the bus at peak hours, conductors could not always return to the entrance at the rear of the bus in time to signal the driver when to move on after a stop. This required the driver to determine when to do so by using his rear-view mirror. This caused delays that were costly to the driver—who was paid according to how closely he adhered to the printed schedule—but had no effect on the conductor. As a result, hostility developed between drivers and conductors. This hostility led to a number of violent confrontations between drivers and conductors, and injuries that were covered by the press. The conflict was fueled by the fact that conductors were usually immigrants of a minority race, whereas drivers were "true blue, and drivers and conductors were represented by different unions."

The local press pressured management of the system to do something about the violence. Management delayed action believing that, given time, the conflicting parties would settle their differences (absolution). They did not. Under further pressure from the press, management then identified the apparent cause of the conflict: the incentive system. Therefore, it announced its intention to return to the previous flat salary for drivers and conductors (resolution).

The separate unions immediately threatened to strike unless management was willing to pay drivers and conductors as much as the maximum they had earned under the incentive system. Management refused unless the unions could guarantee the same performance as had produced that maximum. The unions pointed out this was not possible because weather and drivers of other vehicles affected the performance of the buses, whose crews had no control over either of these. Management and the unions could not reach agreement.

Management then employed two university professors who specialized in management problem solving to attack the conflict. They suggested that the incentive payments to the driver and conductor on each bus be added at the end of the week and divided between the two (solution). This, they said, would force the two to collaborate. They were wrong. Both sides rejected the proposal, insisting that their compensation depend only on their performance, not the other's. They rejected any interdependence of earnings.

A human resource research institute in England was then employed to tackle the problem. The principal investigator assigned to the problem rented a room in a plush hotel in the city center and each evening invited four drivers and four conductors, selected at random, to food and drinks followed by a roundtable discussion of the problem. On each of three such occasions, the discussion ended in physical violence. The hotel threatened to sue the institute for damages.

While the principal investigator was considering alternative approaches to the problem, he showed it to a foreign visitor at the institute. The visitor asked how many buses were in operation at peak hours. The principal investigator said this was not relevant because the problem was independent of this number; it could exist on any number of buses. The visitor persisted. He wanted to know the containing system. Reluctantly, the principal investigator went to his files and found the number the visitor wanted. He then asked for the number of stops in the system, explaining that he needed this to have a picture of the system of which the bus was a part. The principal investigator again said this number was irrelevant because the problem could exist for any number of stops. Again the visitor persisted. Together they obtained a map and counted the number of stops. There were fewer than the number of buses operating at peak hours. Then he suggested that at peak hours the conductors be stationed at the stops, not on the buses. This would enable them to collect fares while passengers waited for the bus and always be in a position to check receipts from disembarking passengers. From their position at the outside rear of the bus, they could signal the driver when he could move out. Then, when the number of buses operating became fewer than the number of stops, the conductors could get back on the bus (dissolution).

The redesign of the system was accepted, and made it possible to provide almost every driver and conductor with eight-hour shifts rather than the four-on, four-off, four-on they had been on. They were delighted and happily went back to a fixed salary. It gave them more time to spend at home with their families, and it gave a number of them an opportunity to take on a separate full-time or part-time job.

It is frequently the case that redesigning a system that contains a part that has a problem can eliminate, dissolve, the problem, not merely solve it. The following example illustrates this point and the importance of looking at problems from a variety of points of view.

IMPROVING PRODUCTIVITY AT COATED PAPERS

The Coated Paper Company was very old. It was formed in the early part of the nineteenth century to produce high-quality papers used in expensive journals and books, usually ones that contain a good deal of color photographs or reproductions of paintings. From its beginning, the company promised its customers that it would never discontinue a paper (so that they could be assured of a supply as long as they wanted it). The paper was produced in a plant in Ohio that consisted of eight continuous production lines.

Although sales remained strong, the vice president of production faced a major problem. The productivity of the plant had declined almost continuously over the past five years. As a result, the plant was no longer profitable.

The vice president had initially suspected that the problem was due to the advanced age of the production equipment. Therefore, he had time studies conducted on the production lines but found no reduction in their rate of output. Then he concluded the lines must be down more often for repair and maintenance. A subsequent study of these activities over the past five years showed that this was not the case. Finally, he found the cause; it was the large number of products that had been added to the product line over the past five years. This required more and shorter production runs and, therefore, more setup time between runs. He was able to show that the increase in setup times exactly matched the decrease in output.

The vice president decided to call in a university-based professor and consultant whom he had worked with before and asked the consultant to meet him at the plant to discuss his productivity problem. The question he put to the consultant was this: "Is there any way of sequencing production runs so as to minimize total setup time?" The consultant told him there was, but the improvement that could be obtained depended critically on the accuracy of forecasts of production requirements. Efficient scheduling for poor forecasts would not yield much improvement in performance. The vice president asked how the potential saving might be estimated before launching a detailed study. The consultant said it could be done using a computer simulation of the plant, assuming a perfect forecast over the past five years and using the improved scheduling method. This would reveal the upper limit of improvement and, therefore, indicate whether the potential improvement was large enough to justify the time and expense of changing the scheduling process. The vice president authorized the simulation.

The simulation showed that the saving with perfect forecasting and improved scheduling was quite large and, therefore, further study was justified. The vice president agreed. However, in the course of carrying out the simulation, the consultant learned that only about 8 percent of the products accounted for all the profit and more than 90 percent of the production. Many of the old products were seldom sold, and when they were, it was usually in very small quantities and unprofitable.

Therefore, the consultant suggested to the vice president that unprofitable products be dropped from the product line because a larger saving could be obtained by doing so than by improving production sequencing. The vice president rejected the suggestion. He pointed out that he did not control the content of the product line; it was controlled by the marketing department. He was unwilling to discuss the possibility of reducing the product line with that department. He explained that he did not want to involve marketing management in production planning in any way. He said this would give that management carte blanche to interfere with production whenever it was so inclined. The consultant, who had also worked for the marketing department, tried to convince the vice president of production to the contrary but did not succeed.

The consultant went back to the sequencing problem but "cheated." He had the company's computing center run off a list of all products in the product line with their sales and production quantities over the past five years. The list was ordered from the most profitable down to the least. The consultant, starting at the bottom and working up, then determined how many of the products would have to be dropped to obtain the same saving the new sequencing procedure and a perfect (but unattainable) forecast would yield.

The consultant found that fewer products, all unprofitable, would have to be dropped than had been added in the past five years. When this was shown to the vice president of production, he reluctantly allowed the consultant to talk with the vice president of marketing at corporate headquarters. He instructed the consultant to make clear his, the vice president's, opposition to the meeting and why.

The consultant met with the vice president of marketing, went through the argument, and suggested a reduction of the product line. The vice president of marketing agreed with the argument but rejected the conclusion. He said that the unprofitable products were sold to profitable customers who might discontinue their purchases if availability of the unprofitable ones was discontinued. The consultant asked whether he had any evidence to this effect. The vice president said he did not, but he was not going to try to test it because of the risk involved. Regardless of how small that risk might be, he argued, it was not worth taking.

The defeated consultant retreated. However, he remained convinced that the problem should not be treated by changing the production scheduling. In desperation he recalled an infrequently used principle of inquiry: "If you can't solve the problem you are facing, you're probably facing the wrong problem." He then reformulated the problem, not as one requiring the reduction of the number of products offered for sale, but as reducing the number of products that had to be produced. He then saw that he had made a restrictive assumption: The only way to reduce the number of different products that had to be produced was to reduce the product line. There was another way: Don't sell as many of the unprofitable products. How to bring this about?

He conducted an idealized redesign of the sales force compensation system. The salespeople were being paid a flat salary plus a commission, a percentage of the dollar value of their sales. To a salesperson, a dollar's worth of profitable sales had no more value than a dollar's worth of unprofitable sales. The consultant came up with the following change in that system. The salespeople would continue to get the same base salary, but their commission would be based on the profitability of a sale. They would receive no commission for the sale of unprofitable products, but their commission for profitable products was raised. This increase was so designed that if the salespeople sold what they had sold the previous year, their income would be the same. Of course, if they sold more of the profitable products, their income would go up. On the other hand, if they sold either more or less of the unprofitable products, it would have no effect on their income.

When this design was shown to the vice president of production, he showed interest in it but pointed out that the vice president of human resources controlled compensation of salespeople. However, he allowed the consultant to talk to this vice president because he was not perceived as wanting to run production. The vice president of human resources was greatly interested in the scheme and said he was willing to try it without modification for six months in one of the five sales regions into which the United States was divided.

The trial was run. About 65 percent of the unprofitable products in the product line were not sold over the trial period in that region. Sales of profitable products increased by about 18 percent. The salesmen's income more than doubled. Company profit from the region also doubled. The resulting improvement in productivity of the plant from the change in this one region was greater than could be obtained with perfect forecasting and the best scheduling procedure known.

This experience revealed that every problem, no matter where it appears, is best approached from a variety of points of view. And the idealized design process opens the problems to a variety of treatments. Because it focuses on performance of the whole, it also prevents improving the performance of a part of a system while decreasing the performance of the whole of which it is a part.

In the next example, we briefly examine a problem of life or death for an organization dedicated to preserving life.

PRESERVING AN ORGANIZATION THAT PRESERVES LIFE

Contact is an organization in Harrisburg, Pennsylvania, that operated a 24-hour, 7-day-a-week, telephone-counseling service for those contemplating suicide. Its objective, of course, was to talk to those who call when thinking about ending their lives. Almost all of its operators were volunteers who had undergone appropriate training. It was financially supported exclusively by the United Way.

The United Way, because of its own financial problems, began to reduce support for Contact. As a result, Contact was threatened with the need to close shop. It asked a research center at the Wharton School for "pro bono" assistance. A team of faculty and students was formed to provide it.

In an idealized redesign session, the employees and volunteers of Contact agreed that the best way of dissolving the problem would make Contact self-supporting. The question was how to do it. The designers began to view themselves from outside, rather than inside, the box. They saw themselves as a facility with people answering phone calls from people needing help. From this perspective, they saw an opportunity to expand the population and purpose they served. Everything was already in place for Contact to begin offering a fee-based telephone-answering service to professionals and businesses. This enabled it to generate enough income to become financially independent and remain a hotline for would-be suicides.

In the next example, we see how the imposition of a market economy eliminated chronic corruption in a licensing system.

ISSUING LICENSES IN MEXICO CITY

Mexico City had a centralized bureau for issuing building licenses in its city hall. Licenses were required for even small changes in structures and, of course, new structures. It took a great deal of time to get an application processed. Efforts to get an application moved up in the waiting line was a major source of what the Mexicans call a *mordida* (a bite, a bribe). Unfortunately, as the number of bites increased, the associated applications formed a new waiting line of many applications that tended to cancel out any time savings. Delays continued. A rising chorus of complaints became more intense. They reached a point at which the mayor felt obliged to do something.

The mayor asked a research group at the National Autonomous University of Mexico to see what could be done about the problem. That group undertook an idealized redesign of the licensing system. It called for decentralizing the bureau and introducing the market economy to the system.

As a result, the city opened a licensing bureau in a storefront in each *colonia* (a ward or borough). One could go to any one to apply for a license. The only income each issuing station received was a fee from the city for each license it issued. Because an applicant could go to any one of the bureaus, the stations had to compete for them. A bureau that could not cover its costs would be closed.

The average time to receive a license was dramatically reduced, and bites were virtually eliminated.

This case shows how effective a market economy can be even in government. It suggests that any service provided by government should, where possible, have two or more sources. The income of these sources, therefore, should depend on the number of those who have a choice of the server that they serve. This forces them to compete for "customers."

SUMMARY

It was once considered desirable to "cut problems down to size." This was advice developed by problem solvers who approach problems analytically. Here we have presented an alternative approach, one that requires enlarging a problem to take in its containing system, a characteristic of problem dissolving. Problem dissolving employs design and, as we have been trying to show, idealized design is an effective way for dissolving problems.

In a related way, it was conventional wisdom to disaggregate the domain of experience into disciplines and then to classify problems by the domain in which they appear. All system problems have to do with the interactions of parts of the system, parts that fall into different, allegedly disciplinary domains. Because all the essential parts of a system interact, to treat any such part as autonomous is to distort the system that contains it. In a sense, therefore, all problems belong to the containing system as a whole, not to any one part of it alone. Therefore, there are always many different ways to approach a problem, but there is no better way than with an understanding of how the containing system works.

In the next chapter, you will see how idealized design is a powerful tool in facilities and site design.

8

Facilities and Sites Design

"I would never feel disoriented—I would always know
exactly where I am in the store, where everything else is,
where the checkout is. . . ."
—Customer specification for home furnishings store

The design of facilities and sites almost always requires
an integration of function and form (the arrangements
of its parts). In a well-designed facility or site, the form
is the servant of the function. Too frequently, the wrong
form prevents a site from functioning as intended. For
example, the higher in rank corporate executives rise,
the larger and more separated from each other are their
offices. This is based on the false assumption that priva-
cy is a perk and the need to interact with others is minimal at the top.

In this chapter, we demonstrate how idealized design
can be applied to the design of facilities and sites, and
we stress the importance of the interrelationship
between form and function.

In the two cases that follow, form is involved as well as
function. In the IKEA example, it is clear that the

malfunctioning of the design of its current stores as perceived by customers derives from the form of the buildings and the arrangement of their interior spaces. In the airline case, the containing form is determined by the shape of the airplane, but the interior space was open to modification.

IMPROVING SALES BY IMPROVING THE LAYOUT OF A STORE

In the mid-1990s, IKEA's Chief Executive for North America, Goran Carstedt, wanted to grow the home furnishings business by gaining an even deeper understanding of, hence better connections with, store customers. He hoped that idealized design would generate breakthrough ideas about stores, products, and services. To this end, IKEA, with the help of consultants, arranged for nine separate small groups of customers to design their "ideal IKEA shopping experience."

It quickly became clear that the participants wanted a store layout that differed significantly from the one IKEA was currently using. Some of the participants complained that the existing stores make them feel they are in a maze; they feel disoriented and suffer from sensory overload. The session facilitators reminded them that they need to start from scratch and focus on what they want rather than what they do not want. Given this guidance and prodding, they came up with breakthrough specifications:

- I would never feel disoriented—I would always know exactly where I am in the store, where everything else is, where the checkout is, and so on.
- If I am buying one item, all of the other items that go with it would be in the same place. I would not have to hunt around the store to find related things. For example, if I'm buying a sofa, then pillows, curtains, carpets, lamps, and picture frames would be nearby.
- Checkout should always be fast, and there should be self-checkout capabilities.
- Shopping at IKEA would be a relaxing, pleasant experience.

After the teams had developed their specifications, they were asked to develop a design that would bring the specifications about. They drew their designs on flip charts. Participants indicated that they wanted to create a "home base" in the store from which they could orient themselves to the vast array of products and departments and not suffer from information overload or disorientation. They came up with an octagon-shaped building with an open, airy central area with a cathedral ceiling. They described and sketched the following additional features that they wanted:

- The central area should be open and multistoried so that shoppers can look up or down, into or out of the center, and see where other departments are.

- The departments around the sides of the central area would be clearly labeled.

- There would be a Guggenheim Museum-like circular central area with a natural-light ceiling.

- At the top would be a restaurant providing an "oasis" where shoppers could relax, have Swedish food, converse, and think about their shopping needs.

- People would be able to go up and down levels using conveyors located in the central area.

In 1998, IKEA opened its Chicago store that incorporated many of the features of the users' designs. The building was 411,000 square feet (roughly seven football fields). The store quickly did twice as much business as expected. Therefore, IKEA added 50,000 square feet in 2001.

Large-sample surveys of customers, conducted by IKEA, reflect the improved design of the Chicago store:

- Fully 85 percent of customers rated the shopping experience "excellent or very good," and 15 percent rated it "good." None rated it "fair or poor."

- 93 percent of customers (purchasers and nonpurchasers) said they would "definitely or probably shop at IKEA again."

- Return visits to the Chicago store are higher than at other IKEA stores. After the store had been open only five months,

25 percent of customers had visited the store six or more times.

■ Shoppers spend an average of one hour longer in this store than do customers of other IKEA stores.

It is important to remember in this example that IKEA was offering the same merchandise in its Chicago store that it offered in all of its other stores. The difference in the sales was due entirely to the redesign of the layout of the merchandise.

The next example is one that all travelers can relate to. A major commercial aircraft manufacturer embarked on a study of the ideal interior of a plane of the future using idealized design.

IMPROVING THE QUALITY OF AIR TRAVEL

When you settle into your seat on a commercial airliner, the flight attendants—either real or on TV—always inform you of "the safety features of this aircraft." They finish by asking you to "sit back and enjoy the flight." But how many of us actually enjoy flying? It is likely that the more frequently we fly, the less we enjoy any given flight.

Knowing this, the Boeing Company undertook a study in 2001 designed to reflect the complaints air travelers have about the airline experience and to point the way toward an airliner of the future that would make it possible again to "sit back and enjoy the flight." The company initiated idealized designs prepared separately by different stakeholder groups. These included flight personnel, aircraft company executives and staff members, and frequent travelers. The description that follows is the result of synthesizing their specifications and designs. There was virtually no disagreement among them, nor were any of the designs identical.

What follows is a mixture of many of the specifications and design elements.

GENERAL OBJECTIVES

■ To make flying a unique and valued experience that exploits its uniqueness

■ To make the company's airplanes clearly and conspicuously different from airplanes manufactured by others

■ To provide users with maximum feasible physical flexibility and choice of activities

■ To facilitate inclusion of airlines' branding and differentiation needs

ENTERING THE PLANE

From the moment a passenger enters a plane, the flight experience begins and should reflect the needs and concerns of the passenger. There should be two entries, each wider than those currently in use. Overhead luggage storage bins should pull down for loading and unloading, with bins assigned to seats. Easily accessible storage space should be located under the floor in front of each seat. Seat numbers should be clearly visible on approach to them. Pillow and blanket storage should not be in overhead bins but should be easily accessible (perhaps, for example, held in the back of the facing seat).

GETTING SEATED

Passengers are going to spend virtually the entire time in a seat that should respond to their needs. Seats should be heated and completely adjustable, including up and down, with wraparound head and neck rest, and the ability to go flat for sleeping. Coat storage should be close and accessible to passengers instead of only to flight attendants. Seats should have the capacity to rotate slightly for changing eye contact and to make it easy to get in and out of. Every seat should have its own armrests. Passengers should be able to control temperature, air, and humidity both for feet and upper body. There should be handholds so that passengers in front of one are not disturbed when someone gets out. Some storage should be available beside each seat (perhaps in an armrest). All seats should have leg rests. Each seat should be provided with a convenient means of disposing waste such as napkins, accumulated wrappers, and so on. Seat belts should have reel-in and -out capacity, as in an automobile. Choice of records, movies, and video games should be available at each seat. Windows should be larger so that passengers can see down and up easily and so that the passenger seated nearest the window does not block the view of others. To give a feeling of intimacy, seating areas should be divided into smaller, flexible compartments that reduce the amount of the interior of the plane visible from each seat. Areas for serenity and socializing should be separated. When the seatback in front of a passenger is in a reclining position, it does not make eating or exit difficult.

IN THE AIR

Designers had a number of suggestions to make the experience aloft more enjoyable. Pilot or first officers should act as a tour guide, pointing out points of interest below over earsets and identifying sights on screens at passenger seats. Food service should be flexible and include a self-service option. There should be significant ability to express airline identity (colors, patterns, services, uniforms, lighting, materials, bar). Washrooms should be accessible forward and backward from all seats. Larger washrooms should be equipped with visible exhaust fans, windows, and automatic replaceable paper toilet seat covers. Cups and drinking water should be available in each washroom. There should be a special room for changing children's diapers. There should be a special room for clothes changes equipped with just a washstand. Cabin air should be filtered to remove risk of infection. A play area for small children should be provided. Instructions and announcements over the speaker system should be audible and comprehensible; if not, passengers should be able to signal the speaker. Interior lighting and window darkening should have the capability of producing the plane's own diurnal cycle (sunrise/sunset, airplane automatically postpones dawn). Immigration processing should be on board.

ONBOARD LOBBY AND BAR

Separate from the seating section, designers called for a lobby that contains a bar that serves hard and soft drinks, snacks, and doubles for duty free sales and catalogue purchases. Foldout seats should be hinged to the bar. Catalogue goods should be on display. Detailed information about the flight should be shown on the walls, including the cockpit control panel (with explanations) and clocks to show different relevant times. There should be washroom entries off the lobby. The lobby can then be used as a waiting area for use of the washroom. The bar should be revenue generating and self-supporting.

Many of these features are being designed into an airliner that Boeing has designated the 787 (now on offer to airlines). Other features are available as options to airlines that purchase the plane. In the hotly competitive world of commercial airline manufacturing, the 787 is "selling like hotcakes," in the words of one of the Boeing designers.

SUMMARY

There is, of course, a large variety of facilities and sites. Therefore, no handbook can be prepared to guide the designs of all of them. The unique characteristics of each must dominate their design. Their uniqueness lies in the functions they perform. We cannot do better than quote ourselves from the beginning of the chapter: "In a well-designed facility or site, the form is the servant of the function."

The next chapter, the last chapter in this part, summarizes the considerable amount of practical, hands-on, experience we have gained over the years in working with the idealized design process. If you are unsure whether it will work for you, this is the chapter you need to read.

9

Take the Plunge

"It is only by risking our persons from one hour to another that we live at all. And, often enough our faith beforehand in an uncertified result is the only thing that makes the result come true."
—William James

It should be clear to you that the wide range of applications we have presented in this book suggests that we believe idealized design has a virtually unlimited potential to "dissolve" the problems organizations face today, or to discover what organizations can do today to prepare for the future. In our experience, we have found that there are two situations in which managers are most open to idealized design.

You may face an intractable crisis here and now. Or you may be in an organization that is doing well but you want your organization to do even better in the future—to move to the frontier of management.

In this chapter, we draw on our experience with idealized design to tell you how both groups of managers, and even those somewhere in between, can benefit from the process. You will also see that individuals can experience great personal success and satisfaction by participating in a design process. And, finally, we tell you about potential obstacles you may encounter and how to overcome them.

The underlying message of the chapter is that after you are convinced that idealized design is what your organization needs, you should be ready to jump right in—take the plunge into applying the process.

OVERCOMING TODAY'S CRISIS

We do not have to tell you whether your organization is confronted with a crisis—small or large. You know that already. What we can tell you is that if your organization has not been able to fix the problem after many attempts, it is a prime candidate for an idealized design. The chances are that the crisis is the result of a *systemic* problem and that previous fixes only affected a part of the overall system. We have argued from the beginning that you cannot fix a systemic problem by fixing only one part. The great power of idealized design is that it identifies a much wider set of possible solutions and opportunities to make changes in the larger system that will make the symptoms in the part disappear.

What can you do as an individual to wake up your organization to the need to undertake an idealized design? Our experience tells us that the answer is to lead by example. Start where you are, the unit or activities you manage. You may not even have to get higher approval. Success in your area will make it clear to others that idealized design might be the answer to the larger problems, too. We have seen this happen often, including in some of the examples in this book. And (dare we say it?) it can enhance your reputation in the organization.

MAKING A GOOD ORGANIZATION BETTER

An organization that is not in the middle of a crisis may not seem to be a candidate for an idealized design. However, there are almost always individuals in successful organizations who are thinking about the future and how they can improve their competitive edge now in a rapidly changing global economy. They perceive idealized design as a tool to make their organizations even better as they confront the future.

Successful organizations use idealized design to generate breakthrough product and service innovations. They use the process to become more organizationally flexible and adaptable. It gives them more proactive control over their future instead of waiting to react to changes in their marketplace.

MAKING WORK MORE SATISFYING

On an individual level, idealized design can reduce the level of fear of being left behind by competitors. People who apply idealized design benefit in their personal and professional development. It makes work more satisfying by producing a greater impact while providing stimulating challenges in thinking about the future. Most people use only a part of what they know in their present jobs, but they are able to use *all* of their knowledge in participating in an idealized design. And, as we have pointed out previously, it can make proactive managers more visible to senior management and can thereby enhance career prospects. Finally, remember the "surprising ingredient" we told you about in Chapter 1, "The Stages of Idealized Design": Participation in preparing such a design is great fun.

If you are in an organization that has never undertaken an idealized design, there will almost certainly be obstacles to overcome. Next we tell you about a number of these and how you can overcome them.

OVERCOMING OBSTACLES TO IDEALIZED DESIGN

Even the best-planned idealized design can run into obstacles that can threaten success. To prepare you for overcoming potential obstacles, we close this chapter by describing the kinds of obstacles you may encounter and tell you how to cope successfully with them.

One set of obstacles is psychological. As with all new processes, some people tend to resist the process of idealized design because of what they mistakenly believe and fear about it. The other set of obstacles arises in the course of the design process.

Here are some of both kinds of obstacles followed by discussions that offer ways of overcoming them.

PSYCHOLOGICAL OBSTACLES

- Belief that it is too complicated.
- Belief that it is too time-consuming.
- Fear that the design will be too pie-in-the-sky and not implementable.
- Fear that the process will raise unrealistic expectations that will disappoint and frustrate the designers.
- In a threatening environment, the belief that they do not have the time to engage in such a process.
- The inability to imagine that the existing system "was destroyed last night."
- The fear that they might lose their jobs in the new design.

PROCEDURAL OBSTACLES

- Meetings are too infrequent and have uneven attendance.
- Some participants dominate the sessions, whereas others don't speak up.
- Some managers love authority and won't relinquish it in an idealized design.
- Some participants can't think outside the box while they are in it.
- The culture of the company has "trained" employees to be passive and they do not believe that they will be granted any control of their future.
- Top management does not support the design process and will not support the final design.

Let's look as these obstacles and explain why they do not stand up to our experience with idealized design in the real world.

OVERCOMING PSYCHOLOGICAL OBSTACLES

- **Belief that it is too complicated.** The first impression of idealized design can make it seem complicated. It is essential at the initial orientation that the facilitator describe the process and emphasize that there is an inherent logic to the design sessions. This impression is usually dissipated when participants understand the complete process.

- **Belief that it is too time-consuming.** With all the meetings people now attend, they understandably worry that more meetings will take that much more time. But the design process reduces the need for other meetings that deal with problems resulting from a lack of design in the past. Furthermore, critical organizational problems are raised in the design process—ones that are not raised in other meetings—and they are treated openly and effectively. In the end, there should be fewer meetings than now.

- **Fear that the design will be too pie-in-the-sky and not implementable.** Before an idealized design is first prepared, there is a natural tendency to think that there is no way that it will ever be implemented. There are simply too many impediments to making it a reality. But it must be remembered that the goal is to approximate the idealized design as closely as possible, not necessarily to implement it exactly. We have found that participants almost always are surprised at how many of the parts of an idealized design can be implemented. A conventional planning process would not result in the implementation of the best elements of an idealized design.

- **Fear that the process will raise unrealistic expectations that will disappoint and frustrate the designers.** Some managers may feel that the process will make their subordinates (or customers) hopeful, only to have their hopes dashed when nothing is changed. What happens in practice, however, is that many creative ideas are generated that are widely supported, and it becomes evident that a number of them can be productively pursued.

- **In a threatening environment, the belief that they don't have the time to engage in such a process.** Instead of dealing with current threats conventionally—solving or resolving them—participants find that in idealized design they can deal with them creatively and dissolve them, and usually in less time than conventional approaches require.

- **The inability to imagine that the existing system "was destroyed last night."** Present reality can make it difficult for people to clear their minds and imagine a new system unencumbered by present conditions. It is up to the design facilitator to keep reminding participants of this liberating assumption.

- **Fear that they might lose their jobs in the new design.** It is natural to worry that it will result in downsizing. To overcome this fear, it is essential that the CEO assure participants that no one engaged in the design process will lose his or her job or be demoted as a result of participation.

OVERCOMING PROCEDURAL OBSTACLES

- **Meetings are too infrequent and have uneven attendance.** Design facilitators must insist on holding meetings no less frequently than once a month. Otherwise, there will be too much redundant updating and repetition of old discussions at each meeting.

- **Some participants dominate the sessions, whereas others don't speak up.** Inevitably, some voluble participants will attempt to dominate the discussions and others will fear to speak up and make "fools" of themselves. The facilitator's role is crucial in calling on the quiet participants—while keeping the vocal ones from dominating—to be sure that all ideas are out for consideration. There is no corner on creativity and the design process should strike a creative spark in all participants—even the quiet ones.

- **Some managers love authority and won't relinquish it in an idealized design.** The prospect of change always threatens the status quo in organizations. Some managers try to hold on to their authority in planning sessions—including withholding their knowledge when knowledge is power. To overcome this obstacle, the design facilitator needs to reiterate the difference between *power over* and *power to* accomplish something. This is especially important when the design gives power to highly educated subordinates, who will always be more attracted to a democratic organization than an autocratic one. When reluctant managers realize that they will gain more than they lose by democratization, they should enthusiastically participate.

■ **Some participants can't think outside the box while they are in it.** Try as they may, they do not seem to be able to see problems from outside their present experience. This can be mitigated by arranging meetings early in the process with stakeholders who do not participate in the design process. By insisting that the stakeholders' suggestions be positive, not negative, the design team members will not only gain an important perspective but also make the idealized design acceptable to those stakeholders outside the design process. In addition, a good facilitator will stimulate out-of-the-box thinking by providing examples of it.

■ **The culture of the company has "trained" employees to be passive and they don't believe that they will be granted any control of their future.** In an organization in which senior management presently sets the direction, often in a command and control fashion, it is quite foreign to many middle managers and staff members that they can use idealized design to think boldly and to proactively contribute to their organization's future. In a well-run idealized design, they come to realize that the process helps them to have an impact on the organization.

■ **Top management doesn't support the design process and will not support the final design.** For a successful organization-wide idealized design, it is essential that the CEO or a relevant senior manager be a part of the design process from the beginning. At the initial orientation, the design facilitator needs to tactfully make it clear to top management that their prestige is at risk if they fail to participate in and support the effort.

SUMMARY

We can best close this chapter on taking the plunge into an idealized design by repeating the quote from William James with which it began: "It is only by risking our persons from one hour to another that we live at all. And, often enough our faith beforehand in an uncertified result is the only thing that makes the result come true."

This ends Part II. The chapters in this part have described idealized design applied to a wide range of businesses and organizations, and this last chapter has provided insights into the conditions that can make or break an idealized design. In Part III, we explore the application of idealized design to some of the major challenges facing the world today.

IDEALIZED DESIGN: NO LIMIT— APPLICATIONS TO WORLD CHALLENGES

10

The Urban Challenge

An Urban Car
A Redesign of Paris and Beyond

"The private motorcar [is] a method that happens to be, on the basis of the number of people it transports, by far the most wasteful of urban space."
—Lewis Mumford

So far in this book, we have focused on applying idealized design to businesses and other related organizations. We are convinced, however, that idealized design can be a powerful tool in responding to many of the major challenges facing the world today. In this part, we apply idealized design to some of these challenges.

In this first chapter of Part III, we show how idealized design can be applied to the perennial challenge of cities and large urban areas. The first example is an automobile design specifically for cities, and the second is a redesign of Paris as a national and international city.

AN URBAN AUTOMOBILE

When the automobile was first conceived and mass produced, it was a luxury item. Therefore, it was designed as a general-purpose vehicle, one to be used for both within- and between-communities movement. But, as Lewis Mumford observed, "The private motorcar [is] a method that happens to be, on the basis of the number of people it transports, by far the most wasteful of urban space."

Not only is space wasted, but also time. The value of the amount of time lost in moving within cities, especially at peak hours, has become large. For example, the time currently required to go to the center of Philadelphia from one of its northern suburbs is as large, or larger, than was required of a horse-drawn carriage a century ago. In one Latin American city, there recently was a gridlock involving thousands of automobiles that could not be moved for hours. During the delay, several people died of heart attacks. Medical treatment could not reach them to provide emergency aid.

Extended delays on urban expressways due to accidents is a common experience. Moreover, the pollution created by idling vehicles is mounting precipitously.

The fact that today most households have more than one automobile makes it reasonable to consider the possibility of designing two different types of automobile, one for intra-urban use, and one for inter-urban use. A small car for intra-urban use promises the possibility of reducing urban congestion, which is reaching crisis dimensions in many cities. Some cities have restricted the use of automobiles within their urban core, but a small urban car would only have to be restricted to, say, Monday through Friday from 6 a.m. to 7 p.m.

Realizing the advantages of such a car, a group of professors and their students decided several years ago to undertake an idealized design of one and then explore its potential with auto manufacturers. Remember, idealized design assumes that the present model was destroyed last night and that designers start with a clean slate. Our design does not look like today's small cars, most of which are little more than shrunken versions of full-size sedans.

The first question to answer is how large should an urban automobile be? Research in American and Mexican cities revealed that the average number of passengers per car was 1.2. Therefore, it was decided to make the urban automobile a two-passenger car.

However, there are times when there is a need to move more than two people. This requirement was delayed for consideration later in the design process. Still, the problem is not a major one because today we often want to move more people with present cars than can fit in one car and we manage to move them—usually with more than one car.

The next step in the design process was drawing a seat for the driver, because it was decided to retain the current assumption that the driver should be in a sitting position (see Figure 10.1). Next, the passenger; in two-passenger vehicles—for example, sport cars—is always seated beside the driver facing forward. But studies have shown that a passenger is safer if sitting facing the rear of the vehicle. Then in the event of a collision, the passenger is thrown against the back of his/her seat rather than into a windshield. This opened two possibilities: Seat the passenger backward beside the driver, or backward behind the driver.

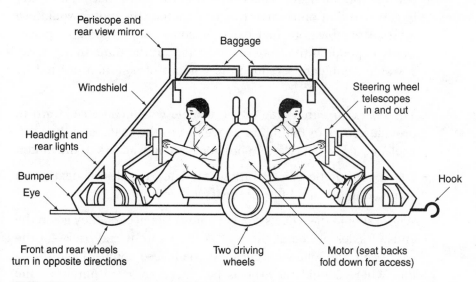

Figure 10.1 A schematic design of an urban automobile

This led to a study of the density of people in moving traffic that could be achieved if all cars were two passenger but were either all side by side, or all one behind the other. The increase in density that could be obtained by the narrower but longer car was several times greater than that which could be obtained by the shorter and wider vehicle. This was due to the fact that all lanes could be divided in half, bearing two of the narrower cars side by side, and half of the shoulders of expressways could be used for this much lighter vehicle. Therefore, it was decided to place the passenger behind the driver.

Now where should the motor go? It could go at either end as it does in current automobiles. But another question challenged conventional thinking: Where should it go to maximize the stability of the vehicle? The answer was "in the middle, between the seats of the driver and passenger."

How fast should the car be able to go? Studies have shown that movement at speeds of about 40 miles per hour made for the greatest density of people on a road. Therefore, the urban car required a motor that would move the car up to speeds of about 50 miles per hour but no faster. This meant that the motor need not be any larger than that on a small tractor. Whether the motor would use internal combustion, fuel cells, or some other source of power would depend on the state of technology at the time. In any case, it would significantly reduce the amount of pollution created by vehicles.

The doors on either side of the vehicle would slide backward to provide access to the motor as well as to the seats, and the seatbacks would fold forward to provide complete access to the motor.

Leaving aesthetic considerations for later, the design next put a simple frame around the two seats and motor.

Where should the wheels go? On conventional cars, they go on the ends of axles placed at the four corners—front and back—of the car. Again, the follow-up question challenged conventional thinking: Where should the wheels be placed so as to minimize the transmission requirements? The answer was clear: two wheels on a driving axle in the middle, directly under the motor. This would enable a direct connection between the motor and driving axle. Then the design placed one wheel at each end of the car. These would be "idler" wheels, not driven by the motor. But they would control the car's direction in a straight line or turning. They could be geared so as to turn in opposite directions simultaneously when the driver wanted them to. This would reduce the turning radius of the car to virtually zero. Otherwise, only one of these wheels would turn to control the direction of the car, while the other "rear" wheel would swivel freely when the car turns.

The vehicle was now symmetrical, the same from either end. Where should the steering wheel and other controls go? The current assumption is "at one end, where the driver is." However, what would happen if it were possible to drive the car from either end, but only one end at a time? Two major advantages would be possible if the vehicle were parked at an angle to the curb so as to extend out into the street no more than a current automobile parked conventionally does. First, a number of these cars could fit into the space currently occupied by one conventional car. Second, this car could be parked without holding up cars coming behind it. It could pull right into an open space without backing up.

However, in pulling out from a parking space at an angle to the curb, the driver would have poor visibility, unless the car could be driven from the other end. Then the car could pull out without holding up traffic. Therefore, the design put controls at both ends with the proviso that the controls would only be operative from one end at a time. The steering wheel would retract at the end at which the controls are not in use.

Luggage, or other items such as groceries, could be placed on a rack on top of the car, and covered in bad weather.

Returning to the question of how to accommodate more than two people, one possible combination was a mother who has, say, three children. To accommodate them, the design would include another vehicle, a cab just like the car but without a motor or controls, and it would hook onto an equipped car. Each vehicle would have a retracting or folding hook on one end and a retracting or folding eye on the other. The mother could pull the kids around at will and not have to listen to them, although it would be easy to place a communication link between the car and cab. Other possible combinations of passengers would be accommodated in a similar fashion.

Now every car would be a potential tractor for any other car. Cars that break down on the road could be pulled to a repair place by any other car. Furthermore, chains of cars could be assembled at designated points and drawn by small tractors to specified locations. Drivers and passengers could relax, even sleep, during the trip.

To maximize the safety of the car, each would have a bumper like that on electrified bumper cars found in amusement parks. Bumper cars reach speeds of well over five miles per hour but, in contrast to current automobiles, they collide head-on with no damage to vehicles or passengers. Therefore, the design provided similar shock-absorbing bumpers all around our car.

To increase safety further, a sensing device would be located between head/taillights. It would signal cars approaching from the rear when they are getting too close by flashing a light at them. They would also signal the driver of the car when he is getting too close to the car in front of him/her. In addition, periscopes would be provided at both ends of the car so that the driver could see over the top of the vehicles in front of him/her. Research has shown that this significantly reduces accidents.

The completed design was discussed with potential manufacturers of such a vehicle, companies not currently manufacturing automobiles. They were asked for estimates of what they might be sold for. Their answers were about one half the price of the lowest-priced automobile currently available. This would open the market for them in less-developed countries where current automobiles are just too expensive.

Because automobiles are currently used for such a small percentage of their available time, the design addressed whether the urban cars should be publicly owned and publicly available. Then they could be made to operate off of credit or debit cards. One could pick anyone up to go wherever one wanted and just leave it on the street or at assembly points where one arrived. It would then be available to anyone else to use. If off-street assembly points were used, it would free streets of parked cars. Such assembly points could be used to keep the cars fueled and maintained.

An economic analysis of public ownership and availability of these cars revealed that even if the cost to users per mile was no greater than it is currently in their own vehicles, they would become by far the largest source of income to cities through the "rental" revenue generated by users.

Since this concept of a small urban automobile was prepared and published, several two-passenger urban vehicles have been produced in Europe. One is the reincarnated Volkswagen New Beetle, introduced in 1998. Another is the Smart Car from Daimler-Chrysler, which has lost money in Europe but still may be introduced in the United States at some future time. Yet another similar car is under development by Pininfarina, called the Nido, the concept car that was introduced at the Geneva auto show in 2004. But each of these has different designs than ours. They have only a few of the advantages designed into this urban car. Still, not all the features in our design would have to be used at once; some could be used to improve conventional automobiles.

It should be borne in mind that continual building of additional urban expressways does not reduce congestion. New and better means of getting from one place to another generally create more new demand than the amount of old demand that new highways satisfy.

A REDESIGN OF PARIS AND BEYOND

Early in 1971, a group at the Wharton School at the University of Pennsylvania was engaged by the French government to do a study of the future of Paris. There was a widespread belief within the French government and among the public that something needed to be done about the capital city. It was suffering from administrative neglect. It had been allowed to grow with nothing other than economic planning; all the other aspects of the city's growth and development had been ignored. Consequently, the city was deteriorating, had no sense of its "role," no sense of its future, no sense of what it "ought to be." Paris was the only city in France without its own government; it was governed by France's national government. The consequences extended beyond the city itself because, as part of a national system, "Whatever happened to Paris seemed to radiate and resonate throughout France; in one way or another it affected the entire country."[1]

The project was organized so as to obtain the widest possible participation by the French authorities and by stakeholder groups selected to represent the widest possible spectrum of opinion. The project was organized into four stages: 1) formulation of the mess; 2) redesign toward a desired future; 3) planning approximations to the design; and 4) organizational and implementation planning.

The project team identified the current "dissonances" within Paris and its national and European environment and projected into the future assuming that then-current governmental policies were not changed. The projection revealed a mess with "catastrophic potentialities hidden in the current situation." The need for fundamental change in existing policies and the lack of policies that were needed became apparent. The project team then conducted a survey to obtain opinions as to what Paris ought to be. The team synthesized the information obtained into a set of specifications for a design of a desired Paris. The dominant values that emerged were *primacy* and *uniqueness*, "both being, in the French mind, historical properties of Paris as an 'ideal city.'"

The design team then established the following goals to realize these values:

- **Political**
  Become self-governing
  Become an open city
  Denationalize
  Become the capital of the European Community
  Become the seat of multinational authorities

- **Economic**
  Develop multinational functional specializations
  Become the seat of less-developed country product associations
  Become the center of marketing specializing in transnational marketing
  Develop worldwide financial management information systems

- **Urban**
  Limit population influx
  Deflect industry to dynamic regions
  Become a world center for environmental research planning services
  Protect the center of the city by regulation
  Become a locus of high-tech industry
  Become a center of information systems design and production
  Become a center of knowledge-based services

The deconcentration of population in Paris required considering its effects on other parts of France. This led to a plan for the regionalization of France. The western regions had resisted industrialization, whereas the eastern regions were rapidly industrializing. So, it was planned to bring new industries into the west based on local traditions (for example, mariculture and tourism) plus natural growth of the existing economic base. Then transnational regions were planned around Lille, Metz, Nancy, Lyon, and St. Etienne as industrial catchment areas.

In redesigning Paris, the traditional types of industries it housed had to be replaced by technologically based enterprises. Paris was also conceived as the capital of the European Community and as a global city. As such, attention had to be given to the *cultural* functions of the city, including the following:

- Regulate new construction in the center of the city
- Eliminate private traffic from the center of the city
- Create multinational accommodation facilities
- Establish a university of development
- Create and establish a university of the world
- Create a center of non-national cultural events

Two of the most exciting ideas to surface among cultural-function-related goals were the university of development, and the university of the world. The former was conceived to support the "*centre mediateur*" idea (Paris as existing in a privileged crossroads and acting as a non-national mediating center of France and beyond), and would be exclusively directed at facilitating the socio-economic development of the Third World. A special curriculum for this institution was outlined, and contains innovations in this long-neglected field.

The second, more ambitious idea was to create at some later date a university that would be "multinational in every sense: curriculum content, faculty, and student body." It was envisioned to be "one of the central nodes of a global educational networks. . . ."

To validate the plan, the Wharton group was asked to conduct an extensive survey covering representatives of all the stakeholders groups, in and out of France. The survey—using a Delphi methodology—was intended to determine whether the concept of Paris as a global city was valid in the opinion of the constituents who had been introduced into the overall design. This was consistent with the principle of participation that the Wharton group had established from the beginning. The survey revealed that the subjects clearly agreed with the concept of Paris as a global city, but not as the only one. They thought New York, São Paulo, and Singapore would follow the same development.

In addition, the meaning of three key terms had undergone significant change as a result of the work on the project. They had become enlarged. What had originally been construed to be Europeanization now appeared to have become the "globalization" of Paris; what had been originally understood as regionalization now appeared to imply the "Europeanization" of France; and the narrow meaning of participatory democracy as a critically acquired property of a desired Paris now seemed to have become akin to the process Ackoff has called "humanization"—something that suggests realms of social, but especially cultural, consonance among peoples. The design played a major role in the subsequent development of Paris and the rest of France. Traffic patterns, building zoning, industrial development and location, population distribution, universities, and many other elements have felt the impact of the design. Even today, more than 30 years after the design, elements of the design are still at work in guiding the way Paris and France evolve.

In the next chapter, we apply idealized design to one of the most intractable problems facing the United States—and other countries—today. This is the fair and equitable delivery of health care to all citizens.

11

The Health-Care Challenge
A National Health-Care System
A Health-Care Mall

"About half the debtors cited medical causes, indicating that between 1.850 and 2.227 million Americans (filers plus dependents) experienced medical bankruptcy."[1]
—Study in Health Affairs: *The Policy Journal of the Health Sphere*

> The disparity between health care available to different members of society is deplorable. In this chapter, we apply idealized design first to a national health-care system that delivers care equitably to everyone, and then to an improved way of delivering it locally.

A NATIONAL HEALTH-CARE SYSTEM

Almost everyone agrees that the U.S. health-care system is not ideal. It is estimated that 45 million people have no health coverage. The result is that health care is delivered unequally, and the costs are borne unequally. A study released in 2005 disclosed that about half of those surveyed who filed for bankruptcy "cited medical causes, indicating that between 1.850 and 2.227 million Americans (filers plus dependents) experienced medical bankruptcy."[1] Among the policy implications of the study was that "The privations suffered by many debtors—going without food, telephone, electricity, and health care—lend credence to claims that coverage was unaffordable and belie the common perception that bankruptcy is an 'easy way out.'"

Many proposals have been put forward to fix the system, but none of the leading proposals would *transform* it; they would only reform it and then only its financial aspects. By itself, changing the way medical care is paid for will not transform its delivery system. Before deciding how health care should be paid for, we should first design a system that is worth paying for.

Although some of the proposals under discussion would improve the current system by covering persons not currently insured, they would not make the changes most needed to make it focus on the preservation of health rather than treatment of sickness or disability. The design that follows was intended to show how unnecessary treatment, excessive administrative costs, malpractice, and fraud might be reduced. It does this by focusing on the needs and desires of those treated before focusing on the needs and desires of those providing the treatment.

The effort was organized and facilitated, in 1993, by a small group of professors from the Wharton School of the University of Pennsylvania. Representatives of all stakeholder groups were organized into a consortium that prepared the following design. These included individual and institutional health-care providers, users of the system, communities in which health care is provided, employers, insurance companies, suppliers serving the health-care industry, and the U.S. government.

The first two design sessions were disappointing in that none of the output was surprising or innovative. A breakthrough occurred when the facilitating group of three—the executive committee of the group—meeting between design sessions, became aware of the fact that the health-care system they were trying to replace was not a health-care system at all but rather a sickness- and disability-care system. The two types of system are not equivalent. The current system was directed at getting rid of or alleviating what we do not want, sickness and disability, not getting what we want, health. When one gets rid of what one does not want, one does not necessarily get what one does want. In fact, one may get something worse. Recall that the effort to get rid of alcoholic beverages in the United States not only failed to do so, but it stimulated the development of organized crime.

When the observation—that a sickness- and disability-care system is not equivalent to a health-care system—was shared with the larger design group, creative design took over. The design that is summarized in what follows departs significantly from the current system. A more detailed presentation of it than what follows, together with an application of it, can be found in Ackoff and Rovin (2003).

THE DESIGN

The system would provide essential health-care services (including preventive, long-term, wellness and optical, auditory, and dental services) to every legal resident of the United States. It would also provide coverage to all employed illegal residents at a cost to their employers. This should discourage the employment of illegal immigrants and even their immigration.

Health-care services would be funded by an annual health-care tax paid by individuals to the Internal Revenue Service (IRS). This tax would reflect the individual's income, age, number of dependents, lifestyle, health status, and environment. Those with a low or no income would pay no tax.

Employers would only pay a health-care tax that would be proportional to the hazards of their employment conditions. In addition, they could elect to pay all or part of their employees' health-care taxes. If they elect not to pay any of these taxes, they would initially be required to increase employees' salaries by the amount they, the employers, currently contributed to the employees' health-care insurance.

The IRS would collect the health-care taxes and issue annual health-care vouchers and wellness stamps to each eligible individual. The value of these vouchers would be independent of the amount of taxes paid; it would reflect the health-related characteristics of the individual (for example, age, disabilities, and lifestyle). Actuarial experts located in the National Institutes of Health or some other appropriate agency, but not in the IRS, would determine the value of the vouchers issued. The wellness stamps could only be used for wellness-related activities.

Individuals would be free to select any primary-care provider who has elected to practice within the system. They would give the providers they select their vouchers.

The primary-care providers would receive monthly payments from the IRS that reflect the number and nature of the people who have submitted their vouchers to them. The primary-care providers would then be required to pay for all essential health-care services and products they provide or prescribe. The personal income of the primary-care providers would be the difference between the payments from the IRS and their costs for the services and products they provide and prescribe. *Therefore, the better the health of those served, the more profitable it would be for the primary-care providers, and the lower would be the tax rate for individuals.* Later we describe why primary-care providers would have no incentive to prescribe fewer services and products, regardless of their patients' needs, to minimize their costs and maximize their residual income. Primary health-care providers might also receive some payment for second opinions as described later.

By offering monetary incentives, the system would encourage the use of preventive services by many who do not use the current system, thereby decreasing long-run costs, for example, for prenatal care and immunization, particularly of children.

Community health-care boards would administer health-care programs in each community. These boards would define essential health-care services, certify health-care providers for practice within the community, and monitor the quality of their services. Such monitoring would reduce the number and intensity of malpractice suits. They would establish courts to adjudicate complaints. In addition, the boards would maintain a medical information system that would be part of a national network. This system would provide its users with such information as they require to make intelligent choices of health-care services and servers.

The National Institutes of Health (NIH) or another appropriate federal agency would establish medical-record and other informational standards to be adhered to by all communities.

The IRS would provide each community health-care board with the funds required to carry out its responsibilities.

Individuals would be able to choose and pay primary-care providers who practice outside the system, but even if they did, they would still have to pay the health-care tax.

Primary-care providers would be able to operate either within or outside the system, but not both. Those operating within the system would have some control over selection and retention of patients.

Wellness vouchers would cover the cost of participation in certified wellness programs. Tax deductions would be available to those who attended such programs regularly.

The system would provide the following checks and balances to ensure that patients received as much service as they require:

- The value of an individual's voucher would increase with each annual renewal with the same primary-care provider.

- Individuals could change primary-care providers once a year with no penalty, and more often with a penalty.

- Individuals could obtain second opinions. If these agreed with those of the primary-care providers', the individual would have to pay for the cost involved; otherwise, the primary-care providers would have to do so.

- The community health-care board would arrange for audits of provider performance and revoke certification or require further education of those who do not meet their standards.

- The community health-care information system would provide information regarding the best practices and the quality of services provided by those operating both within and outside the system.

Primary-care providers would be able to insure themselves against such adverse selection of patients as would reduce their net income below what they consider to be an acceptable minimum. This would cover them only if their net income was less than the specified minimum. Their premiums would be proportional to the minimal income level they selected.

The federal government would provide scholarships to medical students who agree to serve for a specified period of time as a primary-care provider in currently underserved rural or urban areas.

THE EFFECTS OF THE DESIGN

In 1991, total savings produced by this design were estimated to be about $306 billion per year. This would have been enough to cover all those then not covered by health insurance and leave enough to cover optical, auditory, dental, and wellness-program costs. Therefore, the design team did not expect the system it designed to require any additional expenditure.

The design team identified additional effects the design would produce. National health-care costs would be substantially reduced, but the coverage of all legal residents of the United States would be significantly extended. Medicare and Medicaid would be eliminated. The role of the federal government would be significantly reduced. Employers would be required to cover cost of only work-related health care. The system would be market driven with incentives to encourage appropriate behavior and with disincentives to discourage abuse by any of the participants. It would provide health-care services to areas currently underserved. It would encourage the formation of integrated health-care systems.

AN APPLICATION

A version of this national health-care system was adapted and applied to the health-care system operated by the Sisters of Charity of Nazareth Corporation. Seven hospitals—five in Kentucky, one in Tennessee, and one in Arkansas—put the design into practice.

A HEALTH-CARE MALL

Individuals experience health care at the point at which they interact with health-care practitioners. In this example, we offer a design of a health-care facility that delivers high-quality care efficiently to everyone who comes in. It could be a part of the national health-care system previously discussed, or a stand-alone local system.

The organization of the facility is flexible enough that individuals and groups of primary-care practitioners could operate in facilities of their own or out of malls where population density makes them feasible. For simplicity's sake, we call all of these facilities "health-care malls." They can be located in academic or corporate campuses or facilities, near or connected to shopping malls or other places where there are concentrations of people.

New users coming to a health-care mall would go to a reception and information desk where "smart cards" (or equivalent technology) would be prepared for them, or a reading would be taken off the cards they already have (see Figure 11.1). Appointments would then be made with the server(s) selected by the users or to whom they would be assigned if they had no preference. The information on their smart cards would be transmitted to the relevant servers. Walk-ins would be welcome, and they would be accommodated as the schedules of the mall health-care staff permit. Appointments could also be made by phone. The intention would be to make access to the mall as user friendly as possible.

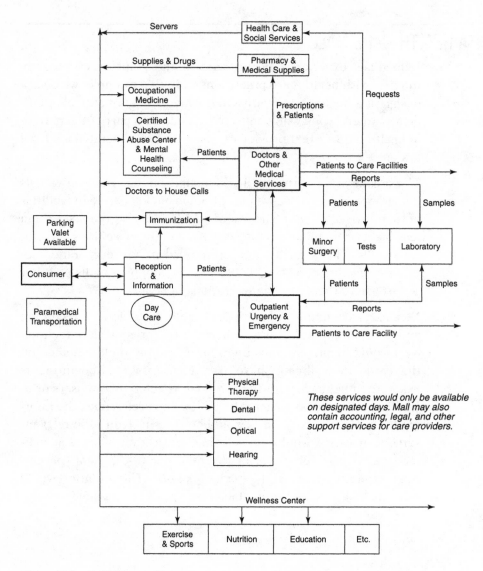

Figure 11.1 Health-care mall

The malls would normally include the following servers and services:

- Physicians

    These would cover general practice, internal medicine, pediatrics, and other such specialists as are justified in the community served. They would be assisted by primary-care nurse-practitioners and nurses. There would be a relatively small number of specialists, only the number and types justified by the area served; for example, one or more gynecologists and orthopedists might be justified. Referrals could be made to specialists inside or outside the mall by primary-care providers.

- An emergency unit

   This unit would take care of emergencies and urgent cases that are not likely to subsequently require inpatient care. However, it would provide beds to facilitate observation and treatment of patients. If a patient required more care than could be provided by this emergency unit, transportation would immediately be provided to a unit that could provide the care required. The mall's emergency unit would be accessible around the clock.

- A surgical and alternative procedure center (for outpatient care)

- Radiology, cardiology, and other testing facilities (to support primary care only)

- A laboratory

- An occupational-medicine consulting center

- A certified substance-abuse, mental health, and genetic-counseling center (which would also make home deliveries)

- A medical ethicist (who would be available on request)

   This and other services listed could be provided on a part-time basis. Servers could rotate among several malls.

- A health-care and social services unit

   This community-supported unit would provide counseling and advice. It would report persons needing but not receiving health care to the community health-care board. It would notify the appropriate primary-care providers of the services it has rendered. It would also provide home care and a mobile diagnostic and care unit for those who could not come to the mall or are better off at home than in a care facility.

- A day-care center for children of patients and employees

- Auxiliary services:

  A physical therapy unit

  Dentists

  Ophthalmologists, opticians, and optical services and products

  Hearing and speech services
- A wellness center, including such facilities as a:

  Health club (exercise and sports)

  Nutrition center

  Health education center
- An immunization unit (to provide essential immunizations and some optional ones for a fee)
- Parking (valet available)
- Paramedical transit (available to and from the mall)

This list of facilities and services is not meant to be exhaustive. Space would be available for such other related facilities and services as medically relevant accounting and legal services, health-book stores, and the sale or rental of athletic equipment.

As with other primary-care facilities, health-care malls could be either privately or publicly developed and owned. Rent would be paid by all servers, public or private, for the space they occupy.

Shuttle busses would connect the health-care malls to higher-level care units. The buses would operate on a regular schedule with designated pickup and drop-off points.

Individuals would not be required to use the mall located in their community; they could use any one of their choice. This would encourage competition among the malls and ensure their responsiveness to consumer needs.

The virtue of health-care malls is that they equalize the quality of the care given to everyone who comes in. They provide "one-stop shopping" instead of shuttling patients between specialists in multiple locations.

We have purposely not discussed the cost to the user of health-care malls. This critical topic is better treated in the design of a national health-care system described previously.

The next, and last, chapter in this part describes how idealized design can be used to cope with some of the major challenges facing governments in the world today.

12

The Challenges to Government
A National Elections System
A New United Nations
A Response to Terrorism

"[Social and economic development] provides economic alternatives to potential [terrorist] recruits, and it creates a new middle class that has a vested interest in maintaining peace."
—Rand Corporation study of terrorism and development

In this third and last chapter of Part III, we apply idealized design to a range of challenges that face the world today. In this chapter, we demonstrate that idealized design can be a powerful tool in dealing with national and international challenges that confront government. We begin with a design for national elections that would ensure the largest participation of eligible voters; we then design an international organization to replace the present United Nations that eliminates the myriad obstacles to its mission; and finally we put forward a design to cope with international terrorism, perhaps the greatest threat to nations today. In contrast to the other examples in this book, these examples are our own designs. They were not commissioned by outside organizations. As such, we offer them not as finished, definitive designs. They are intended to stimulate discussion and generate alternatives.

A NATIONAL ELECTION SYSTEM

When the system of elections in the United States was designed, the number of eligible voters nationally was less than it is today in most cities. In the beginning, voters could feel that their votes "counted." Today, this is no longer true; as a result, too many eligible voters do not vote in most national elections. In the 2004 presidential election, it is estimated that about 60 percent of those eligible to vote did so. Although a little more than 122 million voted, some 80 million eligible voters did not. A turnout of 60 percent might sound impressive, but those 80 million votes that were not cast exceed the total vote received by either major candidate.

What's worse, even fewer eligible voters vote in local elections, where their votes have the potential to affect them more directly than in a national election. Some studies show that 25 percent, or fewer, of eligible voters turn out in many local elections. Candidates in local elections are often completely unknown to most of the electorate, and the responsibilities of the positions for which they are running are equally unknown.

The reasons offered for low turnout are pervasive and varied. Campaigning is too long. It is too costly. The way campaigns are financed makes candidates beholden to special interests. Not enough detail on candidates' positions is provided. There is seldom an opportunity to question candidates about their positions.

A redesign of the election system prepared by Ackoff and Rovin (2003) took these deficiencies and complaints into account. It was a part of a redesign of government itself. Thus, the election system that follows should be considered to be an integral part of a larger system of government that was the result of an idealized design.

BALLOTS

Voters would have a new option in addition to the candidates. After the list of candidates, there would be an entry: *Someone Else* (not a place for a write-in). A vote for Someone Else would register a protest against the candidates listed above. If a plurality of voters voted for Someone Else, new candidates would have to be nominated and the election rerun. The cost of the rerun would be charged to either those who nominated the defeated candidates or to the candidates themselves. To ensure the availability of funds, an amount sufficient to cover the cost of the rerun would be required to be placed in escrow before the election on behalf of each candidate. A candidate who received more votes than Someone Else would have his or her deposits returned. This design should likely improve the quality of candidates seeking public office.

THE OBLIGATION TO VOTE

Even with these changes, it is likely that a significant number of eligible voters might still stay away from the polls. Such failure to vote is treated as an offense against the state in some countries. It can result in a large fine or substantial punishment for nonvoters. It is better, however, to treat voting as an obligation, not a requirement. The proposed election system would require the nonvoter to contribute an amount of time to be specified to social service. The principle is this: If a citizen does not fulfill an obligation to society through voting, the citizen should fulfill it in some other, commensurate way.

POLITICAL PARTIES

The election system would permit political parties, and even encourage them, but they would be required to publish platforms that are more than a group of platitudes.

PLATFORMS

Platforms would include a statement with a justification of the party's objectives. In addition, the platforms would include estimates of the amounts and types of resources required, and their expected sources, to meet their objectives. Candidates at all levels would be required to publish platforms and would have to identify the political party with which they are affiliated, if any. A candidate running as an independent would be required to publish a platform of objectives, or list those special interest groups with which the candidate is affiliated. Elected officials who fail to make a significant effort to fulfill promises made in a platform would be subject to recall by the electorate.

CAMPAIGNS

Election campaigns would be confined to a limited period of time—for example, two months. Candidacy for an office could not be announced earlier than three months before the election. Elections would be publicly funded, and each candidate at each level would receive the same amount of financial support and be given equal access to the media. No private funding of elections would be permitted. Candidates would be required to maintain a website to which questions could be sent. The candidates' answers would be recorded along with the questions so that they would be accessible to everyone on the Internet. A nonpartisan campaign board would be established to ensure that campaigning would be constructive, not devoted to denigrating opponents. The board would have the power to give one warning for negative campaigning and could disqualify a candidate who repeatedly engages in negative campaigning.

TERMS OF OFFICE

All terms, regardless of office, would be for six years. Every 2 years, one third of the members of every legislative body would be elected. Office holders would be limited to 2 terms and could not hold an office for more than 12 consecutive years. In addition, no one would permitted to run again for an office held for 12 consecutive years.

This election system would greatly increase the participation rate of eligible voters and make the U.S. democracy more responsive to its electorate.

We next look at one of the world's great bureaucracies, the United Nations, and offer a design for a new world organization that should be able to accomplish the mission that the present organization has so far failed to deliver.

A NEW UNITED NATIONS

At a time when the United Nations was being subjected to an increasing amount of criticism, Jamshid Gharajedaghi and Russell Ackoff prepared the following design in 2003. This design obviously has not been implemented. It was circulated privately with the hope of initiating discussion of either how to make the U.N. more effective, or what should replace it.

INTRODUCTION

The world is in a mess. This statement hardly needs documentation. The terrible state of world affairs is disheartening, particularly to those of us who hoped the U.N. would be able to bring some order and sense into these affairs. Unfortunately, the U.N. has turned out to provide little more than the now defunct League of Nations after World War I. It is clear that it is only through effective, decisive, and strong international action that any improvement in the state of the world can be brought about. A unilateral approach by any super power not only places a great and unfair burden on its own people, but it does not produce desirable results. In fact, up to now, such interventions have only exacerbated the mess. The only workable solution requires the world community to accept its collective responsibility and act with authority to create a world order that is capable of managing interactions between nations. Therefore, the following idealized design of a potentially effective multinational organization might minimally encourage some productive changes in the U.N. The design does not need to be implementable but, clearly, it should be able to improve the world if it were implemented. However, even an approximation to it may be possible either as a replacement for the U.N. or as a new multinational venture.

First we develop the idealized design and then consider what aspects of, or approximations to it, are feasible. It will become apparent that all the obstructions to implementation of even the idealized design lie in the minds of people, not "out there." But these are the hardest kinds of obstructions to remove. Fortunately, in the past, mobilizing ideas and visions have produced massive mental changes and brought about social revolutions of huge proportions.

Ortega y Gasset has eloquently made the case for this kind of design: ". . . man has been able to grow enthusiastic over his vision of . . . unconvincing enterprises. He has put himself to work for the sake of an idea, seeking by magnificent exertions to arrive at the incredible. And in the end, he has arrived there. Beyond all doubt it is one of the vital sources of man's power, to be thus able to kindle enthusiasm from the mere glimmer of something improbable, difficult, remote.[1] Yogi Berra put it more simply: "You've got to be careful if you don't know where you are going because you might not get there."

The intention of this ideal design is to stimulate a discussion that yields improvements in the way world affairs are handled while generating consensus as to what is most desirable. In other words, the design should raise the level of discussion of global issues to a higher level than that at which such discussion currently takes place. Current discussion tends to accept the global system that exists and asks how parts of it or their behaviors can be changed so as to reduce the mess. Such discussion, although pervasive, is based on an assumption that one can dissolve a mess by patching or attacking its parts separately. But the underlying premise of this book is that improving the performance of parts of a system may not improve the performance of the system of which they are part.

DESIRABLE PROPERTIES OF A NEW UNITED NATIONS

Certain important properties should be designed into the organization. These must provide nations with a good reason for joining; that is, there must be a significant advantage to membership in the organization. Therefore, the following properties should be established:

1. It should be a voluntary association of autonomous nations committed to democracy, pluralism, the protection of human rights, and the promotion of development of its member nations and those that are external to it. A suitable name of the organization might be the *Union of Democratic Nations*.

2. It should have the ability to dissolve or manage conflicts a) between its member nations, b) between its members and nonmembers, and c) between nonmember nations when invited to do so or when such conflicts endanger one or more of its members.

3. It should provide security for all member nations by protecting them against aggression from any internal or external source.

4. It should facilitate unrestricted economic, cultural, educational, and technological exchanges between its members.

5. It should make possible completely free communication and movement of individuals, goods, and capital among member nations.

6. It should prevent exploitation within member nations of any group that is based on discrimination and/or segregation by race, nationality, religion, language, sex, or age.

7. It should help eradicate poverty, illiteracy, genocide, tyranny, health hazards, and environmental deterioration all over the world.

8. It should assist nations that are not eligible for membership but want to join the Union in becoming eligible for it.

GOVERNANCE OF THE UNION

There would be two policy-making bodies. One, the Council of Heads of State, would consist of the elected presidents or prime ministers of all member states with their deputies (for example, vice presidents or deputy prime ministers) serving as alternates. The other, the Chamber of Representatives, would consist of representatives of each member nation, the number proportional to their population and their GNP per capita.

The Union would have an executive director elected for a nonrenewable term of six years. At least three persons would be nominated by the Chamber of Representatives, and be elected by a majority of the Council of Heads of State.

- Any elected executive of the Union could be dismissed from office by a two thirds vote of both the Council of Heads of State and the Chamber of Representatives.

- The Union would have a court whose function is to handle issues between member nations and between member and nonmember nations. Members of the court would be nominated by the Council of Heads of State and selected by majority vote of the Chamber of Representatives. The court would consist of nine members each of whom serves one nine-year term. One member of the court would leave each year and be replaced.

- Nominations to the court would be made by the executive director of the Union but selected by a two thirds vote of the Council of Heads of State. Nominees would be drawn from former heads of state or national supreme courts.

- The executive director would have a cabinet consisting of the head of each division of the Union, these appointed by the executive director, but requiring approval of two thirds majority of the Council of Heads of State.

GETTING INTO THE UNION

Membership in the Union would be open to all nations irrespective of their location, race, religion, and size as long as they meet the following conditions:

- Members must have been an autonomous pluralistic democracy for at least 20 years with at least 2 peaceful transitions of administrations (that is, transfers of power).

    A "democracy" exists in a nation if 1) everyone who is affected by a decision has an opportunity to participate in making it either directly or indirectly (through elected representatives), 2) anyone in a position of authority over others individually is subject to their collective authority, and 3) anyone can do anything they want to providing that it has no effect on anyone else's ability to do the same, otherwise they require the agreement of those affected.

"Pluralism" exists in a society that permits any and every point of view on any issue to be expressed and acted on unless it restricts the ability of anyone else to do the same thing.

An "autonomous" country is one not subject to any external source of control.

A "peaceful transition of an administration" occurs when the transfer of authority at the top of the nation's government is the result of an election that passes power from one elected person or set of persons to another elected person or set of persons.

- Application for membership must be approved by a majority of its eligible voters.

- Members must accept and fully meet requirements of the Universal Declaration of Human Rights without any exceptions, including allowance of no discrimination or segregation based on race, sex, religion, national origin, language, or age.

- Members must accept the role of the Union and commit to making the changes necessary to conform to the transfer of responsibilities from the nation to the Union.

- Members must not be at war with any other nation, nor be experiencing a civil war, and not be engaged in any territorial disputes.

- Members must not belong to any other association of nations, obligations to which take precedence over those to this Union.

- Members must not harbor or support terrorism in any form.

- Members must abolish all forms of capital and physical punishment.

- Members must provide all nationals (except prisoners and those awaiting trial) with the freedom to emigrate.

- Members must provide free public education to all residents for a minimum of eight years, also universal health care and unemployment insurance along with incentives to work.

SEPARATION FROM THE UNION

Membership would be suspended if any of the criteria for membership were violated. Members would lose their membership with three violations and or refusals to honor the Union resolution. Any member nation of the union could be expelled from the union by a two thirds vote of both governing bodies. Any member nation could secede from the Union with support of a majority of that member's eligible voters. Any part of a member nation may secede from that nation by a majority vote of its population. Once separated, it would have to go through normal procedures to reenter the Union.

CONDITIONS OF CONTINUED MEMBERSHIP

The conditions for continued membership would be strict and enforced by the Union. Members would not maintain a national military force; the Union would provide a military force to protect all members against aggression from within or without.

Each member would pay dues annually consisting of a per-capita assessment that would be proportional to average per-capita income in that nation. Members would provide complete freedom of movement within the Union. They would facilitate free trade within the Union. They would limit nonrenewable terms of all elected officials to six years, and the relevant government would finance all campaigns for public office and limit them to three months. The Union would adopt an official language that would be taught as a second language in all schools in member nations. No member of the Union could ship into any other member of the union goods or services outlawed in the receiving member (for example, guns or drugs).

SERVICES PROVIDED BY THE UNION

In addition to providing and maintaining a military force, it would provide a range of services to member nations. Operate a Food and Drug Administration and an Environmental Control Service. Establish and maintain a Center for Disease Control directed at prevention or control of epidemics originating both within and outside the Union. License products and services and establish and administer safety standards and grading systems applicable to these in all member nations. Operate a conflict-resolution service available both internally and externally to the Union. Establish and maintain a commission to monitor all nations in and out of the Union for presence and development of weapons of mass destruction. Provide a patent office, registration of trademarks, and copyright facilities. Provide a stock market and a Security and Exchange Commission. Provide custom and immigration services. Establish, maintain, and operate a fund and consultation service to encourage and facilitate development of nations both within and outside the Union. Establish and support (but exercise no control over) a news agency that would publish a daily newspaper and would broadcast the news over radio and television; the output of this agency would be available in all member nations and, on request, by nations outside the Union. However, newspapers within nations would still function and provide a diversity of opinion and treatment of the news.

THE RIGHTS OF MEMBER STATES

The design would make no effort to force all the member states to behave in the same way. The amount of autonomy of members of the Union is maximized in the design by minimizing the authority members are required to relinquish. The intention is to give all nations the greatest incentive to tailor their governance to the requirements of membership. Such an organization should be able to achieve the absence of wars and other international conflicts among member nations.

Next we look at terrorism and a way to reduce one of its prime causes.

A RESPONSE TO TERRORISM

The wave of terrorist attacks that marked the beginning of the twenty-first century shows no sign of abating. Countries have responded by creating or augmenting security organizations to protect themselves from future attacks. However, efforts to protect potential targets of terrorists from attack are futile for two reasons. First, there are many more such targets than can possibly be effectively protected and, second, it is always easier to destroy something than prevent its destruction, particularly when terrorists are willing to sacrifice themselves in a destructive act. It is virtually impossible to protect against suicide bombers and assassins.

This is not meant to imply that we should not make terrorists attacks as difficult as possible and that we should not prepare to minimize the harm caused by their attacks when they occur. But such efforts will not "solve" the problem.

The ways currently used to combat terrorism address its effects rather than its causes. On the contrary, we believe that it is the inability to promote development within a society that makes it susceptible to terrorism. *A principal—but not the sole—producer of terrorism is the inequitable distribution among and within nations of wealth, quality of life, and opportunities to improve either.* This is reflected in a recent study by the Heritage Foundation, the 2002 Index of Economic Freedom,[2] which found that the production of terrorists by nations is negatively correlated with the economic freedom which, in turn, is correlated with their economic development. The bottom six nations are Iran, Laos, Cuba, Libya, Iraq, and North Korea. A Rand study (Cragin and Chalk 2003) found that although social and economic development does not eliminate terrorists, "it provides economic alternatives to potential recruits, and it creates a new middle class that has a vested interest in maintaining peace."

The ability of individuals and groups to cope emotionally and conceptually with the increasing demands of a turbulent environment is directly related to their level of development. We use the term *development* to refer to an individual's and group's ability to effectively utilize available resources to satisfy their needs and legitimate desires, and those of others.

In the long run, the *ideal way* to deal with terrorism requires facilitating the development of disadvantaged communities in both more- and less-developed countries. Such facilitation involves five conditions:

1. The more-developed communities and countries should make available to those less-developed a pool of *resources*—financial, human, and equipment—that can be used in development efforts, but *only in ways the recipients see fit, not the donors.*

2. These resources should only be used for *development.*

3. Decisions on how to use these resources should be made *democratically* by those who would be directly affected by the decisions, and they should be approved by others who would be indirectly affected by them.

4. No *corruption* should be permissible. Its presence should be a sufficient reason for discontinuation of a development effort.

5. The effort should be *monitored* and evaluated by an objective group whose members are acceptable to both the recipients and the donors of the aid.

Now consider these conditions in some detail.

RESOURCES

Each more-developed country should have an agency to administer development programs. It should receive and process applications for aid. A U.N. agency could help by directing applications to appropriate national and international sources. Action should be prompt. Negative responses should not preclude a proposal from being submitted to a different source.

A percentage of the income tax collected in each more-developed country should be designated for investment in equalizing development among nations. Institutions and organizations receiving aid or contracts from the government of more-developed countries should provide human resources as required. Personnel time and expenses, as well as the cost of equipment, should be paid out of project grants.

DEVELOPMENT

As noted previously, by *development* we mean an increase in the ability and desire to satisfy one's own needs and legitimate desires and those of others. A legitimate desire is one the fulfillment of which does not obstruct the development of any others and a need is a requirement for something necessary for maintenance of health or survival.

Development, then, is an increase in *competence*. *Omnicompetence* is the ability to obtain whatever one legitimately wants or needs. It is an unattainable but continuously approachable ideal in which means and ends converge. It is necessarily an ideal for all mankind (past, present, or future) because no one can want anything without wanting the ability to obtain it.

Development is a matter of learning, not earning. The standard of living is an index of earning; quality of life is primarily a matter of learning. Robinson Crusoe is a better model of development than J. Pierpont Morgan.

DEMOCRACY

Democratic decision making involves three principles:

1. Everyone who is directly affected by a decision can participate in making it either directly or indirectly through representatives that they select. Those who cannot make such a selection should be represented by advocates of their interests; for example, parents should represent children, and psychiatrists should represent the mentally ill.

2. Anyone in a position of authority over others in a decision-making body is subject to the collective authority of the others. That is, authority is circular, not linear, flowing up collectively as well as down individually.

3. Every decision-making individual or group can do whatever it wants provided it does not affect any other individual or group. If what it wants to do can have such an effect, then approval of those affected must be obtained before it can be done. This implies that there would be no victimless crime.

CORRUPTION

Corruption consists of the appropriation for personal gain of resources intended for use in development of a group and its members. Corruption is rampant in many less-developed countries, where it is a major obstruction to development. It also produces a feeling of futility in many and thus provides a fertile soil for terrorism. It should be disallowed, and those guilty of it should be treated as criminals. Its presence in a development project should be sufficient ground for discontinuing that project.

MONITORING

Monitoring should be directed at facilitating learning by those whose development is intended. To do this, a record should be prepared for each development-related decision. The record should include 1) who made the decision, when and how; 2) the intended effects of the decision and when they are expected; 3) the assumptions on which these expectations are based; and 4) the inputs that were used in making the decision: the data, information, knowledge, understanding, and/or wisdom used.

The monitors should then track the expectations and assumptions. When a significant deviation from these occurs, it should be diagnosed to find what produced it. Corrective action should then be taken. A record should also be prepared for each such correction and should be processed just as the original decision was. This makes it possible not only to learn from a mistake, but also to learn from mistakes made in correcting mistakes—therefore, *to learn how to learn.*

COLLABORATIVE DEVELOPMENT REDUCES TERRORISM

Development programs should involve a global collaborative effort. One of the characteristics of the world that terrorists exploit is its division by political boundaries. As long as the world remains politically fragmented, it remains possible to find safe havens for terrorists. The reduction or elimination of terrorism requires a global response that addresses the roots of injustice and inequities within and between nations. If every citizen of every nation in the world is well fed, has suitable medical care, has an opportunity to rise economically through productive work, and is free to pursue activities limited only by the requirement that they do not impinge on the rights of others, the number of terrorists will diminish and terrorist attacks should decline.

But there is more to be done to reduce terrorism. We are confident that using the tools of idealized design, we can better understand and combat the root causes of terrorism. Our hope is that this design will stimulate others to take up the challenge and look for other measures that will further reduce the threat of terrorism to all nations.

This ends Part III. In Part IV, we provide three complete idealized designs. These are for a complete business enterprise, a not-for-profit organization, and a government agency, each of which was described more briefly in earlier chapters. Readers who are considering undertaking idealized designs in similar organizations may find it valuable to have the details of these complete designs.

IV

COMPLETE IDEALIZED
DESIGNS

13

Energetics
(Business Enterprise)

This is the complete idealized design of a business enterprise, Energetics, described in Chapter 4, "Business Enterprises." It provides a detailed design that should be of interest and value to anyone who is considering undertaking an idealized design of an entire business organization.

INTRODUCTION

Energetics is a company that produces, distributes, and markets natural gas. In April 1999, Energetics' total enterprise value was $39 million. At the end of 2003, it was $210 million. Its market capitalization in 1999 (adjusted for a reverse stock split) was $17 million. At the end of 2003, it was $165 million. This improvement was due in part to its planning activity, including its idealized design.

The following description is taken from the record of the company's idealized design. The italicized paragraphs contain the reasons given by the designers for the design elements they have selected:

Nothing provides employees at all levels of an organization with as much opportunity to learn and develop as participation in decisions that affect them, nor does anything else raise their morale and dedication to work as much. Conventional organizations that provide such opportunities usually disrupt hierarchical relationships essential for effective management. The design that follows maintains the necessary hierarchy while providing the opportunity for participation in critical decision making to all personnel at all levels of the organization.

Units that adopt the following type of organization—the democratic hierarchy—will be able to modify it to suit their needs and desires. For example, they need not initially give the boards all six functions identified below, but only a subset of them. They could later add functions initially omitted. Each unit would establish the frequency of its board's meetings, their duration, and its rules of procedure.

The Company aspires to provide its users with the most advanced and cost-effective products and services. To do so, it must increasingly attract and retain employees with the most advanced, relevant knowledge and understanding. It has become increasingly apparent that the more educated and skilled a work force, the less effective a command-and-control style of management is. Participative democracy is necessary (but not sufficient) to attract and retain most of those who are on the leading edge of relevant technologies.

The performance of a system, and the Company is a system, depends more on how its parts *interact* than on how they act taken separately. However, hierarchy must be retained in order to coordinate and integrate the interactions of the Company's parts. Therefore, it is the interactions, rather than the actions, of subordinate individuals and units that should be effectively managed. Here too a democratic type of management is required.

Every manager will have a board that will minimally include that manager (as chairman), his/her immediate superior, and each of his/her immediate subordinates. Each board will be able to add additional members as it sees fit, as full or partial members, voting or nonvoting, and so on. However, the number of representatives of any "outside" interest group should be less than the number of subordinates on the board. (The subordinates should constitute a plurality on each board.)

This means that every manager except the one at the top and those at the bottom will participate on boards at three levels: their own, their boss's, and those of each of their immediate subordinates. Therefore, most managers will interact with five levels of management: two levels above them, their own level, and two levels below.

Boards will normally meet once or twice per month for about two to three hours per meeting.

Board meetings should reduce the number and frequency of other meetings by more than the amount of time they require. Where the members of a board are geographically disbursed, meetings should be arranged to coincide with other normally held get-togethers.

Each board may have the following functions:

- **Policy making.** Each board will formulate policies [decision rules] that apply to units subordinate to it. However, it will not violate any policy made by a higher-level board.

  Policies are laws and regulations, not decisions to act. Congresses and parliaments make policies; presidents and prime ministers make decisions. A manager may consult his/her board about a decision requiring action, but however such a decision is made, responsibility for it lies with the managers.

- **Planning.** Each board will prepare strategic, tactical, and operational plans for the units whose board it is. Its plans will have to be consistent with higher-level plans, but it can appeal to the appropriate higher board for a change in these. Every board and its unit will be able to implement any part of its design that does not affect any but its own subordinate units for which it has the required resources. Otherwise it will have to obtain the necessary agreements and/or resources from higher-level units or boards.

- **Coordination and integration of policies and plans.** Each board will take steps to assure coordination of plans and policies of the lower-level units for which it is responsible, and for assuring no violation by itself or lower-level units of higher-level plans or policies.

Note that coordination of the immediate lower-level units is done by the managers of these units together with the two immediately higher-level managers. Note also, that since all boards except those of the top and bottom contain members who are exposed to units two levels down, they are not likely to make decisions that negatively affect lower-level units. If they do, the affected board can launch a request for a change through its members who participate in one and two higher-level boards.

- **Quality of work life.** Each board will be free to make decisions that affect the quality of work life of its members provided such decisions affect only members of the board. If they affect others, approval of the others is required.

- **Performance improvement.** Each year the subordinate members on each board will meet to determine what their immediate superior can do to enable them to do their (subordinate) jobs better. They will prioritize their suggestions and present them face to face to their boss. The boss will have three options: 1) to agree; 2) to disagree but give the reasons for it; or 3) to ask for more time (not to exceed a month) to consider the issue.

In addition, the manager whose board it is will also formulate suggestions to his/her subordinates as to what they could do to improve his/her performance. The subordinates will have available the same types of response to these suggestions as the manager has to theirs.

■ **Tenure of managers.** Every board can remove the manager whose board it is from his/her position. It cannot fire him/her; only his/her boss can do that.

This means that no manager can hold his/her position without the approval of his/her immediate superior and immediate subordinates.

Each board will formulate its own rules of procedure, but operate only by consensus.

A person designated by the manager whose board it is will accumulate agenda items submitted by members of the board between meetings and distribute a finished agenda before the meeting. S/he will also take minutes of the meeting, which, after approval by the manager whose board it is, s/he will distribute to board members.

Finally, each manager's responsibilities will include the following:

■ Enabling subordinates to do their jobs better in the future than they can now

■ Seeing to it that they develop continuously by encouraging and facilitating their continuous education and training

■ Managing the interactions 1) among those who report to them, 2) of their units with other units within the company, and 3) of their units with relevant entities outside the company

■ Leading subordinates in carrying out the Company's mission

THE INTERNAL ECONOMY

Because of increasing size and complexity, organizational economies become increasingly difficult to manage effectively from a centralized position. This was also the case in the Soviet Union, causing it to move toward a market economy, *perestroika*. One of the difficulties that confront management is exemplified in a conventional organization in which transfer pricing is often used. This is the price charged to internal units for use of the output of other internal units. Such pricing almost always produces conflict between the internal units involved. The supplying unit usually thinks it can sell its good or services more profitably externally, and the other thinks it can buy them for less from outside suppliers. In a sense, there is no such thing as a fair transfer price, one that precludes conflict between the affected units. Because transfer pricing is endemic to a centrally controlled internal economy, another type of economy is required to avoid its consequences.

Internally used services and goods in a conventional organization often are supplied by internal monopolies. If these monopolies are supported, as they frequently are, by subsidies supplied from above, they tend to bureaucratize. They become less responsive to the needs of the internal units that they serve. It becomes apparent that goods and services that are used internally and are provided by internal bureaucratic monopolies are often more costly than goods and services that can be obtained externally. This, too, produces pressure for change toward an internal market economy.

In an internal market economy, every organizational unit (with exceptions noted below) that serves more than one other organizational unit or serves one or more external units operates as a profit center. It is free to sell its goods or services at whatever price it wants and to buy whatever goods or services it desires from any source, internal or external, that it wants. However, these decisions are subject to an override by the manager to which the unit reports. The overriding manager must compensate the unit he/she constrains for the profit it loses or the increased cost it incurs. This means that no internal unit will have to pay more for what it buys, or receive less for what it sells, than it would in a completely free market economy.

An internal unit that provides other internal units with goods or services that gives the organization a competitive advantage in the marketplace is generally prevented from selling its services externally—for example, a product-design or research unit. Therefore, such units are usually made cost centers but are assigned to profit centers, which then become responsible for their effectiveness. The same is true of units that are confined to the organization for security reasons.

The following example of a design of an internal market economy is also taken from the record of Energetics' idealized design:

> As many units as possible will be profit centers; each of the others will be a cost center attached to a profit center.
>
> *This does not mean that profit centers must be profitable. They may be retained because of some other type of advantage they provide (e.g., prestige). Where this is the case, the company will know and should attempt to know how much this advantage costs.*
>
> Units that should not sell their output for security reasons or because they provide a distinctive competitive advantage can be treated as cost centers. However, they should be part of a profit center so that their costs are monitored and controlled, and they are prevented from becoming unresponsive internal monopolies.
>
> Every unit will be able to sell its products or services to whomever it chooses at prices it establishes. Decisions to sell the products or services of input units to external customers can be overridden as described below.
>
> Every unit will be able to consider the purchase of any product or service it requires from either internal or external sources. Purchase decisions can also be overridden as described below.
>
> Whenever an internal unit considers a quotation of a price from an external supplier of a product or service that is also provided by an internal unit, the internal unit will be given the option of meeting the external price before the external purchase is consummated. However, even if the internal price quoted is the lowest, the buying unit may, with the approval of a higher-level manager, choose an external supplier for

other-than-cost reasons (for example, quality or delivery or dual-source considerations).

Whenever a unit has a legitimate business desire to purchase products or services externally that a unit within the company provides, the manager to whom the unit reports can prevent that unit from using the external source. However, the overriding manager must compensate the buying unit for any increase in its cost that results. When the cost of the constraint cannot be determined, the overriding manager may still require the internal source be used but must negotiate a settlement with the head of the unit involved.

Whenever a unit has a legitimate business reason for not wanting to sell a product or service to another internal unit at a price that is the only price acceptable to the buying unit, the lowest-level manager to whom both units report can override the decision but must compensate the selling unit for the difference in price.

The compensation allowed to the constrained unit by an overriding manager will be a cost to that manager.

Each profit center will pay [internally imposed] taxes on its profits. The tax rate will be estimated for each profit center at the beginning of the tax year and adjusted when corporate [externally imposed] taxes are determined. The taxes collected internally should not exceed the tax bill of the corporation as a whole.

The executive office of the corporation will also be a profit center. The after-tax expenses of this unit will be offset against its income. Since it is treated as the owner of the profit centers, it collects a share of their profits and interest on the capital it provides to them.

Generally, input and output units will be responsible for the capital invested in them together with the operating capital that they use. Each profit center will be assessed a charge for the net capital employed in their operations. These payments will be accrued to the executive office.

Every profit center will be allowed to accumulate profit up to a specified limit. It will be permitted to use this money with the approval of its board and in a way that is consistent with higher-level policies. Capital accumulation above the specified limit will be turned over to the manager to whom the unit reports. He/she will compensate the unit for the capital at the same rate at which he/she makes it available to other units.

The limit is set for each unit with the belief that investment of additional funds will not produce a satisfactory return, and that the manager to which the unit reports can use the funds more profitably.

ORGANIZATIONAL STRUCTURE

Many organizations reorganize every few years. This is often costly. It consumes large amounts of time, and has negative effects on the morale of many of those affected. Nevertheless, such changes appear to be necessary for the organizations to adapt to internal or external changes. Awareness of this has given rise to the question: Is it possible to organize in such a way as not to require reorganization in order to adapt to such changes? W. C. Goggin (1974), CEO of Dow-Corning, found a way to avoid reorganizations. It consists of organizing multidimensionally. Conventional organizational structures are represented in a two-dimensional chart, up and down (the allocation of authority) and across (the allocation of responsibility). The multidimensional organization has three dimensions.

To organize is to divide labor functionally and to coordinate the divided labor. Regardless of the nature of an organization, there are only three ways of dividing labor functionally: inputs (functions), outputs (products and/or services), and users (markets). Input units consist of units whose outputs are primarily (if not exclusively) consumed within the organization (for example, accounting, research and development, purchasing, mailroom, computing, and personnel).

Output units consist of those units whose outputs (products or services) are principally consumed externally to the organization (for example, at General Motors, the Chevrolet, Pontiac, Oldsmobile, Buick, and Cadillac divisions).

User units are defined by classes of customers defined either geographically (for example, North America, Europe, Asia) or by the means by which they are reached (for example, catalogue, Internet, retail stores, television), or demographically (for example, by age, occupation, race, sex, and income).

In every organization, the relative importance of the three criteria used in dividing labor is expressed by the level of the organization at which they are applied. The first level below the CEO may be organized by using any one or more of the criteria, the next level similarly, and so on. More than one criterion can be used at any level.

Most reorganizations consist of a reordering of the criteria used in dividing labor so as to adapt to changing internal or external conditions. By placing units of all three types at every level of the organization, the need to restructure in order to adapt is eliminated (see Figure 13.1). In such an organization, adaptation is accomplished by reallocating resources among the units. An organization can make its strategy operational in this way.

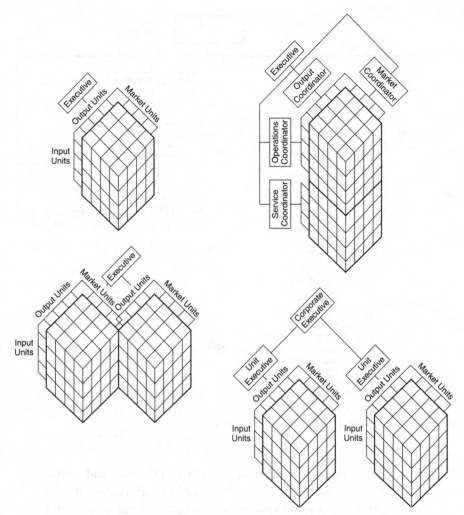

Figure 13.1 Multidimensional organizational designs

Like internal democracy and market economies, the multidimensional organizational form has been adopted by a number of organizations, including Energetics. This company's description of it in its idealized redesign follows:

> Energetics will be organized multi-dimensionally. Its units will have input (functional) units, output (product or service) units, and user (market) units. It will also have an executive office with appropriate staff support (see Figure 13.2).

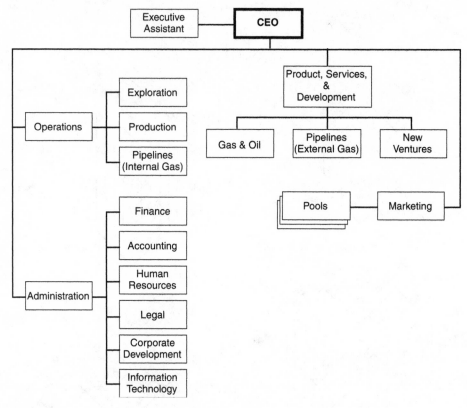

Figure 13.2   Multidimensional structure of Energetics

The Executive Office. In addition to a CEO, there will be four other executives in charge of 1) line input units (operations), 2) staff input units (administration), 3) output units (products and services), and 4) marketing. These four executives together will make up the CEO's board.

Output Units. There will be three output units: gas and oil, pipelines, and new ventures. These units will consist of management and a small supporting staff with scarce and uniquely required expertise and services. They will have fixed assets and operating capital.

Output units will be responsible for the profitability of their products and/or services. They will arrange all activities required for getting their products/services to the market and for receiving payment for them.

Input Units. Input units will develop and provide the personnel, facilities, equipment, and services required by output units. All input units will serve at least two output units. A functional unit that serves only one output unit will be part of that output unit. [For example, a producing facility that produces only one type of product can be a part of that output unit responsible for that product.]

This arrangement ensures that the output units, unconstrained by inputs for which they are organizationally responsible, can easily adapt to changing conditions. Therefore, output units have only a small staff, no facilities or equipment, and require no investments, only operating capital.

Input units will have facilities and equipment as well as personnel; hence, will require both investment and operating capital. There will be three line input units: exploration, production, and pipelines. There will also be six staff units: accounting, finance (tax, treasury, and audit), information technology, human resources, industry and public relations, and legal.

User (Market) Units. Initially there will be pool-defined [gas reservoir] units that will market, distribute, and transport the outputs of the Company and other companies to different customers in the areas in which the pools are located.

The user units can sell products obtained from other producers. They will represent the Company to its existing and potential customers. They will also monitor emerging customers and the emerging needs and desires of actual and potential customers of the output units. They will convert these needs and desires into requests and suggestions for new services and products. In their advocacy role, user units will be responsible for observing environmental conditions and their trends, and exploring the expectations others have of the Company. They will represent those outsiders who are affected by the Company, advocating their points of view inside the Company. They will provide feedback on user reactions to the Company's products and services.

ORGANIZATIONAL LEARNING AND ADAPTATION

Most organizations focus on the acquisition, processing, and retention of data and information. Recently, however, some organizations have become concerned with knowledge. But data, information, and knowledge are not all that can be learned; there is also understanding and wisdom.

- **Data** consist of symbols that represent the properties of objects and events. Data has little value until it has been processed into information. Data is to information as iron ore is to iron. Little can be done with iron ore until it is processed into iron.

- **Information** consists of data that has been processed so as to be useful. It is contained in *descriptions,* answers to questions beginning with such words as *what, who, where, when,* and *how many.*

- **Knowledge** is contained in *instructions,* answers to *how-to* questions.

- **Understanding** is contained in *explanations,* answers to *why* questions.

- **Wisdom** is concerned with the value of outcomes, effectiveness, whereas the other four types of mental content are concerned with efficiency. Efficiency is concerned with doing things right; effectiveness is concerned with doing the right thing.

These five types of mental content form a hierarchy of value; data have the least value, wisdom the most. In general, however, organizations, especially educational organizations, allocate time to the five types of learning inversely to their value. Most time is spent on data and information, the least on understanding and wisdom.

The "righter" we do the wrong thing, the "wronger" we become. If we make a mistake doing the wrong thing and correct it, we become "wronger." If we make a mistake doing the right thing and correct it, we become "righter." Therefore, it is better to do the right thing wrong than the wrong thing right.

Most of the serious problems confronting organizations, including governments, arise from focusing on doing the wrong thing "righter." For example, the alleged health-care system in the United States is not a health-care system at all; it is a sickness- and disability-care system. Its members derive their income primarily from the treatment of sickness and disabilities, not from preserving health. Therefore, despite individually good intentions, the system maintains the alleged need for treatment and prolongs and produces sickness and disabilities. The health-care system as currently motivated would go out of existence if everyone were healthy. Compensation for treating sickness is the wrong thing; compensation for producing and maintaining health is the right thing. If the care providers in the current system had to pay all the medical expenses of their patients out of a fee they received for maintaining their health, the system would be turned into doing the right thing.

We do not learn anything from doing something right. We already know how to do it, but it may provide confirmation of what we know. We can only learn from making mistakes, and identifying and correcting them. But all through school, and subsequently in most organizations, we are taught and told that making a mistake is a bad thing. Therefore, we tend to deny or hide mistakes. This, of course, prevents learning. Unless mistakes are acknowledged and corrected, we cannot learn from them.

There are two types of mistakes: **errors of commission**, doing something that should not have been done; and **errors of omission**, not doing something that should have been done. For example, acquiring a company that turns out to be costly is an error of commission; not acquiring a company that would have been profitable is an error of omission.

Organizations are more likely to get into trouble because of errors of omission than errors of commission. Computer manufacturers that failed to enter the desktop and personal computer market early suffered seriously, as have film producers that failed to enter the digital photography market. Nevertheless, accounting systems identify only errors of commission. Therefore, in organizations that, like schools, treat mistakes as bad and punishable, the best way to maximize job security is to *do nothing.* This is the major contributor to the reluctance of employees at all levels to initiate change. Unfortunately, in an environment that is increasingly unpredictable and turbulent, doing little or nothing is a sure path to death.

Individuals within an organization can learn and adapt without their organization doing so. An organization learns only when everyone in it has access to the learning of any others when they need it, even after the others are no longer accessible. This requires capturing what individuals learn and storing it in a memory that is accessible to others who have a need to know.

It follows from all this that an organization's learning and adaptation requires the following types of support:

- Coverage of all five types of learning—from data to wisdom
- Coverage of errors of omission as well as errors of commission
- Retention and provision of access to relevant learning to every member of the organization who has a need for it
- Identification of mistakes (of both types), determination of their sources, and correction of them

All important decisions should be monitored to detect deviations from their associated expectations and the assumptions on which these expectations are based. The deviations should be diagnosed to determine their causes; then corrections should be prescribed. The corrections themselves involve a decision that should be treated as original decisions are. Correcting correction-decisions makes learning how to learn possible. It accelerates the learning process.

The detailed design of a Learning and Adaptation Support System that was included in Energetics' idealized design follows.

The numbers and letters in parentheses that follow refer to Figure 13.3. The boxes shown represent functions, not individuals or groups. As will be seen, they may be performed by individuals or groups and (in some cases) even by a computer and related technologies.

Because the support of learning should be continuous, a description of the system that supports it can begin at any point. The choice is arbitrary.

DECISION RECORD Date: _____

Identification Number: _____

Report Prepared by: _____

Report Checked by: _____

KEY WORDS _____

DESCRIPTION OF ISSUE _____

_____

_____

ISSUE PRIMARILY AN __Opportunity __Threat (check one)

OUTCOME (check one)

__No Decision __Decision to Do Nothing

__Decision to Do Something (Describe) _____

_____

ARGUMENTS PRO _____

_____

ARGUMENTS CON _____

_____

EXPECTED CONSEQUENCES OR EFFECTS AND WHEN
THEY ARE EXPECTED _____

_____

_____

ASSUMPTIONS ON WHICH EXPECTATIONS ARE BASED

_____

_____

_____

INFORMATION USED: _____

_____

_____

WHO PARTICIPATED IN THE DECISION? _____

_____

THE DECISION-MAKING PROCESS _____

_____

_____

WHO IS RESPONSIBLE FOR IMPLEMENTATION (if anyone)?

_____

IMPLEMENTATION PLAN _____

_____

_____

OBSERVATIONS AND COMMENTS _____

_____

_____

_____

_____

Figure 13.3 An example of a decision record

We begin with the generation of *Inputs* (1) Data, Information, Knowledge, and Understanding of the behavior of the ORGANIZATION being managed and its (internal and external) ENVIRONMENT. These inputs are received by the INPUT SUPPLY SUBSYSTEM. The inputs may come in a variety of forms—for example, oral or written, published or personal.

The INPUT SUPPLY SUBSYSTEM should filter incoming messages for *relevance* and condense them so as to minimize the times required to absorb their content.

Data should be processed to convert them into information, knowledge, or understanding; therefore, data processing is a necessary part of the INPUT SUPPLY SUBSYSTEM. *Inputs* (2) (Information, Knowledge, or Understanding) are transmitted to the DECISION MAKERS in response to their *Requests* (3).

When the DECISION MAKERS receive the inputs, they do not always find them useful, complete, or even correct. They may find them unreadable or incomprehensible or they may doubt their validity or question their completeness. Therefore, the receipt of information often leads to additional *Requests* (3). Such requests require two additional capabilities of the INPUT SUPPLY SUBSYSTEM. This subsystem must be able to generate new data—that is, *Inquire* (4) into the ORGANIZA-TION and its ENVIRONMENT so that additional Inputs can be obtained. It must also have the ability to use data, information, knowledge, or understanding previously received or generated. This means that it must be able to store data+ in retrievable form. A data+ storage facility is a FILE whether it resides in a drawer or computer. It should be a part of the INPUT SUPPLY SUBSYSTEM.

The request-fulfillment cycle—(1) to (4)—may continue until the DECISION MAKERS either have all the information, knowledge, or understanding they want, or have run out of time and must make a decision with whatever they have. In some cases, they may believe that the time and cost of further inquiry is not justified by the improvement or increase of information, knowledge, or understanding that they believe is possible.

The output is a decision either to do something or not; it consists of *Instructions* (5) and is addressed to those in the ORGANIZATION whose responsibility it is to carry them out.

An instruction is a message to others or oneself that is intended to increase or maintain the efficiency of the organization. A decision, of course, may be to do nothing as well as to do something.

A *Decision Record* (6a) is required for all significant decisions whether to do something or nothing.

Every decision has only one of two possible purposes: to make something happen that otherwise wouldn't, or to keep something from happening that otherwise would. In addition, there is always a time by which the effect of the decision is expected. Therefore, to control a decision, its expected effects and the expected times at which they should be realized should be made explicit and recorded. All this is equally true of decisions involving the implementation of a decision. If, for example, a decision has been made to build a new factory, there are expectations about when it should be completed, what if should cost, and so on.

All this should be recorded in the *Decision Record* (6a) that should be placed and stored in an inactive MEMORY and COMPARATOR. [An example of a decision record is shown in Figure 13.3.]

Because human memories over time are inclined to modify their content, especially forecasts and expectations, it is important that the memory employed be completely inactive. Inactive storage of information may be the only thing a computer can do that a human can't.

Monitoring Instructions (6b), a version of the *Decision Record* (6a), should be sent to the INPUT SUPPLY SUBSYSTEM, which has responsibility for checking the validity of the expectations, assumptions, and inputs used in making the decision and its implementation. When obtained, information about the validity of the expected effects, the relevant assumptions, and the inputs used should be sent to the MEMORY AND COMPARATOR in the form of *Monitoring Inputs*

(7). Then, using the information in the *Decision Record* (6a) stored in the MEMORY, and the *Monitoring Inputs* (7), a comparison should be made of the actual and expected effects, and the assumptions on which they are based.

When the COMPARATOR finds no significant difference between expectations and assumptions, and the performance actually observed and reported in the *Monitoring Inputs* (7), nothing need be done other than enter a *Report on Comparisons* (8b) in the FILE for future reference.

This record preserves what is known or believed. Therefore, it should be stored in an easily retrievable form; for example, by the use of key words.

If significant differences are found, *Deviations* (8a) are reported to the DIAGNOSIS and PRESCRIPTION function.

Such deviations indicate either that what was expected did not occur or what was assumed turned out to be wrong. A diagnosis is required to determine what has, and what should be done about it. The purpose of the diagnosis is to find what is responsible for the deviations and to prescribe corrective action. In other words, the diagnostic function consists of explaining the mistake, and therefore, producing understanding of it

There are only a few possible sources of error, each of which requires a different type of corrective action:

- The Inputs (2) used in making the original decision were in error, and therefore the INPUT SUPPLY SUBSYSTEM requires *Correction* (9b) so that it will not repeat that type of error. The information used in decision making can also come from the SURVEILLANCE function, which is described next. Therefore, it too may require *Correction* (9e).

- The DECISION MAKERS may have been faulty. In such a case, they should be *Corrected* (9c).

- The decision may have been correct, but it was not implemented properly. In such a case, *Corrections* (9a) are
  required for the behavior of those in the ORGANIZATION
  who were responsible for implementing the decision.

- The internal or external ENVIRONMENT may have
  changed in a way that was not anticipated. In such
  cases, what is needed is either a better way of anticipat-
  ing such changes, decreasing sensitivity to them,
  reducing their effects, or an attempt to *Influence* the
  ENVIRONMENT (9a).

Through these types of corrective actions, the DIAGNOSIS
and PRESCRIPTION function assures both learning and adaptation.

Consider how threats and opportunities that are not related
to previous decisions are identified and formulated. A "symp-
tom" indicates the presence of a threat or an opportunity; it
is one of a range of values of a variable that usually occurs
when something is exceptionally right or wrong, but seldom
when things are normal. For example, a fever is an abnor-
mally high body temperature that is seldom associated with
good health but frequently with illness.

Variables used as symptoms are properties of the behavior of
the ORGANIZATION or its ENVIRONMENT. Such variables
can also be used dynamically as presymptoms or omens: indicators of future opportunities or problems. A presymptom is
nonrandom normal behavior; for example, a trend, a (statistical) run, or cycle. For example, a trend of rising body temperature, each of which is separately within the normal range,
is a predictor of a coming fever. There are many statistical
tests for nonrandomness, hence presymptoms, but the naked
eye can't identify many of them.

A complete Learning and Adaptation Support System regularly obtains information on a number of internal and external performance indicators. Inputs (10), some of whose values are Symptoms (indicators of current changes) and
Presymptoms (indicators of future changes) are used to Alert

(11 a) the DIAGNOSIS and PRESCRIPTION function. A copy, Findings (11b), is filed with the INPUT SUPPLY SUBSYSTEM.

Analysis of the Deviations (8a), and the Symptoms and Presymptoms in the Alert (11 a), may reveal Threats and Opportunities (12), which are transmitted to the DECISION MAKERS.

Whenever the DIAGNOSIS and PRESCRIPTION function prescribes a change, a diagnostic and prescriptive Decision Record (13) of it should be prepared. This record (which differs from the decision record of the original decision [6a]) is sent to the MEMORY and COMPARATOR where its content can be compared with the Monitoring Inputs (7) supplied by the INPUT SUPPLY SUBSYSTEM in response to the monitoring request of its decisions (prescriptions)

Deviations (8a) are then reported to the DIAGNOSIS and PRESCRIPTION function where corrective action should be taken. Such corrective action may involve Correction (14) of the DIAGNOSIS and PRESCRIPTION function or making any of the types of change previously referred to.

Such changes are what makes possible learning how to learn and adapt.

If every document in the FILE is characterized by key words drawn from a glossary prepared by the INPUT SUPPLY SUBSYSTEM, and if all individuals provide the SUBSYSTEM with key words that reflect their interests, Profile Information (t5), then they can be supplied with a list of all documents relevant to them each week or month. Abstracts and full texts can be provided to them on request.

HUMAN RESOURCES DEVELOPMENT

In addition to the four recurrent idealized designs that have just been described, there are usually a number of smaller sections dealing with personnel matters, community relations, and facilities and equipment. Energetics' treatment of these follows:

The Company will provide all personnel with 1) a clear under-standing of and mutual agreement on what is expected of them; 2) opportunities to acquire the skills that enable them to do their jobs better and increase their employability; 3) the authority and resources required to do their jobs as well as they know how; 4) regular feedback on their performance; and 5) work that is satisfying, challenging, and fun.

EXPECTATIONS

Every manager and supervisor will establish with each subor-dinate exactly what is expected of him/her. This will be done collaboratively with, and agreed to by the subordinate. Once agreed upon, subordinates will be free within corporate poli-cy to select the means required to meet these expectations.

Every employee will be given the opportunity to develop a career development plan with the help of his/her immediate superior. When completed, it will be retained by that superi-or for monitoring its implementation.

This plan will not be a promotion schedule but will focus on professional development of the subordinate.

The Company will provide the time and money required to obtain certification, accreditation, or licensing of skills required by the company. It will provide time and money for development of other skills that can be used in the com-pany, with the approval of the CFO and the director of oper-ations. Finally, it will provide some financial support but no time off for personal development that has no relevance to the company, with the approval of the CFO and the director of operations.

Should employees' career paths in the company be interrupt-ed by agreement, they will be provided with the retraining required to provide the skills needed and expected by the Company.

Personnel at all levels of the organization will encourage, recognize, and reward innovation and be tolerant of failure of innovative efforts. Such failures will be regarded as opportunities for learning. Failure to learn will be taken as a serious mistake.

All personnel with direct reports (other than the CEO) will be expected to record and submit to the director of human resources their recommended successor or possible successors, and notify and discuss this with their immediate superior. If they cannot designate one or more successors, they should indicate this so others can initiate appropriate planning for an eventual replacement.

FEEDBACK ON PERFORMANCE

Supervisors and managers will provide effective and timely feedback on performance to their subordinates, and encourage their subordinates to provide them with feedback of their (the supervisors' or managers') performance.

There will be a formal (minimally) annual separate face-to-face review of each employee's performance and progress relative to his/her personal plans by his/her immediate superior. Where possible, evaluation of the subordinate's performance will be obtained beforehand from his/her peers, their subordinates, and "customers" (if any), and used during the review by the superior.

Every manager's evaluation by his/her superior will include an evaluation of his/her conduct of evaluations of subordinate performance and the assistance they provide subordinates in realizing their personal development plans.

COMPENSATION AND BENEFITS

Base salaries will be based on the market and value to the company. Incentive compensation will be based on individual and corporate performance.

There will be a 20% cap on bonuses for superior performance. Flexible competitive benefit packages will be available to all employees. Individual needs will be met by flexibility in the design of benefit packages. Sabbaticals will be offered to outstanding performers. These will involve full salary for six months or half salary for a full year.

RECRUITING AND HIRING

The Company will encourage development and acquisition of critical skills, including those that will broaden and enhance its intellectual capital.

All employees will be encouraged to identify, develop, and maintain external contacts to provide an inventory of related candidates bringing new or advanced skills to the Company.

If it is practical, initial interviews of external employment prospects will be conducted by the supervisor/manager to whom the prospect would report if hired. For key hires, senior managers will be available for discussion with the candidate to provide information about the company. In addition, in both the hiring of internal and external prospects, the prospect would also be interviewed by those who would be his/her peers and subordinates (if any) if hired. The opinion of all levels involved in the interviewing would be taken into account in hiring decisions.

All persons hired will be evaluated after an appropriate period of time (for example, six months), at which time an explicit decision to retain or dismiss will be made.

Summer internship for students will be initiated and encouraged. All internship employees and co-op students should be carefully managed and overseen by both human resources and the manager responsible for the intern. The intern should be assigned to meaningful work and have the opportunity to develop his/her skills. Human resources should maintain records of their performance, but the manager to whom they are responsible should prepare reviews.

New hires will be put through an orientation to the corporation and introduced to corporate-level managers. This may be either in person or through a video presentation. These sessions will be designed and managed by human resources.

The manager to whom the person hired would report will initiate recruiting of new personnel. This would not require approval from above if the manager involved heads a profit center. If he/she doesn't head a profit center, he/she would require the approval of the manager of the profit center of which his/her unit is a part.

JOB POSTINGS

Whenever applicable, most openings other than those created by the need for redeployment will be posted in and/or outside the Company, where there is no explicit succession plan. To the extent possible, redeployments will be voluntary. All transfers will require the joint approval of the two supervisors/managers involved and not be unreasonably withheld.

TERMINATION, RESIGNATION, AND RETIREMENT

Their immediate superior will give dismissed employees an explanation of their dismissal.

Most salaried personnel who resign or are dismissed and have been employed for two years or more will receive an exit interview by the human resources department to determine the reasons for their leaving. Where practical, there will also be a follow-up interview after about one year to solicit suggestions for improving the Company's operations and practices. The results of these interviews will be shared with the relevant manager(s).

Human resources will analyze demographic and other relevant characteristics of those dismissed and those who leave voluntarily to determine if and how company practices might be improved. It will produce and distribute at least one report each year covering these analyses.

Retiring personnel will receive an exit interview by human resources again to determine whether improvements in personnel policies are possible. A report on their finding will be included in the annual report referred to above. Retirees will be given opportunities when possible to do part-time work for the Company. Programs to maintain retirees' connection to the company will be developed and administered by human resources.

In the case of involuntary termination, a severance package will be offered at the management's discretion. If the termination is because of bad performance, there will not usually be a payment, but there may be one at the discretion of the relevant manager. In the case of elimination or reduction of the size of a unit (downsizing), there will be a severance package.

PERSONNEL POLICIES AUDIT

At least once each year, human resources will audit all personnel policies to ensure their correct implementation and to assess their effectiveness. Where found deficient, suggestions for change or modification should be made. This report should be submitted to the CEO's board.

COMMUNICATIONS

All managers and supervisors will be readily accessible to subordinates through either face-to-face meetings or electronic media. Questions addressed to managers by any means will be responded to within three days where possible. Managers who receive a very large number of communications will be able to use an assistant to filter out the ones to which they should reply personally. The assistants would reply to the others.

There will be at least one annual communication session with the employees at each of the company locations. These will provide a "state of the company" report and opportunities for employees to question a corporate executive.

There will be a quarterly newsletter that will invite signed (not anonymous) inquiries. They will be responded to by the one to whom they are addressed.

Terminals to access e-mail will be available to all personnel.

The Company will have ombudspersons at each company location. They should not be normal employees of the company but persons of relevant professional competence who are retained for this activity—for example, local academics or members of the clergy. They will have no authority over others and will only produce change where indicated through persuasion. They will analyze complaints received and propose changes to appropriate managers.

The office of the ombudsperson should be off-site in order to provide anonymity to employees using this service.

Visits by Company employees at all levels to suppliers, customers, or other relevant organizations will be encouraged.

COMMUNITY RELATIONS

The Company will continue to encourage and support employee activity directed at improving the quality of life in the communities in which it has operations. It will give recognition to those employees who engage in such activity and publicize their efforts in the community. The company itself will engage in such activities as a corporation.

The field locations should be given discretion for their community relations.

Participation in industry associations and relevant engineering associations and support groups will be encouraged and supported.

The CEO's board will have responsibility for allocating funds for use in community relations (including industrial and professional communities). The individual location will have their own funds allocated for such activities.

FACILITIES AND EQUIPMENT

In an ideal situation, the Company would be located where travel is easy (to minimize transportation) and a high quality of life is provided to employees.

All the locations should be of equal quality in terms of building and equipment.

The building and reception area should be attractive. In general, there should be open offices with easy access to all personnel. In addition, there should be some closed areas with glass partitions for those who prefer closure or for meetings.

14

Academy of Vocal Arts (Not-for-Profit)

This is the complete idealized design of a not-for-profit organization, the Academy of Vocal Arts in Philadelphia described in Chapter 5, "Not-for-Profit and Government Organizations." It provides a detailed design that should be of interest and value to anyone who is considering undertaking an idealized design of a not-for-profit organization.

INTRODUCTION

Participative planning is often used to promote organizational change. Although there have been numerous participatory planning initiatives in the past several decades, most of them, according to Allen (1999), are islands of success, not models that have been widely imitated. In addition, some of what is presented as participative planning is so in name only (Roth, 1997, p. 42). For example, in describing the planning effort at Oxford University, Kay (2000, p. 27) noted that it is widely believed to have failed because it was participative only in appearance, not in reality.

There are few reported cases in which participative planning has produced the amount and intensity of commitment required to carry a plan through to successful implementation. Organizations need to learn how to generate the support required from all stakeholders to effectively execute a plan. As Wilcox explains:

> Commitment is the other side of apathy: people are committed when they want to achieve something, apathetic when they don't. But what leads to commitment? Not, in my experience, telling people "you ought to care," inviting them to public meetings or bombarding them with glossy leaflets. I think people . . . become committed when they feel they can achieve something. (Wilcox, 1994)

What follows is a description of an organization's participative planning effort that was implemented successfully and an examination of the reasons for it.

THE ORGANIZATION INVOLVED

Throughout its 67-year history, the Academy of Vocal Arts (AVA) has focused exclusively on tuition-free advanced training, including performance experience, for young singers showing the potential for careers in the world's leading opera houses. Reasonable success came early, in the form of a growing worldwide field of applicants for audition-only admission to AVA. A respectable proportion of graduates enjoyed successful careers as opera singers in the United States and abroad, among them an occasional international star. By the early 1990s, AVA had settled into a rather self-satisfied stability. However, by being known only among the cognoscenti as "the best-kept secret in Philadelphia," it had achieved less success in fund-raising than desired.

THE PLANNING PROCESS

A decision in 1996 to embark on a "long-range [strategic] planning" project was quickly followed by adoption of the interactive planning approach. Getting the organization to embark on a strategic planning effort was a multifaceted decision, influenced partly by the requirements imposed by funding institutions and partly by the desire of leadership to use this opportunity to improve organizational performance. More than 100 stakeholders (faculty, students, managers, subscribers, donors, and board members), representing a wide variety of interests, participated in a six-month effort to redesign the organization, using professional facilitation and guidance.[1] The process used was Russell L. Ackoff's *interactive planning* methodology. Planning is as much an art as it is a science (Ackoff, 1999, p. 55). For this reason, it is not easy to specify a set of steps that guarantee attainment of a good plan. The most that can be done is to suggest a procedure that serves as a guide—a theme on which variations should be written to suit the unique characteristics of the planners, the organization, and the conditions under which the planning is conducted.

Interactive planning is not an act but a process involving six phases that form a cycle that has no arbitrary endpoint in time, but continues to adapt to changing internal and external conditions. All of the phases interact and can be initiated in any order, but must be completed together:

1. Formulating the mess (situational analysis)

   The aim of this phase is to determine how the organization could destroy itself if it were to continue behaving, as it is currently—that is, if it failed to adapt to perfectly predictable aspects of a changing environment.

2. Ends planning

   This phase determines what the organization would like to be and identifies the gaps between this vision and the current reality. The remainder of the planning process seeks to remove or reduce these gaps.

3. Means planning

   The point of this phase is to determine what should be done to remove or reduce the gaps; it selects the courses of action, practices, projects, programs, and policies that should be implemented.

4. Resource planning

   This phase examines how much of each type of resource—facilities and equipment; materials, energy, and services; personnel; money; and information, knowledge, understanding, and wisdom—will be required to implement the means selected.

5. Design of implementation

   This phase identifies who should do what and when it should be completed.

6. Design of controls

   This phase determines how to monitor these assignments and schedules and to adjust for failures to meet the schedules or meet expectations.

Interactive planning clearly differs greatly from "expert planning," in which a series of projects and programs is based on the perceptions of a few individuals considered to be experts. Contrary to conventional planning, which is retrospective, interactive planning is prospective. In the former, planners are preoccupied with identifying and removing deficiencies in the past performance, or at best in the forecast performance, of existing system components. Getting rid of what one does not want is not equivalent to getting what one wants; in fact, what results may be worse than the deficiency removed. Contingency planning treats assumed possible futures in the design process. Every issue is addressed systemically—that is, by taking into account *all* the relevant interactions within the system and between the system and its environment. No improvement in a part's performance is planned unless it produces a demonstrable improvement in the performance of the whole system.

In interactive planning, the most important product is the process, not the plan. Those who engage in it come to know the system planned for and to understand why it works as it does—that is, interactive planning leads to holistic treatment of the organization, with all its internal and external interactions.

The vision prepared in ends planning may not be attainable, but it must be continuously approachable. The vision is *not utopian* because it is subject to improvement over time. Therefore, it is *not* a description of an ideal system, but of an *ideal-seeking* system, the best one can conceive at the time.

The process of designing an ideal-seeking social system usually brings about the following results:

1. It facilitates the direct involvement of a large number of those who hold a stake in the system. No special skills are required because no one is an expert on what ought to be; all value-based opinions are equally relevant. The process encourages thoughtful attitudes and opinions and provides an opportunity to put them into operation.

2. Agreement tends to emerge among participants and other stakeholders. Within an organization, disagreements often arise with respect to means, not ends. The idealized design process focuses on ends, not means, and can incorporate tests of alternative means to reduce conflicts and disagreements.

3. The idealization process forces those engaged in it to formulate explicitly their conception of organizational objectives. This opens their conceptions to examination by others and thus facilitates progressive reformulation of the objectives as well as the development of consensus.

4. Idealized design aims to promote creativity; it encourages those participating to become conscious of self-imposed constraints, hence making it easier to remove them. It also forces reexamination of externally imposed constraints that are usually accepted passively. Ways of removing or evading them are explored, often successfully.

5. The process reveals that system designs and plans, each of whose elements appear to be unfeasible when considered separately, can become feasible when considered collectively.

THE APPLICATION

In the discussion that took place, very early on, between the management and the facilitation team, the following decisions were made:

1. Because of numerous constraints, including the deadline for grant applications to the potential funding organization and the fact that the board and the management were steadfast in their commitment to the interactive planning process, the "mess" formulation (situational analysis) phase was left out. (It was limited to what was known by the organization at that time.)

2. The ends planning phase would be done in one day, and more than 100 stakeholders would be involved.

Having made the decision to involve more than 100 stakeholders in the ends planning, the team made detailed preparations regarding the "requisite variety" in the mix of participants, the venue (free use of the facilities of Deloitte Touche), and the organization of the session (including having four subgroups, as well as four facilitators who were familiar with the interactive planning process and the systems-thinking paradigm and, specifically, skilled in preparing and assisting the participants to become designers for a day).

In addition, a number of preparatory sessions among the facilitators resulted in these subsequent agreements (ground rules):

1. Facilitators were free to exercise their own judgment as to how they would facilitate the dynamics of the group they were moderating (usually it is the same as the organization for any group event, mostly directing the flow of the session in meeting its objectives), with the goal of providing equal opportunity for participation, consensus building, and an entertaining experience.

2. Participants were encouraged to share ideas rather than debate them, and there was room for everyone to contribute. All contributions were recorded on large sheets of paper that were hung on the walls of the breakout rooms. Doing so provided a sense of progress and allowed the facilitators to be perceived as resource people present to assist rather than to direct the design activity.

3. Every session ended by allowing participants to reflect on what had been contributed thus far. This allowed for evaluation and

greater awareness of the values and ideals expressed by the whole group.

4. The first hour of the session was spent on participants speaking about the current reality as it applied to the organization and its relevant business environment (usually becoming a sort of a whining session).

5. The design session was started by creating a "discontinuity" in the thinking process of the participants. (A tape on which Ackoff describes his Bell Lab experience was used to set the stage for the transition from the first session to the design segment.)

6. Every facilitator was to ensure that, during the design process, participants were not permitted to say what they didn't want; only what they did want. They were told specifically not to dwell on the existing system, as this was contrary to the stage-setting caution that "the system was destroyed last night." They were told that they were free to replace the existing system with whatever they wanted, right at that time.

7. The commitment to specific design elements was to be delayed until participants had developed appreciation for everyone's contribution. Emphasis would be placed on the interrelationships among issues, and everyone would have the opportunity to modify his or her views in light of what was learned from one another (Schön, 1992, p. 3).

The session began with introductory remarks by the executive director and a brief explanation, made by one of the facilitators, of the planning objectives, the nature of the engagement, and the proposed phases that would lead to achievement of the day's objectives. The introduction led directly into the first session, which focused on discussing the current reality and lasted about an hour. Just before the break, the tape in which Ackoff explains his experience with redesigning the telephone system at Bell Labs was played. This tape set the stage for what was to follow—that is, asking the participants to become creative (through discontinuous thinking) and to design their ideal system. Thereafter, the large group was broken up into four smaller groups, and a facilitator was assigned to each group for the purpose of starting the work of idealizing the future of AVA. The first design session was to last until the lunch break.

At the break, the facilitation team and the members of management got together to see how the groups were doing and whether there were problems that had to be dealt with (Schön, 1983). In the discussion that ensued, it became clear that there were some people who were uncomfortable with the format and really had difficulty in understanding the task at hand and its overall relevance. In addition, some groups had individuals who were trying to dominate the discussions, and a few were presenting themselves as experts and trying to tell the fellow designers what to do.

As is typical with such work, some participants had difficulty in understanding the role of the facilitators. It was hard for them to distinguish the facilitators from consultants, who typically have the task of listening to clients and designing solutions. It was agreed that the facilitation team would continue to play their role by recording all the contributions, provoking critical discussion of each point, and trying to stimulate the group by occasionally asking for clarification that would generate further contributions.

One group, in particular, reported a case of near conflict and polarization. The facilitator dealt with this situation by reframing the issue and taking it out of an "either/or" formulation, showing that after the issue is reframed, the two design ideas become complementary in an *and* relationship, creating a strong synergy between them.

Every group was asked to have its work reviewed during the plenary session in the afternoon. They were told to have a reporter who would present their work in the plenary. (Some chose to have a subgroup present in the plenary.) Every group was encouraged to consider the plenary session as an "idea" market and to "borrow" ideas from one another. Each group was given 15 minutes to present and answer a limited number of questions. After the first plenary session, the groups were sent back to complete their work in view of what they had learned from the others and then asked to come back to the final plenary session in a couple of hours.

After the afternoon break, the groups returned and presented what they considered to be their idealized design of AVA. As the presentation was in progress, it became apparent that there was a lot of similarity in the four designs presented. After the presentations were completed, the facilitation team, in a participative manner, synthesized the four designs into one.

The mission of the "new" organization, as synthesized and approved by the planners, read as follows:

> The mission of the Academy of Vocal Arts is to be the world's premier institution for training young artists for careers as international opera singers. AVA operates by:
>
> ■ Accepting only the highest-quality resident artists
>
> ■ Providing each artist with a full-tuition and fellowship award
>
> ■ Presenting the resident artists in concerts, oratorios, and in fully staged professional opera performances
>
> ■ Making performances accessible to a wide community

Next, AVA developed a description of what it would be now if it could be whatever it wanted, without any internal (but with externally imposed) constraints. The planners sought to envision a system in which *all* the stakeholders could achieve their objectives for AVA.

When the vision was completed, the participants identified the gaps between the vision and what was then the current reality and formulated a set of comprehensive strategic/tactical actions to approximate its vision as closely as possible. Over the next five months, a number of teams, each chaired by a member of the board's Long-Range Planning Committee, proposed actions geared toward closing the gap and realizing the plan. The recommendations were reviewed and revised by the full committee, which then constructed a strategic plan for review and adoption by the board.

Some of the planned actions were innovative and new. Many, perhaps most, of the actions selected for inclusion in the ultimate plan had been thought of by various participants for a considerable time, but they either lacked, or thought they lacked, the authority and resources to pursue them. In particular, through dialogue and facilitation, the planning process enabled participants with a strong vision for the organization to inspire and influence others whose support was critical.

WHAT HAS BEEN DONE

Since the plan's adoption in 1997, a large percentage of the planned actions have been implemented, including some of the most ambitious and supposedly difficult to accomplish. Of the more than 40 actions planned for the first 3 years, more than 30 were fulfilled within that period. Prominent among these were the following:

- Establishment of 13 fellowship awards (living stipends to supplement tuition-free training)
- Purchase of the (architecturally identical) adjacent building to meet critical needs for additional space
- Increase in endowment funds by $7 million (over $10 million from which AVA previously received operating income)
- Conducting of regional auditions
- Institution of an oratorio training program
- Securing of expanded media attention, including regional National Public Radio broadcasts

Other planned actions, delayed largely as a result of the limited number of available staff, are still in the process of implementation as time permits. In the case of the few delays attributable to resistance, or attempted "pocket vetoes," by occasional nonbelievers, the deep overall organizational commitment to the strategic plan resulted in their continued pursuit and accomplishment.

RESULTS

Although it is still too early to evaluate the long-range impact of these activities on the organization's mission, early indicators are favorable. For example, organizational resources—professional, physical, and financial—have been expanded. AVA has been named by a major philanthropic foundation as one of the region's cultural leadership agencies. It has achieved unconditional accreditation by the National Association of Schools of Music. Most important, an increasing number of graduates are achieving early success in the world of opera.

Monitoring implementation and periodic environmental scanning and updating of the plan have enabled AVA to stay on track, but some issues remain unresolved. As a voluntary organization committed to maintaining its vitality partly by continual replacement of the members of its governing body, how and when should the organization invite new members into its planning process?

AVA has decided that five years is the limit for implementing an existing strategic plan. Therefore, it is currently preparing to launch a new interactive planning effort in January 2002.

IMPACT ASSESSMENT

In comparison with other applications of interactive planning, this project, right from the beginning, benefited from a number of critical conditions that contributed to its success:

- The management had a clear understanding of and a firm commitment to the proposed methodology.
- There was no indication of a "hidden agenda," by either the participants (including the management) or the facilitators.
- No party had any concealed political purposes, as far as the facilitators could establish.
- There was no element of distrust between the various segments of the AVA organization and the leadership, including the relationship between the executive director and the board (in particular, the chairman of the board).
- All of AVA's stakeholders may be considered in one sense a self-selected universe, their common passion for opera creating an environment, which may have facilitated achievement of a shared vision.

Because such intervention is rare at AVA, the whole process had tremendous credibility, in contrast to situations in which managements try different approaches according to the "flavor of the month."

Good things are happening to AVA. Recently, to determine as accurately as possible whether the planning process had produced the intended effects, a number of AVA stakeholders who had participated in the planning process were asked by the authors[2] to describe the high and low points in AVA's life and to list the contributing factors.

The majority of respondents considered the interactive planning process to be a highpoint in the life of the organization and to have had a positive impact on its operations. Analysis of the responses generated and the follow-up questions revealed the following themes:

- Interactive planning produced a radical change in AVA by involving all the stakeholders in the planning process and by changing their understanding of the organization and its environment. ("Board members understood who the students were.")

- Multiple perspectives were brought to bear on the decisions. ("They even heard from the students.")

- The interactive planning process created a critical mass of people behind the plan. ("It got everybody on the same page.")

- The dynamics among the stakeholders improved. ("One idea sparked another idea.")

- AVA became proactive. ("Some of the ideas were floating around for some time.")

- The list of topics open to discussion widened. ("People who want to do things were able to get a hearing.")

- The faculty came to understand why fund raising is important.

- The organization was successful in meeting the objectives. ("Buying the building next door was a great achievement.")

There was a subsequent probing of the respondents to obtain a deeper assessment of the impact. Additional themes came to light:

- A consensus was created around the vision. ("Elements of the vision became enriched while there was a buy-in from the participants.")

- The organization became empowered to do things. ("People who wanted to do something were legitimated and energized; for years we wanted to buy the building next door.")

- The power was redistributed. ("The board altered its role, executives altered their role, and so did the staff.")

- The objectivity of the facilitators was important for the process. ("Researchers were not paid and had no axe to grind.")

- The process had a positive effect on content. ("[For] everybody in the room, the process affected you personally.")

It became apparent that, although inspired discoveries are often attributed to talented individuals, it is more often the case that the planning team creates the solutions (Northcraft et al., 1990, p. 302). The combined intellects of team members, often representing different disciplines, can create an intellectual environment in which truly new ideas emerge. The important thing is to provide the right mix of experience and skills so that the combined knowledge and understanding of the individuals can be focused on the problem. Realistically, this condition is made possible by the interplay among the different factors, such as the participants, venue, facilitators, and the catalyzing effect of the interactive planning process itself.

Clearly, the outcome of the participative interactive planning process may be affected by a set of factors peculiar to the social system in question. However, despite the idiosyncratic features of each intervention and the special characteristics of the organization involved, certain processes are generic, contributing to success in all such applications of interactive planning.

CONCLUSION

The best way to ensure that the design will serve the organization's purpose is to include as many stakeholders as feasible in formulating that design. Hence, the success of a design is related directly to stakeholder participation in its development. But stakeholder participation by itself will not guarantee the commitment that was created in this project. Participants need an environment that nurtures talent, they need a way to communicate across professional boundaries, and they need leadership. They also require the capacity to integrate the skills and ideas that generate success. An effective facilitation can do a great deal to make all this possible.

The planning process positively affected the ongoing social processes in AVA, specifically interactions among individuals, as well as decision-making, policies, norms and values, attitudes, authority, and responsibility.

The interactive planning process increased enthusiasm and commitment. Most important, it increased the level of motivation among the stakeholders by empowering them (Blanchard, 1996, p. 90). It gave them the opportunity to redesign their future, and thus AVA's future, based on the desires of all parts of the organization. The stakeholders thus *owned* the plan.

By increasing their interest in AVA's future, the stakeholders were motivated to advance the development potential of the organization of which they are a part. Thus, their role in the design process increased their concern for the future welfare of the AVA, which was closely linked to their individual self-interest. Consequently, it could be said that the opportunity to design a future for AVA and then to work toward its realization instilled in the stakeholders the desire to act—it motivated them by focusing on the advantages of the new system rather than on the problems with the old one.

Although we have presented *mobilizing commitment* as the major outcome of the participative planning process, trust is required to sustain the commitment created by the planning process. As Harkins (2001, p. 46) writes: "Trust begins with candor. It is expanded when people are clear with each other. It is as simple as following through on what you say you will do."

Change of paradigm together with building trust are necessary for what Ackoff (1999, p. 274) calls organizational development and transformational leadership.

Transformational leadership requires the ability to encourage and facilitate the formulation of an inspiring vision, but it also requires the ability to implement pursuit of that vision. "Inspiration without implementation is provocation, not leadership. Implementation without inspiration is management or administration, not leadership."

Judging from the continued success enjoyed by AVA, one could conclude that the leadership and process required to accomplish an organizational transformation have been provided—through enabling inspiration and then implementing the plan.

REFERENCES

Ackoff, R. L. 1999. *Re-Creating the Corporation: A Design of Organizations for the 21st Century.* New York: Oxford University Press.

Allen, W. 1999. Participatory Planning and Management, NRM Changelinks, http://nrm.massey.ac.nz/changelinks/co_man.html (2/27/01).

Blanchard, Ken. 1996. *Empowerment Takes More Than a Minute.* New York: MJF Books.

Harkins, P. 2001. How to use powerful conversations to drive systems thinking, *Journal of Innovative Management,* Volume 6, Number 2: 45–53.

Kay, J. 2000. A lost cause, *PROSPECT,* December: 22–27. Bristol, England BS32 OPP.

Northcraft, Gregory B. and Neal, Margaret A. 1990. *Organizational Behavior—A Management Challenge.* The Dryden Press. p. 302.

Roth, William F. 1997. Going all the way with empowerment, *The TQM Magazine,* Volume 9, November 1, pp. 42–45.

Schön, Donald A. 1983. *The Reflective Practitioner.* New York: Basic Books.

—— 1992. Designing as reflective conversation with the materials of a design situation, *Knowledge-Based Systems,* Vol. 5, No. 1.

Wilcox, D. 1994. The Guide to Effective Participation, Partnerships Online, UK, http://partnerships.org.uk/guide/index.htm (3/12/01).

15

White House Communications Agency (Government)

March Laree Jacques

This is the complete idealized design of a government organization, the White House Communications Agency, described in Chapter 5, "Not-for-Profit and Government Organizations." Written in 1999, it provides a detailed design that should be of interest and value to anyone who is considering undertaking an idealized design of an agency or other organization of government.

INTRODUCTION

Among the symbols of American democracy, such as the flag, the Liberty Bell, the Constitution, and the Declaration of Independence, one symbol—the White House—is an organization. Like the others, the White House is a visible, physical representation of American ideals. Unlike the others, the 18-acre White House complex is a human network, home to the numerous inter-related agencies and services that support the office of the president of the United States. The complex is head-quarters to, among others, the Secret Service, a medical office, food service, and an 800-person communications agency. The White House, symbol of freedom and democracy, is also the ultimate command-and-control organization.

In 1992, the first organizational transformation effort in the history of the White House began when the White House Communications Agency (WHCA) hired Dr. J. Gerald Suàrez to establish an office of organization and process improvement. Late December that year, Suàrez became the archetypical lone ranger. A civilian with a Ph.D. in industrial-organizational psychology and a background in research, Suàrez was cast in a fast-paced, high-tech, military organization. Today [1999], Suàrez's business card still reads "Director, Presidential Quality Management, White House Communications Agency," and the agency's office of presidential quality/organization and process improvement has grown to eight people. It is still charged with helping the agency improve. Significantly, the agency has made enough progress over the last six years to be willing now to talk about its transformational efforts. The journey has taken the agency from continual process improvement initiatives, following an approach espoused by Dr. W. Edwards Deming, through the implementation of a total organizational redesign, using systems thinking precepts championed by Dr. Russell Ackoff.

For practitioners, the agency's story shares numerous insights about how one organization met and dissolved obstructions to organizational transformation. The barriers that the agency met will be especially familiar to change agents who work with skilled, high-tech work forces, as well as those who work in government agencies or in any organizational environment that is top heavy in terms of managerial hierarchy, or that serves critical customers, or that makes decisions which are highly visible to the public. For researchers, the agency's story suggests a need for further study into the relationship between social systems theory and quality management, especially as related to discontinuous improvement. It also suggests a need for further investigation into the factors that affect the transferability of quality improvement and organizational design concepts between commercial and guardian organizations.

MEET WHCA

The White House Communications Agency (WHCA, pronounced "walk-a") is the unit of the federal government responsible for fulfilling the communication needs of the president and presidential staff. From relatively mundane, nonsecure phone calls, to highly visible public speeches, to unique, high-security encrypted messages, the agency supports the office of the president by fulfilling all aspects of communications, instantaneously. This includes an enormous amount of detail that citizens take for granted.

For example, when the president gets a phone call, wherever he may be, someone in WHCA makes the connection. (Imagine disconnecting Gorbachev or asking Yeltsin to hold!) When the president takes the presidential limo through the streets of Washington, someone from the WHCA checks the mobile phones. When the president gets top-secret telecommunications aboard Air Force One, WHCA is at work. When the president gives a speech in Afghanistan—or anywhere else in the world—WHCA provides public address systems, videotaping, photographic processing, audio and video editing and archiving, cable distribution, audio and video distribution, teleprompting support, plus an official, presidential lectern, and much, much more. Moreover, if the vice president or first lady acts in official capacity as an emissary of the president, WHCA's responsibilities extend to them as well. Radio frequency systems, information systems, and network infrastructure all fall within the agency's domain.

In the narrowest sense, the agency's customers are the president, vice president, and first lady of the United States. But it also supports the chief of staff, the office of administration, National Security Council (NSC), Defense Information Systems Agency (DISA), the U.S. Secret Service, and the presidential staff and "others as directed." In the broadest sense, the agency's customers are the citizens of the United States and the free world.

Organizationally, the agency is part of the Department of Defense. Established in 1942 as the White House Signal Detachment, its mission during the Roosevelt administration was to provide normal and emergency communications to support the president. The detachment's first jobs were to provide mobile radio, teletype, telephone, and cryptographic services in the White House and Camp David (then known as Shangri-La). In 1954, during the Eisenhower administration, the detachment was reorganized under the Army Signal Corps and renamed the White House Army Signal Agency. In 1962, it was transferred to the Defense Communications Agency and took its current name. The agency is under operational control of the White House Military Office (WHMO), with administrative oversight provided by the Defense Information Systems Agency (DISA). Agency personnel come from all branches of the armed forces. The agency commander is a one-star flag officer.

SETTING THE STAGE

By the late 1980s, quality management was making inroads into government. The Reagan administration created a Federal Quality Institute and an annual quality award—the President's Quality Award—that used a modified version of the Baldrige Award criteria. Many of the early success stories came from the Department of Defense (DoD), which also garnered by many of the Presidential Quality Awards. The Defense Department tended to see quality much the way its contractors did, as a valuable management philosophy and a set of quantitative tools and techniques that should be widely disseminated. In the late 1980s, the department committed resources and internal expertise to provide management directives and guidance, self-assessment processes, and training materials to DoD organizations wanting to start down the quality path (Hyde, 1997). Also in the 1980s, the Defense Department began to send personnel to Deming's seminars and had Deming present his famous Four-Day Seminar at the Pentagon. According to one participant, Del Nelson, Project Officer, 1983–1990, for the Pacer Share U.S. Civil Service Demonstration Project conducted at McClellan Air Force Base, Deming's seminars and subsequent advice to project leaders at McClellan were pivotal in shaping the Pacer Share Project, which in turn became part of the torrent of influences that eventually became Vice President Gore's federal reform initiative (Nelson and Gilbert, 1991).

By the late 1980s and early 1990s, quality was in the air. Synchronous quality initiatives were underway in private telecommunications companies, a happenstance that encouraged benchmarking and sharing of best practices with their counterparts in the public sector. The U.S. General Accounting Office conducted a study of quality in government that concluded that by 1992, quality management in some form had been introduced into most federal agencies. The study also indicated, however, that direct worker participation was significantly smaller with just 17 percent of the work force directly involved in quality activities (Hyde, 1997). The 1992 presidential election ushered Bill Clinton into the presidency. With him came promising reports about a history of quality management initiatives in state government during his term as governor of Arkansas. Later, expectations about the future of federal quality initiatives increased again with Clinton's choice of cabinet members such as Robert Reich and Donna Shalala (Jacques, 1993a, 1993b). Then, came Vice President's Gore initiative to reinvent government. Quality, it seemed, was poised for a big step forward.

ENTER THE CHANGE AGENT

In December 1992, as the White House Military Office was preparing for a new president, a hiring process which had started at WHCA during the latter days of the Bush administration was winding down. The agency finished culling through more than 125 candidates to find the person who would be tasked with establishing an office of process improvement for the agency. On Christmas eve, they offered the job to Dr. J. Gerald Suàrez. On paper, his selection sounds at first like a mismatch: The agency is a military command. Suàrez is one of only four civilians employed in the 800-person agency. Suàrez has a Ph.D. The agency has an environment in which a doctoral degree is often seen as "academic" (interesting but irrelevant). At the time he was hired, Suàrez had no experience in telecommunications, yet WHCA was, and is, overwhelmingly staffed with communication professionals whose work language is peppered with high-tech jargon. For those who hold to the theory that a change agent should offer an outside view, Suàrez had the right stuff.

In reality, the fit was better than it sounds. Suàrez had worked extensively with military personnel, specifically with the Department of the Navy (DoN). While in graduate school at the University of Puerto Rico, where he earned both his Masters and Ph.D. in industrial and organizational psychology, Suàrez had the opportunity, in the summers of 1984 and 1985, to work with the research staff of the Navy Personnel Research and Development Center (NPRDC) in San Diego, California. There he got his first introduction to quality when he was assigned to read *Quality, Productivity, and Competitive Position* (Deming, 1982b). He recalls the book and others by Deming as having a powerful, but confusing impact on his intellectual progress. "Here were ideas that were almost the exact opposite of what I had been taught in industrial-organizational psychology. To give you an example, Deming said in essence, 'Get rid of performance appraisals' (Deming, 1982a)—I was learning how to design them!"

In 1987, Suàrez joined the center full-time as a personnel research psychologist and as an instructor and consultant for both the Navy and the DoD. There, he did research related to developing educational strategies and training plans for Total Quality Leadership (TQL), the Navy's approach to quality improvement. In 1991, he joined the Office of the Undersecretary of the Navy's TQL office as a technical advisor, researcher, and instructor. He was a member of the faculty responsible for training the Navy's TQL specialists and the instructors of the Navy's "Senior Leaders Seminar" series. A 1992 report Suàrez prepared for the Navy's TQL Office provides an in-depth comparison of the approaches expounded by three of the most prominent quality gurus of the day: Crosby, Deming, and Juran. The textbook-quality report, titled "Three Experts on Quality Management" (Suàrez, 1992), is noteworthy for its concise but detailed examination of the similarities and differences among their philosophies. As part of his investigation, Suàrez attended Crosby's Quality College, Juran Institute seminars, and Deming's Four-Day Seminar.

In studying the Deming approach, he became intrigued with Deming's admonition to "drive out fear" in the workplace. From a psychological point of view, Suàrez understood that absence of all fear would be a sign of pathology, much like absence of all stress. To understand how fear manifests itself in the workplace and how it affects performance, he began to research the kinds of fear and their impact from a psychological point of view—social psychology, clinical psychology, industrial-organizational psychology. His conclusions appear in "Managing Fear in the Workplace" (Suàrez, 1993), a free Navy publication that offers guidelines for dealing with fear in the work environment. The work also is the basis for a three-volume video series (Suàrez, 1996). In both, he argues that fear cannot be eliminated, but must be understood, coped with, managed, and channeled. He discusses several types of fear and behaviors associated with them: fear of failure, fear of reprisal or of receiving poor appraisals, fear of change, fear of success, fear of math, fear of speaking up, and fear of not making a mark on one's watch.

The research would prove valuable at WHCA. On his first day with the agency, a long-time employee predicted, "When you leave the White House, you will be a young man with a promising past. If you do the right things right while you are here, you will have a promising future. But, while you are here, you will know intimidation, fear, and pain."

UNDERSTANDING THE CULTURE

The organizational culture into which Suàrez had stepped was unpredictable and pressure filled. He sometimes describes the White House as a clock, "hermetically sealed with an internal structure and precise movements and interactions that affect us all," a place "where the monumental and the mundane coexist." Yet, as he would learn, there are no typical days at the White House. It is always unpredictable and dynamic. Nonetheless, it is also rigidly structured. There is a plan, a backup plan and a contingency for everything. It is, Suàrez says, "the ultimate military command structure."

Cast as the change agent, Suàrez set out to understand organization, but his "outsider" credentials distanced him from other people in the agency, making it difficult to develop trusting relationships. Typically, people bond with the familiar. "For example," Suàrez explains, "if you are Army and I am Army, we bond because we have Army in common. Or I'm Navy, you're Navy. Or you are a communicator, I am a communicator. Or I have a Masters in engineering, you have a Masters in engineering. Well, I had none of that. I had to build coalitions. I had to bring people together. I had to trust people, and they didn't trust me. So, it was challenging, just to get that portion of it going." Even Suàrez's natural wit and easy, gregarious style did not mesh at first with the stiff, intense agency environment. Then, too, there was the security issue. After all, this was the White House. "I felt paranoid at first," he recalls. "They briefed me on so many things—if you do this, this will happen. I had this feeling that—I think they are watching me—and of course they were. From a quality perspective, that was a barrier. You need to have an openness. You need to have a dialogue and 'invite people in.' It was hard to develop synergy in work."

Suàrez began by observing and by interviewing people, especially those with ten years or more with the agency. Later, he did a formal climate survey, but first he did lots of lunches and had lots of talks with old timers. They all seemed to agree; to understand the agency, he needed to go on the road with the president. He needed to do the work and feel the pressure. "Altogether, probably my first 18 months were spent learning to understand the agency," he says. "Every time I would think, 'aha, I've got it,' another window would open. My first presidential trip, my first this, my first that, you hang around here for two or three years and there just is no typical day. So it took a long time to really understand the business environment. Yet, within a month or so, I was ignorant enough to write a memo saying these are the things that need to happen."

"Looking back on it now, I think it was one of my earliest mistakes. I tried to make an impact too soon. I started to shake some trees that I should have left alone until I knew exactly why they were doing things that way. I was very proactive. People come here to survive it. They don't come here to make it better. I came here to make it better and that was a big challenge."

Memo in hand, new employee Suàrez learned that the agency was not ready to have some civilian Ph.D. tell them how to do business. Today, many of his first recommendations have been implemented, but early in 1993 the agency was not ready for those kinds of changes. Suàrez remembers that the commander at the time, Colonel Thomas Hawes, USAF, had a "strange look in his eyes" when he finished reading the memo. "I asked him, 'Sir, is everything okay?' He said, 'Where did you get that information?' I said, 'Well, I've been here observing and this is what I perceive.' And he said, 'But it's been less than a month, and you already know too much about what is wrong with the agency.' Coming from the outside, I could see room for improvement all over the place. They were so close to it, they were used to it. They were coping with it. It had become their way of life. Then here I come saying, your way of life is not good enough. They resented that and said, essentially, 'it's not good enough but it *is* our way of life and you've got to learn it if you want to be part of us.'"

Eventually, he would understand. The old timers had predicted that traveling with the president was the key to the agency mentality, so Suàrez took his show on the road. He went on lots of trips. He did communications work and discovered firsthand what it was like to have a razor-thin margin for error. It was different from teaching the win-win concept, which he was doing about the same time. His wake-up call came in Spain. One day in Madrid, something went wrong. Things were not working. Pressure built and it was Suàrez who transformed in front of everyone, pounding the table and throwing win-win out the window. "I was almost yelling, 'This how it's got to be done. We've got to do this. There is no time . . .' Everyone cracked up and someone said, 'You are finally one of us. You broke the code.' And even though it was a good thing—I was in, I had the secret handshake—it was a bad thing. I thought, this is scary. If I am getting like you are, then I won't be effective. And the story spread. Pretty soon, everyone knew about it because it was so out of character. I was so autocratic and emotional. When I reflected on that, I realized that if I continue to do this, I won't be able to do what I came here to do."

Suàrez refocused. Today, he believes he has a solid appreciation for the traditional agency point of view and is functioning in a way that feels very comfortable and effective. The stories of his first change memo and his own change in Spain echo a principle of social systems theory articulated below by Jamshid Gharajedaghi (1999, in press).

> Open (living) systems, not only preserve their common properties but jealously guard their individualities. . . . the cultural code becomes the social equivalent of biological DNA, those hidden assumptions deeply anchored at the very core of our collective memory. Left to be self-organized, these internal codes, by default, act as organizing principles that invariably reproduce the existing order.

In hindsight, the incidents foreshadowed the likelihood that it would take more than training and more than process improvement to achieve breakthrough organizational improvement at WHCA. Although Suàrez got past his culture shock, the agency's distinctive cultural traits continue to impact the transformation effort.

KEY CULTURAL INFLUENCES

- **Fear of making a mistake.** The agency's environment demands constant, high-level performance. Pressure for perfection permeates the atmosphere. A huge percentage of the decisions made at the White House have national and international implications. Mishandling a phone call or having an open microphone at the wrong moment can create an international incident. On high-security tasks, the margin for error is thinner yet. People try to conceal mistakes.
- **Constant public scrutiny and hoopla.** The press have a permanent encampment on the White House lawn. Reports from White House (especially of mistakes) are on the news within minutes—or live. The hoopla that constantly swirls around the White House is a distraction for the work of improvement.
- **Lack of democratic processes.** The White House is run autocratically. Introducing participative teamwork is a contradiction.
- **Military synergy.** WHCA personnel are military people. Their first loyalty is to their own branch of the service. Loyalty to WHCA must be encouraged and nurtured.

- **Mobility of personnel.** The average tour of duty is four years. WHCA has requirements and specifications that its people may never have use for again. The agency must find ways to provide people with experience that will be useful to them after they leave.

- **Pride.** Agency personnel take considerable pride in the words "presidential quality" because their work supports what they call the "ultimate customer, the leader of the free world." Within the agency, "presidential quality" means providing the highest product and service possible to enable the president to lead the nation.

- **Lack of bottom-line incentives.** Unlike commercial organizations, agency improvement efforts are not driven by financial considerations. WHCA supports the president and, by extension, the free world; ergo, the agency gets what it needs to accomplish the job. In any tradeoff between effective and efficient, effective wins. The agency is subsidized by the DoD. What Suàrez calls "the fallacy of the third party which pays for everything" is a mixed blessing for improvement work.

- **Access to top people.** The agency has the luxury of being able to access the top people in any field. This includes top communication experts and top management consultants.

GETTING STARTED

The transformational effort underway at WHCA is one that would move the agency from an autocratic organization—which it is—to an democratic social system—which it is not. The agency's organizational culture presents huge challenges, but also huge opportunities. Major among them is the opportunity to work with world-class people in all areas, including the areas of quality and organizational development. In the course of its journey, WHCA first explored Deming's approach to continuous improvement, engaging several of Deming's prominent associates as consultants and trainers, and then explored Ackoff's approach to organizational design, engaging his associates and Ackoff himself as a consultant and mentor.

Total organizational redesign was not what WHCA had in mind originally. Like much of the federal government in the early 1990s, the agency was feeling pressure to optimize its processes. Prior to hiring Suàrez, WHCA engaged external consultants to help start a process improvement initiative, but the nature of the agency limited the effect an external consultant could have. There were spotty success stories of improvement, an administrative process here, a personnel process there, but not systemic improvement. Suàrez talked with a consultant from Process Management Institute (PMI) who had worked with WHCA on process improvement prior to 1992, and learned that he had not had the security clearance necessary to impact critical operations. Suàrez explains, "Most of our key processes by nature are sensitive or classified. He literally could not get to things that would fundamentally change how we do business. To be effective, you have to have access. That is what generated a need for having an in-house person versus using an external consultant."

CHANGING THE SYSTEM

With the addition of an in-house quality and process improvement officer, the agency had a resource that could help move quality methodology and concepts into its core business processes. It had teams, empowerment, improvement projects, just-in-time training, and more. What it didn't have was the effect it was looking for.

> Changing the *system* will change what people do. Changing what people do will not necessarily change the system. (Scholtes, 1998)

By 1994, the agency's process improvement projects still were not having the impact they wanted. Every time WHCA made, or tried to make, an improvement, it had a ripple effect. Suàrez notes, "It is easy to say, from an academic point of view, that processes are cross-functional, but when you are actually working on improvements, you can literally see the boundary expanding. Every time that we would get better—make an improvement—it was like we also got worse because now we had a bigger problem. Now, we had to involve 'those people' and 'you know how they are.' The other thing was that we had fallen pretty much into what Brian Joiner calls 'whack-a-mole' behavior (Joiner, 1994). We were just hitting at problems and they would go away but another one would pop up. We were burning a lot of energy, consuming our people like fuel. We were throwing people at problems."

The agency was growing rapidly and asking for still more people at a time when DoD was shrinking everything. Process improvement projects were not enough. The agency's traditional organizational structure (see Figure 15.1) had too much complexity, too much redundancy. Technological changes meant it no longer made sense to have separate departments for AV, paging, and so on. The agency needed a radical transformation, a fundamental change in the way it operated. Suàrez began to talk with the agency's leaders about social systems theories and radical redesign. He says they thought it was impossible: "We just couldn't make a phone and say, 'Mr. President, can you please stay in town? Don't go anywhere; we're going to redesign.' I continued making presentations on systems thinking and over time a small group of people came to believe it made sense. But how could we do it? We needed help."

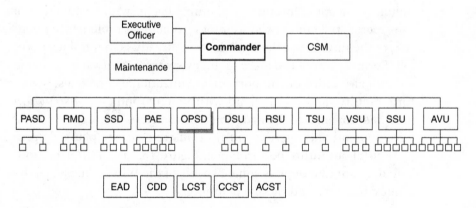

Figure 15.1 Organizational diagram

ORGANIZATIONAL REDESIGN

In the fall of 1994, the Republicans took Congress. At WHCA, the budget-chopping attitude in Congress added clout to the case for changing the agency's structure. For the redesign effort, the agency chose to use the interactive planning and idealized design concepts articulated by Dr. Russell Ackoff (Ackoff, 1981, 1994). Dr. Suàrez and the office of process improvement facilitated the redesign team; Ackoff and his associates, including John Pourdehnad and Jamshid Gharajedaghi, mentored the agency and provided strategic advice. The new structure, however, was created by the people within the agency. According to Suàrez, "We guided them to the realization that an ideal-seeking system is better than an optimal system." The theory behind WHCA's change effort focused on the use of the following:

- Synthesis as a way of thinking about the organization
- Democracy and participation
- Interactive planning
- The board structure

Ackoff's concept of interactive planning begins with formulation of the "mess," the complex system of interacting problems that constitute the future that the organization already is in if it does nothing. Formulation of the mess includes *systems analysis* to provide a detailed picture of the current organizational processes, structure, culture, and relationship with its environment; *obstruction analysis* to surface obstructions or barriers to organizational development; and *reference projections* to generate plausible projections about future performance. Figure 15.2 is an interrelationship diagram that depicts some aspects of the WHCA "mess" as the agency began its interactive planning.

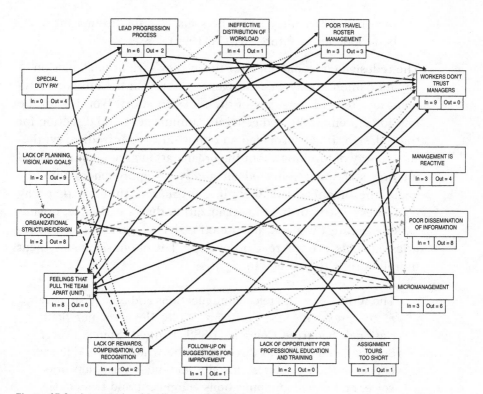

Figure 15.2 Interrelationship diagram of WHCA issues

The redesign team used surveys, off-site sessions with all unit commanders, and numerous one-on-one conversations to gather information, formulate the mess, and lay a foundation for the redesign work. An internal document describes the agency's approach to redesign. It echoes Ackoff's writings (WHCA 1996, iii):

> An idealized design of a system is the design its stakeholders would have *right now* if they could have any system they wanted. The design is subject to only two constraints: it must be technologically feasible (no science fiction), and it must be operationally viable (capable of surviving in the current environment if it came into existence, with or without modification). The design has one requirement: it must be capable of rapid and effective learning and adaptation, and therefore be able to change. It is called idealized because it is the best ideal-seeking systems its designers could imagine at the time,

recognizing that they and others may be able to imagine a better one in the future (WHCA, 1996).

The redesign effort did not alter the agency's traditional mission in any fundamental way, but the agency did revisit the mission statement and reword it as part of the redesign effort. Working on the mission statement helped generate commitment and direction for the redesign. It also provided an opportunity to introduce synthesis as a way of thinking about the organization as a system. The old mission statement reflected an analytical approach to thinking about the organization. According to Suàrez, thinking that way translates to structuring the organization that way. Hence, organizations create divisions and functional boundaries. The boundaries, he adds, are where fear develops. The old mission statement literally broke the agency into parts:

> The WHCA provides telecommunications and related support to the president, vice president, White House Senior Staff, National Security Council, USSS [United States Secret Service], and others as directed by the White House Military Office. WHCA operates, installs and maintains networks, voice, and data communications equipment and technology. Our support to the POTUS [president of the United States] includes non-secure voice, secure voice, record communications, audiovisual services, automated data processing support, and photographic and drafting services both in Washington, DC and on trip sites worldwide.

The systems approach, which the agency was striving for, called for synthesis to be used to develop the mission statement. Synthesis asks: What are we part of? WHCA is part of the presidency. What is the presidency part of? The presidency is part of the nation. The new mission statement focuses on both:

> The White House Communications Agency's mission is to provide premier communications systems that enable the president and the presidential staff to lead the nation effectively.

The refocused mission statement provided direction and focus for a systemic way of looking at the organization (see Figure 15.3).

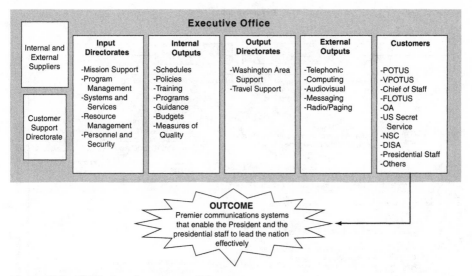

Figure 15.3   WHCA viewed as an extended system

WHCA's redesigned structure (see Figure 15.4) is led by the agency commander and the executive office. It is organized into eight directorates, each with its own specialized mission that supports the agency's overall mission. The directorates are divided by inputs (skills/functions), outputs (products/services), and markets (customers/users). Input units are mission support services. Output units are mission fulfilling units. Market units are customer support units. Agency materials describe the new structure is the "foundation for coordination and integration of WHCA as a whole. It is through this structure that the agency executes its operational tasks and achieves its mission. It is through our participative management style that we will deliberately and continuously improve the overall WHCA system." (WHCA, 1997)

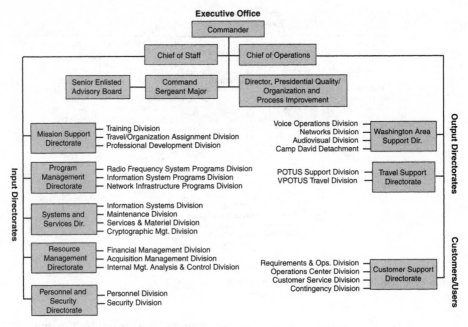

Figure 15.4 WHCA's interactive structure

BOARD STRUCTURE AND PARTICIPATION

The concept of participative management is not compatible with the traditional style of military management, which continues to be a key characteristic of WHCA's culture. That the agency, in 1997, could talk about having a participative management style is an indication of how far it had come since 1992. Some of that progress must be assumed to be the result of the ongoing continuous quality improvement initiative. Some of the progress also must be attributed to the realities connected with leading well-educated, skilled workers who do specialized high-tech work. None-the-less, without an organizational mechanism to support participative management, it would be consistent with systems theory to predict that the agency might not hold this progress against an ingrained command-and-control culture. To provide such a mechanism in its redesign, the agency incorporated the board structure, prescribed in Ackoff's concept of the circular organization (Ackoff, 1994).

In the circular organization, each person in a position of authority is provided with a board. At WHCA, each agency supervisor has a board that includes himself, his immediate supervisor, and each of his immediate subordinates (see Figure 15.5). The board structure ensures that supervisors interact with two levels of management above them, their own level, and two levels below. In this way, the board structure opens and strengthens communication and supports interactions between levels. Boards set policy, conduct planning, and provide coordination and integration of plans and policies. The people at the top still make decisions, but people at all levels set policy. According to Suàrez, people in the lower ranks of the agency have used the boards to change policies and procedures, including some activities that had existed since 1942 when the agency was established. He credits the board structure with ensuring that those at the top are subject to the collective opinion of those at the bottom.

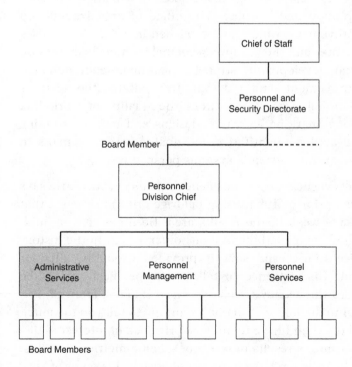

Figure 15.5 The branch chief's board

The boards, he explains, "include your immediate subordinates, your peers, your boss. This provides vertical and horizontal integration. Boards can do whatever they want so long as it doesn't affect anyone else's job. Boards determine whether an issue needs to be addressed at another level." Initially, people tended to think that the number of boards would increase the number of meetings a person must attend to an impossible level. In practice, the board structure reduced the number of meetings, as well as the number of memos, e-mails, and miscommunications. Suàrez says, "Team skills are necessary, but not sufficient, to manage interactions. The boards are how the agency manages interactions."

RESULTS

In an October 1998 interview, Dr. Suàrez says the implementation of the redesign is approximately 80 percent complete, though he quickly adds that it will never be finished, but will always be subject to adaptation and learning. The office of organization and process improvement, which he established in 1992, now houses a resource center and the agency's principal technical advisers on organizational development, strategic planning, team building, process improvement, and redesign. It facilitates the agency's strategic planning process, monitors the quality of work life, assists in benchmarking activities, designs and delivers training courses, and applies quantitative and qualitative instruments to assess the organization from a systems perspective.

Suàrez speaks vaguely about the agency's quality metrics. He says that a survey, prior to 1994, using Baldrige criteria revealed that the agency was weak in the results area. He notes that by mid-1997, they had completed the first customer survey in the history of the White House, and says it provided useful insights for improvement. His reticence to talk more specifically could be attributable to the agency's sensitive mission. This, after all, is a man who pointedly jokes: "You don't want me to tell you too much because, if I do, then I have to kill you." His lack of interest in discussing the agency's results in terms of specific metrics also illustrates what he calls a relatively recent change in his point of view about the value of measuring results. An observer might speculate that it constitutes something of a paradigm shift for a research academic now engaged in a world driven by practical application.

As preface to his changed view, Suàrez points out that he teaches tools and methods in basic statistics, and was a student of the Deming approach, accustomed to Deming's often repeated question: "How could they know?" So, when the agency had finished its redesign, he began to query Ackoff. "I said, 'We have a multidimensional design now. How do we know we are better off? We need to measure it. I need to show progress somewhere so I can say to everyone, *look.*' [Ackoff] looked at me and said, 'If you really need to measure to know how much progress you've made, then you have made no progress.'"

"It's true," Suàrez continues. "Progress should be obvious. It should be evident. People should feel good. They should talk about it. You should see it in their interactions." Today, he says he hears the voice of progress in the language of the agency. He sees it in the people's interactions. Now, when there is an issue to be addressed, the board structure gives them a way of knowing who they need to interact with to address it. "This does not mean that we are flying without looking at the instrument panel," he emphasizes. "It means that not everything that counts can be quantified. Not everything that counts can be counted." He briefly mentions that they have reduced the number of meetings by 40 percent, that they have customer surveys and internal customer surveys, and that they are developing additional metrics, but he emphasizes that their measurements are used to enhance the process, not drive it.

OTHER CHANGES

- **Customer support.** The redesign created a Customer Support Directorate to provide two-way liaison between the agency's customers and WHCA personnel. Creation of the directorate provides a centralized, proactive approach to understanding and fulfilling customer requirements.

- **Personnel evaluations.** The agency uses its board structure as a mechanism for performance evaluation, both up and down. Each year subordinate members of the boards meet to determine what their immediate supervisors can do that will enable them to do their jobs better. They prioritize the suggestions and present them to their supervisors who may agree, disagree but give reasons, or ask for more time to consider the matter. The process also works in reverse with the same three options. Feedback from clients is also factored into personnel evaluations. (In the new structure, workers have one boss and multiple clients.)

- **Training.** In the previous structure, someone who was good at a job could become locked into it. If someone was good at the switchboard or the teleprompter, for example, a boss could "secure" him in that job. The one-boss-multiple-clients structure changed that. Now, client feedback identifies skill gaps and triggers the agency's just-in-time approach to training. During the redesign, the agency also came to grips with the issue of how to deliver training to people who were constantly on the road. The result has been new instructional design packages that take the learning environment to the people wherever they are. The new emphasis on training and development, Suàrez says, is helping make the WHCA a good tour of duty.

- **Fee for service.** One change that, at the time of this writing, is still meeting considerable resistance is an initiative to "bill" the multiple internal clients a fee for service. The controversial effort is an attempt to challenge the "fallacy of the third party" that pays for everything.

- **Newcomer's orientation.** The agency now has a newcomer orientation program to introduce new personnel both to the information systems and to the agency's mode of interacting and participative management. The orientation also serves as a bridge to help new people extent their existing loyalty to their branch of military service to include a loyalty to the agency.

MANAGING FEAR

Today, newcomers to the agency do not know they are entering a redesigned organization. The structure they meet during orientation is simply the way the agency works. Initially, however, the redesign left people feeling disenfranchised from their previous departments and operating units. Over time, loyalties have shifted from the parts to the whole, and that, Suàrez says, is one of the big benefits of the new design. "In the new structure, problems no longer exist in isolation," he says. "It's not just AV's problem if the lights on the president are wrong." This attitude of shared responsibility helps the agency manage the negative impact associated with the fear of making a mistake that still permeates the agency's culture. WHCA's margin for error is just as razor thin as ever, but the changes at the agency make it a little easier for people to acknowledge mistakes and get past them.

Dr. Suàrez argues that it is impossible to eliminate fear completely. Drive out one fear, he says, and another will take its place like weeds in a garden. Someone running a teleprompter, for example, may master that job to the point of being very comfortable with it, but given a different responsibility will find the fear of making an error returns at a different level. In the context of the White House, Americans probably would prefer that the people who work there to have some fear of making a mistake. The problem lies in too much fear, too much pressure for perfection, and the corresponding pressure to conceal mistakes. To manage the negative impacts of fear, WHCA puts emphasis on building trust: trust in competencies and trust that mistakes will not be used to embarrass or persecute people.

The first way leaders build trust, Suàrez says, is by providing the technology, training, and education that workers need and then putting them in responsible positions that allow them to use their competencies. This continual investment in human development builds the workers' confidence and demonstrates the leaders' trust. The next step is creating an environment in which it is safe to admit to a mistake. To do this, the agency tries to allow the people who made a mistake to be the ones to correct it, share the learning from the mistake without mentioning who did it, and reverse the direction in which bad news travels.

At the White House, attempts to conceal mistakes are futile. "We are going to find out anyway," Suàrez says. "If they didn't tell us, there is a gap in the trust." If someone does attempt to conceal a mistake, the psychology of rumor can take over. Say a glitch takes place during a presidential trip. The president is unhappy. He tells the White House chief of staff, who tells the executive officer in the presidential office of administration, who tells someone within WHCA. By the time the agency tracks down the error, the soldier who made the mistake is devastated. It went all the way down from the president to him.

WHCA's current commander, Brigadier General Select Joseph J. Simmons IV, has been adamant about changing that. He has made it well known within the agency that he wants to be the first one to hear about something that goes wrong for the key customers. He has let everyone know that as soon as a glitch occurs, whoever is on site is to proactively report the problem and take action. This allows information to pass up the chain so that when the president says, "I was unhappy with this," the chief of staff can say, "Yes sir, we are aware of it, and this is what we have done." It reverses the order in which the bad news travels.

ROLE OF LEADER

In an interoffice memo announcing the implementation of the redesign, Simmons described himself as "committed to creating an environment conducive to cooperation, teamwork, joy, and pride in work." (WHCA, 1996) Apparently, it was not just talk. The agency's previous commander was supportive, Suàrez says, but Simmons is beyond supportive; he drives the transformation effort.

Yes, he does talk the talk. He says things Suàrez did not hear when he first came to the agency. For example, Simmons talks about the importance of being proactive and "managing the interactions versus managing the actions." More important, Suàrez says that Simmons "deploys that the values we agreed we stood for, the integrity, the trust, honesty, speaking truth to power. He lectures you on speaking truth to power. You see him actually protecting people from the heat that comes from the House. When people see that, it's inspiring. In the past, we were running for cover and then pointing fingers. Now, it's different. If AV went down, we all went down. And, if any one receives high praise, we all celebrate!"

HOLDING THE GAINS

It is hardly surprising to learn that, after accomplishing a total organizational redesign, WHCA is still engaged in continual process improvement activities, especially as related to standardizing its newer processes. More than 30 years ago, Dr. Joseph M. Juran wrote that an "unvarying sequence" underlies all human progress, and that control is the inevitable final step occurring both during and after attainment of a breakthrough in performance or a breakthrough in a cultural pattern. "*All* managerial activity is directed at either Breakthrough or Control. Managers are busy doing both these things, and nothing else. There is nothing inconsistent about a manager conducting both of these activities simultaneously." (Juran, 1964) So the agency continues to improve its processes and to reach ever higher. An internal benchmarking study revealed that people loved being on the road because of the cohesiveness of everyone pulling together. One goal then is discover how to maintain that synergy and cohesiveness when people are at headquarters. The bigger challenge, however, is to hold the gains the agency already has made and, possibly, to expand the initiative to the agency's containing system, the White House Military Office.

For some time, the big question has been what would happen when Simmons moved on. According to Suàrez, there have been only two other examples of a redesign of this type in military organizations, one at an Army base in Germany and the other at a Naval base in Pensacola. Both floundered when the number-one person left. The other efforts, he says, were not as advanced as WHCA's, but nonetheless rotation of leadership has been a major concern. In November, however, Simmons moved, but not out. He was appointed deputy assistant to the president and director of the White House Military Office. As such, he will select his own replacement at WHCA and continue to influence its direction. (At the time of this writing, a new agency commander has not yet been appointed.)

WHCA has made what appear to be very fundamental system changes, and Suàrez is optimistic about the future. "The board structure has given a voice to the people. We have given people democracy. In a military structure, that is a profound shift. Initially, people were very skeptical because they lost their own power. Now they see that no one can 'back door' them by getting the commander's ear and having him approve a policy." If someone wants a change, that person must make a presentation to the appropriate board. Policy changes require consensus, in practice not in principle, that the change supports the common good. This, he says, has reduced "maneuvering" and turf battles. The board structure, he says, makes people focus on what is good for the agency, not what is good for their units.

"People have seen their ideas implemented. They've had a taste of democracy." That, Suàrez believes, is one thing that will help keep the transformation alive. "Another thing is the indoctrination to the newcomers which is very strong. When they arrive, they have two weeks of orientation, which includes boards training and training in Covey's seven habits (Covey, 1989). So that should help, too." He hesitates, "Will it survive over time? I don't know. Ackoff says, even if it fails, there will be a great many lessons learned. I think anyone reading our story will see how much potential there is. If it dies, maybe a future WHCA director will read our story and revive it. Maybe that never happens. Maybe it never dies." For now, the work goes on.

FURTHER STUDY

What will happen at WHCA over the next several years? With an average tour of duty of four years, the agency seems a good place to examine theories related to the impact of changing the system versus the impact of changing the people, and especially the impact of a change in leadership. It would be interesting to compare the agency's experiences with those of other organizations that have taken a similar path, moving from an emphasis on continuous quality improvement via the Deming approach to a total organizational redesign via Ackoff. What commonalities exist? Do they support an argument that there exists a natural progression in participative management practices? How has it been different for the commercial organizations that followed the same path?

As for Suàrez, WHCA's redesign raised still more questions about how to further improve the agency. The issues he and the agency identified suggest several areas where research data would be useful to practitioners who are working to improve their organizations.

ORGANIZATIONAL DESIGN

What are the organizational conditions and attributes that encourage people to document and share ideas?

What factors positively and negatively impact the design and use of organization-wide incentives to stimulate the documentation and sharing of ideas?

What are the conditions and infrastructure that stimulate the interactive flow of relevant data, information, and knowledge through an organization?

What organizational design elements facilitate the development of a knowledge culture or knowledge community within the organization?

What metrics and methodologies are useful in assessing an organization's collective wisdom?

What are the indicators that anticipate an inability on the part of an organization to develop stability and/or flexibility?

What actions are useful in removing systemic blocks that prevent organizations from developing stability and flexibility?

What organizational design structures promote stability and flexibility?

ORGANIZATIONAL PSYCHOLOGY

What planned, intentional activities or structures are useful in building trust between people within an organization? Between the people in the organization and the organization as an entity?

What characteristics and behaviors identify various levels of trust?

How do various levels of trust impact organizational synergy and the sharing of ideas?

How do various levels of trust affect a group's capacity to achieve consensus?

Is resistance to change a function of personality? Of perceived likely effects? Of whether or not the change is imposed or voluntary? Is resistance to change an inherent human trait?

What planned, intentional actions and/or structures are effective in enabling an organization manage interactions in ways that deflect, disarm, and defuse resistance to change?

NOTE

This article has been reviewed and approved for public distribution by the White House Communications Agency. Unless otherwise attributed, Dr. Gerald Suàrez's observations about the transformation effort at the White House Communications Agency are drawn from his public presentations in May 1997 and June 1998 at the Hunter Conference in Madison, Wisconsin, and from a personal interview with the author in October 1998.

REFERENCES

Ackoff, R.L. 1981. *Creating the Corporate Future*. New York: Wiley.

———. 1994. *The Democratic Organization*. New York: Oxford University Press.

Covey, Stephen R. 1989. *The Seven Habits of Highly Effective People*. New York: Simon & Schuster.

Deming, W. Edwards. 1982a. *Out of the Crisis*. Cambridge, MA: Massachusetts Institute of Technology, Center for Advanced Engineering Study.

Deming, W. Edwards. 1982b. *Quality, Productivity, and Competitive Position*. Cambridge, MA: Massachusetts Institute of Technology, Center for Advanced Engineering Study.

Gharajedaghi, Jamshid. 1999. *Systems Thinking: Managing Chaos and Complexity*. Woburn, MA: Butterworth-Heinemann Publishers.

Hyde, Al. 1997. A decade's worth of lessons in continuous improvement, *Government Executive* (July).

Jacques, March Laree. 1993a. "National Know-How," *The TQM Magazine* (May/June): 41–46.

——. 1993b. "Not Such a Sorry State," *The TQM Magazine*, September/October: 27–31.

Joiner, Brian L. 1994. *Fourth Generation Management*. New York: McGraw-Hill.

Juran, Joseph M. 1964. *Managerial Breakthrough*, 2nd ed., 1995. New York: McGraw-Hill.

Nelson, Adel E. and G. Ronald Gilbert. 1991. *Beyond Participative Management: Toward Total Employee Empowerment for Quality*. Westport, Conn.: Quorum Books.

Scholtes, Peter R. 1998. *The Leader's Handbook*. New York: McGraw-Hill.

Suàrez, J. Gerald. 1992. *Three Experts on Quality Management: Philip B. Crosby, W. Edwards Deming, Joseph M. Juran*. Arlington, VA.: U.S. Department of the Navy, Total Quality Leadership Office, TQLO Publication No. 92–02.

——. 1993. *Managing Fear in the Workplace*. Arlington, VA: U.S. Department of the Navy, Total Quality Leadership Office, Publication No. 93–01.

——. 1996. *Managing Fear, Better Management for a Changing World,* Vols. 5–7, Silver Spring, MD: CC-M Productions.

———. 1996. Creating the Future: an Idealized Redesign of the White House Communications Agency (WHCA). Washington, DC: White House Communications Agency.

———. 1997. The White House Communications Agency: Building for the 21st century. Washington, DC: White House Communications Agency.

The text of this chapter is a slightly edited version of the author's 1999 article, "Transformation and Redesign at the White House Communications Agency," *Quarterly Management Review* (American Society for Quality) Vol. 6, Issue 3, and reprinted by kind permission of the author. The figures were cleared for use by Dr. Gerald Suàrez by the Department of Defense counsel and White House Security and are used here by kind permission of Dr. Suàrez.

Endnotes

CHAPTER 4

[1] Ackoff, Russell L. 1999. *Re-Creating the Corporation: A Design of Organizations for the 21st Century*. New York: Oxford.

CHAPTER 5

[1] Jacques, March Laree. 1999. Transformation and redesign at the White House communications agency. *Quarterly Management Review* (American Society for Quality), Vol. 6, Issue 3.

CHAPTER 10

[1] Ozbekhan, Hasan. 1977. The future of Paris: a systems study in strategic urban planning. *Philosophical Transactions of the Royal Society of London*, A387: 523–544.

CHAPTER 11

[1] Himmelstein, David U., Elizabeth Warren, Deborah Thorne, and Steffie J. Woolhandler. 2005. Illness and injury as contributors to bankruptcy, *Health Affairs: The Policy Journal of the Health Sphere,* February 8, 2005. http://ssrn.com/abstract=664565.

CHAPTER 12

[1] Ortega y Gasset, Jose, 1956. *Mission of the University.* New York: W. W. Norton.

[2] O'Driscoll, Gerald P., Jr., Kim R. Holmes, and Mary Anastasia O'Grady. 2002. *2002 Index of Economic Freedom.* Washington, D.C.: Heritage Foundation.

CHAPTER 14

[1] The team that provided the facilitation and guidance voluntarily, in addition to one of the authors, included Susan Ciccantelli, Jason Magidson, and Don Wilson.

[2] One of the authors has been a "participant observer" throughout the process.

Annotated Bibliography

This bibliography contains a listing of books for further reading on idealized design and systems thinking.

Ackoff, Russell L. 1981. *Creating the Corporate Future.* New York: Wiley.

A new, highly participatory approach to planning, interactive planning. Description of its philosophical and theoretical foundations as well as derivative practical procedures that synthesize operational, tactical, and strategic planning into the design of a desirable future and the invention of ways of realizing it.

———. 1999. *Re-Creating the Corporation: A Design of Organizations for the 21st Century.* New York: Oxford.

Covers planning, organizational democracy, internal market economy, multidimensional structures, and organizational learning.

———. 1994. *The Democratic Corporation.* New York: Oxford University Press.

The changing concept of a corporation, from mechanism to social system and its implications for internal politics and economy, and organizational structure. It also looks at business education critically.

——. 1994. *Ackoff's Best*. New York. John Wiley & Sons.

A collection of the author's most controversial, influential, and wittiest work. The essays explore the nature and implications of systems thinking for management and organizational design.

——, and Fred E. Emery. 2006. *On Purposeful Systems*. New Brunswick, New Jersey: Transaction Publishers.

An interdisciplinary analysis of individual and social behavior as a system of purposeful events. Concepts are operationally defined and form a conceptual system.

——, and Sheldon Rovin. 2003. *Redesigning Society*. Stanford, California: Stanford University Press.

Using systems thinking, redesigns are presented of the structure and functioning of government, cities, transportation, health care, education, welfare, criminal justice, and leadership.

——, and Johan P. Stumpfer. 2003. Terrorism: a systemic view. *Systems Research and Behavioral Science*, 20, 287–294.

An analysis of the causes of terrorism and consideration of what might be done about it.

Barabba, Vince, Pourdehnad, John and Russell Ackoff, "On Misdirecting Management." *Strategy & Leadership*, 2002, Emerald/MCB Journals.

The authors argue that consultants are of two types: self-promoting gurus and educators. Gurus that pontificate and promote their proprietary problem-solving techniques do not educate their clients. They promote maxims that define rules of behavior but do not increase the competence of managers. They promote their proprietary solution as a fix for all problems instead of trying to increase managerial understanding of a particular corporate puzzle.

Beer, Stafford. 1966. *Decision and Control.* London. Wiley.

A classic explanation of the field of operations research written in a witty and jargon-free manner.

Bertalanffy, Ludvig von. 1968. *General Systems Theory.* New York: Braziller.

The seminal discussion of systems thinking applied to a number of disciplines including language and psychology but focusing on biology. It seeks properties of systems and laws they obey that apply regardless of type.

Capra, Fritjof. 1982. *The Turning Point.* New York: Simon & Schuster.

A vision of a holistic paradigm of science and spirit that allows the forces transforming the world to flow together as a positive movement for social change.

Checkland, Peter. 1981. *Systems Thinking, Systems Practice.* Chichester, England: John Wiley & Sons.

Provides a useful history of systems thinking and makes a distinction between "hard" and "soft" thinking. Hard systems thinking leads to engineering models that the author considers reductionist. Soft thinking is more philosophical but results in solving real-world problems.

Churchman, C. West. 1968. *The Systems Approach.* New York: Delacourte Press.

A classic work on the foundations of systems thinking.

——. 1979. *The Systems Approach and Its Enemies.* New York: Basic Books.

Several "not rational" but powerful approaches to understanding the human experience, the author claims, are ignored with the result that many planning efforts are sterile, unsatisfying, and irrelevant. A way to overcome these deficiencies is developed.

——. 1971. *Design of Inquiring Systems*. New York: Basic Books.

An in-depth discussion of the basic philosophical aspects of the systems approach. An examination of the great philosophical systems of the past from the perspective and in the language of modern systems thinking.

Cragin, Kim, and Peter Chalk. 2003. *Terrorism & Development: Using Social and Economic Development to Inhibit a Resurgence of Terrorism*. Santa Monica: Rand.

Examines the social and economic development policies enacted by Israel, the Philippines, and the United Kingdom to inhibit a resurgence of terrorism within their jurisdictions, with the aim of informing U.S. decision makers as they develop policy to counterterrorism.

Emery, Fred E. (ed). 1969. *Systems Thinking: Selected Readings, Volumes 1 and 2*. New York: Penguin.

Selected readings of historically important articles covering methods, models, and planning of and for systems; applications to individuals and groups, communication, hierarchical systems, systems management, ecosystems, redesigning systems, ideal-seeking systems, and a search for common ground among these diverse applications.

Gharajedaghi, Jamshid. 1999. *Systems Thinking: Managing Chaos and Complexity*. Boston: Butterworth-Heinemann.

A defense of systems thinking that deals with the art of simplifying complexity, managing interdependencies, and understanding choice using a novel scheme called "iterative planning."

Gharajedaghi, Jamshid, and Russell L. Ackoff. 1985. Toward systemic education of systems scientists. *Systems Research*, Vol. 2 No. 1: 21–27.

A description of the non-systemic way in which most educational programs for systems thinkers are designed. A systemic-oriented educational program—one that avoids the deficiencies identified—developed in the Wharton School is described.

Goggin, William C. 1974. How the multidimensional structure works at Dow Corning. *Harvard Business Review*, 52 (January–February): 54–65.

The development of an unconventional corporate structure, the representation of which involves at least three dimensions, not the conventional two, authority and responsibility. The result is a flexible organization that can respond quickly to even major changes in its environment.

Halal, William E., Ali Geranmayeh, and John Pourdehnad, eds 1993. *Internal Markets: Bringing the Power of Free Enterprise Inside Your Organization.* New York: John Wiley & Sons.

Demonstrates how to design an organization using an "internal markets" model to create the entrepreneurial company and provides an effective response to reshaping a business. Describes how to break up the bureaucracy and make a company work more productively by bringing the logic of the market system and free enterprise into the organization. Case studies from MCI, Control Data, Esso, and Alcoa illustrate successful management practice.

Himmelstein, David U., Elizabeth Warren, Deborah Thorne, and Steffie J. Woolhandler. 2005. Illness and injury as contributors to bankruptcy, *Health Affairs: The Policy Journal of the Health Sphere,* February 8, 2005. http://ssrn.com/abstract=664565.

Report of a survey of personal bankruptcy filers in five federal courts. About half of the filers cited medical causes, indicating that between 1.850 and 2.227 million Americans (filers plus dependents) experienced medical bankruptcy. Even middle class, insured families often fall prey to financial catastrophe when sick.

Hirshman, A. O., and C. E. Lindblom. 1969. "Economic Development, Research and Development, Policy Making: Some Converging Views." In *Systems Thinking* (F. E. Emery, ed.), Hamondsworth, Middlesex, England: Penguin Books.

Although the principle guiding management of separate but correlated systems seems to be that of "joint optimization," their evidence seems to suggest that management of the relations between, and the performance of the parts of each system needs to be guided by the principle of "the leading part": optimizing the leading part even at the expense of other parts.

Jackson, Michael. 2003. *Systems Thinking: Creative Holism for Managers*. Chichester, England: John Wiley & Sons.

A particularly good introduction to systems thinking and the principal ways of conceptualizing it, their strengths and weaknesses, and an effort to formulate an approach that avoids their shortcomings.

Jacques, March Laree. 1999. Transformation and redesign at the White House communications agency. *Quarterly Management Review* (American Society for Quality), Vol. 6, Issue 3.

Detailed description of the application of an idealized design to improving the performance of the White House Communication Agency. This article is reprinted in a slightly edited form as Chapter 15, "White House Communications Agency (Government)."

Kauffman, Jr., Draper L. 1980. *Systems 1: An Introduction to Systems Thinking*. Minneapolis: Future Systems.

An elementary introduction to the basics of systems thinking, including a feel for the common patterns of organization and behavior that characterize most dynamic systems. It is effectively illustrated.

Kuhn, Thomas S. *The Structure of Scientific Revolutions*. Chicago: University of Chicago Press.

The producers, nature, and necessity of scientific revolutions. The priority and persistence of paradigms: crisis and the emergence of revolutions as changes of world view scientific theories.

Lazlo, Ervin. 1972. *The Systems View of the World*. New York: Braziller.

It is argued that there is no better way to understand the world than by the use of contemporary science. The problems, both for science and the widest communities of concerned persons, is to explicate the inherent natural philosophy of the contemporary sciences. Although difficult, this is an attempt to explicate one that is, the systems view of the world emerging.

O'Driscoll, Gerald P., Jr., Kim R. Holmes, and Mary Anastasia O'Grady. 2002. *2002 Index of Economic Freedom*. Washington, D.C.: Heritage Foundation.

An annual survey of economic freedom in the nations of the world. Makes the case that developing countries that fail to embrace economic liberty, which is the solution to poverty and desperation, provide a fertile environment for terrorists.

Ortega y Gasset, Jose, 1956. *Mission of the University*. New York: W. W. Norton.

A set of lectures delivered at the University of Madrid on Ortega's return from exile necessitated by Franco. It focuses on the role universities should play in the progressive development of a nation. In particular, he shows that important revolutions in our history are consequences of the development of mobilizing ideas—an activity to which universities should be devoted.

Ozbekhan, Hasan. 1977. The future of Paris: a systems study in strategic urban planning. *Philosophical Transactions of the Royal Society of London*, A387: 523–544.

A report of a planning project conducted at the Wharton School for the government of France. It involved a redesign of Paris and, of necessity, spread to a regional plan of France. The process and politics of the planning procedure are described.

Rifkin, Jeremy. 2000. *The Age of Access*. New York: Tarcher/Putnam.

Rifkin argues that the compulsion of ownership of resources that satisfy our needs and desires is gradually being replaced by access to them. By payment for the use of resources, not owning them, considerable savings are realized through more efficient use of resources.

Rovin, Sheldon, Neville Jeharajah, et al. 1994. *An Idealized Design of the U.S. Healthcare System*. Bala Cynwyd, Pennsylvania: Interact.

A consortium consisting of representative of each of the participants in the national health-care system produced an idealized redesign of the current system. They argue that the current system is dedicated to caring for illness and disability, not health, because the providers are compensated for the former not the latter. The core idea in the redesign is compensation of servers for the maintenance of health.

Schön, Donald A. 1971. *Beyond the Stable State*. New York: Random House.

Schön presents workable proposals for living in a world of rapidly accelerating change that is undermining the stability of our entire society. Established institutions tend to keep things as they are. Nevertheless, disruptions occur continually. To avoid them, businesses, government, and social institutions must become "learning institutions." In this way, they can maintain the flexibility required to adapt to new situations as they arise.

Senge, Peter. 1990. *The Fifth Discipline*. New York: Doubleday.

Senge identifies five disciplines: systems thinking, personal mastery, mental models, building shared visions, and team learning. He places systems thinking first on this list, yet he calls it "the fifth discipline" because it is the conceptual cornerstone that underlies all of the other learning disciplines. As he points out, all are concerned with a shift of mind from seeing parts to seeing wholes, from seeing people as helpless reactors to seeing them as active participants in shaping their reality, from reacting to the present to creating the future.

Snow, C. P. 1964. *The Two Cultures: and a Second Look.* New York: Mentor Books.

A description of the split between our literacy and scientific communities and a warning that, because of it, the West could lose the race in science and technology. He argues that science, tradition, and art have no choice but to unite.

Suárez, J. Gerald. 2002. Unpublished manuscript.

A memoir of his life that includes a detailed look at the dynamics of his experience in installing an idealized design in the White House Communication Office. Discusses the importance of a champion in management to the success of a design.

Warwick, David R. 1992. The cash-free society. *The Futurist,* November–December: 19–22.

A discussion of how new technology makes it possible to eliminate the use of cash for economic transactions. Consideration is given to some of the social, political, as well as economic implications of such a change.

INDEX

 Wharton School Publishing

Bernard Baumohl
THE SECRETS OF ECONOMIC INDICATORS
Hidden Clues to Future Economic Trends and Investment Opportunities

Randall Billingsley
UNDERSTANDING ARBITRAGE
An Intuitive Approach to Investment Analysis

Sayan Chatterjee
FAILSAFE STRATEGIES
Profit and Grow from Risks That Others Avoid

Tony Davila, Marc Epstein, and Robert Shelton
MAKING INNOVATION WORK
How to Manage It, Measure It, and Profit from It

Sunil Gupta, Donald R. Lehmann
MANAGING CUSTOMERS AS INVESTMENTS
The Strategic Value of Customers in the Long Run

Stuart L. Hart
CAPITALISM AT THE CROSSROADS
The Unlimited Business Opportunities in Solving the World's Most Difficult Problems

Lawrence G. Hrebiniak
MAKING STRATEGY WORK
Leading Effective Execution and Change

Jon M. Huntsman
WINNERS NEVER CHEAT
Everyday Values We Learned as Children (But May Have Forgotten)

Eamonn Kelly
POWERFUL TIMES
Rising to the Challenge of Our Uncertain World

Doug Lennick, Fred Kiel
MORAL INTELLIGENCE
Enhancing Business Performance and Leadership Success

Vijay Mahajan, Kamini Banga
THE 86 PERCENT SOLUTION
How to Succeed in the Biggest Market Opportunity of the Next 50 Years

Alfred A. Marcus
BIG WINNERS AND BIG LOSERS
The 4 Secrets of Long-Term Business Success and Failure

Robert Mittelstaedt
WILL YOUR NEXT MISTAKE BE FATAL?
Avoiding the Chain of Mistakes That Can Destroy Your Organization

Peter Navarro
THE WELL-TIMED STRATEGY
Managing the Business Cycle for Competitive Advantage

Kenichi Ohmae
THE NEXT GLOBAL STAGE
Challenges and Opportunities in Our Borderless World

Mukul Pandya, Robbie Shell, Susan Warner, Sandeep Junnarkar, Jeffrey Brown
NIGHTLY BUSINESS REPORT PRESENTS LASTING LEADERSHIP
What You Can Learn from the Top 25 Business People of Our Times

C. K. Prahalad
THE FORTUNE AT THE BOTTOM OF THE PYRAMID
Eradicating Poverty Through Profits

Michael A. Roberto
WHY GREAT LEADERS DON'T TAKE YES FOR AN ANSWER
Managing for Conflict and Consensus

Arthur Rubinfeld, Collins Hemingway
BUILT FOR GROWTH
Expanding Your Business Around the Corner or Across the Globe

Scott A. Shane
FINDING FERTILE GROUND
Identifying Extraordinary Opportunities for New Ventures

Oded Shenkar
THE CHINESE CENTURY
The Rising Chinese Economy and Its Impact on the Global Economy, the Balance of Power, and Your Job

David Sirota, Louis A. Mischkind, and Michael Irwin Meltzer
THE ENTHUSIASTIC EMPLOYEE
How Companies Profit by Giving Workers What They Want

Thomas T. Stallkamp
SCORE!
A Better Way to Do Busine$$: Moving from Conflict to Collaboration

Glen Urban
DON'T JUST RELATE — ADVOCATE!
A Blueprint for Profit in the Era of Customer Power

Craig M. Vogel, Jonathan Cagan, and Peter Boatwright
THE DESIGN OF THINGS TO COME
How Ordinary People Create Extraordinary Products

Yoram (Jerry) Wind, Colin Crook, with Robert Gunther
THE POWER OF IMPOSSIBLE THINKING
Transform the Business of Your Life and the Life of Your Business

An Invitation from the Editors:
Join the
Wharton School Publishing Membership Program

Dear Reader,

We hope that you've discovered valuable ideas in this book, which will help you affect real change in your professional life. Each of our titles is evaluated by the Wharton School Publishing editorial board and earns the Wharton Seal of Approval — ensuring that books are timely, important, conceptually sound and/or empirically based and — key for you — implementable.

We encourage you to join the Wharton School Publishing Membership Program. Registration is simple and free, and you will receive these and other valuable benefits:

* **Access to valuable content** — receive access to additional content, including audio summaries, articles, case studies, chapters of forthcoming books, updates, and appendices.
* **Online savings** — save up to 30% on books purchased everyday at Whartonsp. com by joining the site.
* **Exclusive discounts** — receive a special discount on the Financial Times and FT.com when you join today.
* **Up to the minute information** — subscribe to select Wharton School Publishing newsletters to be the first to learn about new releases, special promotions, author appearances, and events.

Becoming a member is easy; please visit Whartonsp.com and click "Join WSP" today.

Wharton School Publishing welcomes your comments and feedback. Please let us know what interests you, so that we can refer you to an appropriate resource or develop future learning in that area. Your suggestions will help us serve you better.

Sincerely,

Jerry Wind
windj@wharton.upenn.edu

Tim Moore
tim_moore@prenhall.com

Become a member today at Whartonsp.com

The Design of Things to Come
How Ordinary People Create Extraordinary Products
BY CRAIG M. VOGEL, JONATHAN CAGAN, AND PETER BOATWRIGHT

The iPod is a harbinger of a revolution in product design: innovation that targets customer emotion, self-image, and fantasy—not just product function. This book uncovers the stories behind Swiffer's mops, OXO's potato peelers, Adidas' intelligent shoes, BodyMedia's SenseWear body monitor, Herman Miller's Mirra Chair, the new Ford F-150 pickup truck, and many other winning innovations. You'll meet the innovators and learn how they inspire and motivate their people as they shepherd their visions through corporate bureaucracy to profitable reality. The authors take you through the entire process of design innovation, showing how it really works, and how today's smartest companies are innovating more effectively and faster than ever before. *The Design of Things to Come* will fascinate you—whether you're a consumer who's intrigued by innovation or an executive who wants to deliver more of it.

ISBN 0131860828, © 2005, 272 pp., $26.95

Why Great Leaders Don't Take Yes for an Answer
Managing for Conflict and Consensus
BY MICHAEL A. ROBERTO

Executives hear "yes" far too often. They get groupthink, not reality, and don't hear bad news until it's too late. They think they've achieved consensus, then find their decisions undermined or derailed by colleagues who never really bought in. They become increasingly isolated; even high-risk or illegal actions can begin to go unquestioned. Inevitable? *Absolutely not.* In this book, Harvard Business School Professor Michael Roberto shows you how to promote honest, constructive dissent and skepticism...use it to improve your decisions...and then align your entire organization to fully support the decisions you make. Learn how to test and probe the members of your management team...discover when "yes" means "yes" and when it doesn't...and build real, deep consensus that leads to action. This acclaimed book delivers important new insights into managing teams, mitigating risk, promoting corporate ethics through effective governance, and much more.

ISBN 0131454390, © 2005, 304 pp., $26.95